TABLE OF CONTENTS

Introduction
Definition of Terms
Selling Out: Background and a Brief History of Aunt Jemima
Jemimas Assemble! A Form of Self-Hate?
Jemimas Assemble! The Cast of Clowns

- **Diana Ross**
- **Diamond and Silk (Lynette Hardaway and Rochelle Richardson**
- **Geraldine Alexis, author - "The White Man's Purpose"**

  - ❖ Table of Contents/Overview
  - ❖ "Chapter 1: God's Children";
  - ❖ Chapter 2: Our Purpose in Life;
  - ❖ Chapter 3: White Mans' Purpose;
  - ❖ Chapter 4: White Man's Purpose In Relation to Minorities
  - ❖ Chapter 5: Conclusion.

- **Star Parker**
- **Whoopi Goldberg**
- **Candace Owens**
- **Iman**
- **Ezola Foster**
- **Sheryl Underwood**
- **Stacey Dash**
- **Raven-Symone**
- **Omarosa Manigault**

  - ❖ Entrance into Trump World
  - ❖ Exit Out of Trump World

INTRODUCTION

The African world sees Black people in America as a group that they are related to, but as a group that is passive and opportunistic. Many of them wonder "why don't you have any power?" or "why aren't you doing better?" The fact is that black people have become passive and smugly satisfied with the crumbs from the white man's table. So beaten down from over 300 years of enslavement – an experience that would have eliminated most other groups – Africans trapped in America nevertheless survived but a part of that enslavement experience was a dehumanization process that included a massive brainwashing. No other slave system in history was as brutal and as psychologically damaging as the one that white people placed on African people in the Americas.

Today in 2018, black people are still staggering from the effects of that dehumanization process. There are those of us out there seeking to provide information and motivate, answering questions that are people pose out of ignorance and fear. You hear the same questions time and time again, and even when solutions are provided – such as those in my books – fear takes over and black people scurry to the one institution that has duped them for centuries and that they continue to be beholden to: the black church.

If the brainwashing from enslavement provided the recipe, the black church provides the oven, the kitchen and the materials needed to mix up a batch of "colored stupidity" which permeates the race. This, African brothers and sisters on the continent, is the answer to your questions and concerns. So when you come over here to study, or if you're fleeing from a civil war, or if you just think that you can come here and partake in the myth of the American Dream, then don't expect any help from your black brothers and sisters over here. They suffer from a subliminal "Tarzan mentality" and view you in the same way a white man would view you: with "disdain-and-how-dare-you."

As the books I produce continue to speak truth to power, do not expect that from the "negroes" in America who claim to be "black leaders." Not on the local, the regional or national basis. They are in positions of visibility because they lack viability. In 1964 one of our leading warrior-leaders saw what was going on as plain as day, and he warned us numerous times as he did in his "house slave and negro slave" statement which I mostly agree with, although I do not accept the concept of blacks ever having been "slaves." In fact, LaRue Nedd (2009) makes this clear in his work, *Why We Shouldn't Call Our Ancestors Slaves*. In this masterful work Nedd makes it clear that we were not slaves and to accept that definition is a form of blasphemy against our ancestors. He further asserts:

> Calling our ancestors slaves is a form of blasphemy because it is
> not true and because in the context of our history it dehumanizes
> and implies that our ancestors were inferior by comparison to the
> Europeans who project the idea that they "would rather die than
> accept being a "slave." And, history clearly shows that we resisted
> slavery with a vengeance. Therefore, we should not call our
> ancestors slaves (p. 80).

Agreeing wholeheartedly with what Nedd postulates, references to black people being "slaves" does not sit well with me. But Malcolm is nevertheless correct in his differentiation and designation between the "house negro" and the "slave negro," two different types of black people that were used by white folks and whose "types" continue to exist to this day. I will prove this as we continue with Malcolm's discourse and further demonstrate when it comes to the black person in America and his/her "brainwashing," what was past is also prologue.

Malcolm put it like this:

> To understand this, you have to go back to what [the] young
> brother here referred to as the house Negro and the field Negro --
> back during slavery. There were two kinds of slaves. There was the
> house Negro and the field Negro. The house Negroes - they lived
> in the house with master, they dressed pretty good, they ate good
> 'cause they ate his food -- what he left. They lived in the attic or
> the basement, but still they lived near the master; and they loved
> their master more than the master loved himself. They would give
> their life to save the master's house quicker than the master would.
> The house Negro, if the master said, "We got a good house here,"
> the house Negro would say, "Yeah, we got a good house here."
> Whenever the master said "we," he said "we." That's how you can
> tell a house Negro.

White folks, partially out of ignorance, partially out of denial and partially because they are the products of the "negationism" that permeates their thinking and writing when it comes to the topic of enslavement, do not quite understand what Malcolm is talking about. So let me contemporize his designations and show how these same syndromes continue to exist today in 2018 America.

You see them in every city and scenario: the so-called "black leaders" (known back in the day as "negro leaders"). These people are either self-appointed or they somehow get the white stamp of approval from some white man. If they help out with an election, they'll get a position, a title and maybe a set of keys that don't fit anything. If they side with the white man publicly, they'll be rewarded. If they're ministers or represent a bunch of passive black people in some religious setting, they'll get paid under the table to continue to do the bidding of the system. Milwaukee is full of them, from the state legislatures to the common council; Dallas has them at the Congressional level as well as the county and city council; and Omaha even has a few. In all these cases these opportunistic people can openly sell out the black community and continue to get away with it. These are today's "house negroes."

As I stated earlier, Malcolm saw it in 1964 and called them on it by describing them to the grass roots masses:

> If the master's house caught on fire, the house Negro would fight
> harder to put the blaze out than the master would. If the master got
> sick, the house Negro would say, "What's the matter, boss, we
> sick?" We sick! He identified himself with his master more than
> his master identified with himself. And if you came to the house
> Negro and said, "Let's run away, let's escape, let's separate," the
> house Negro would look at you and say, "Man, you crazy. What
> you mean, separate? Where is there a better house than this?
> Where can I wear better clothes than this? Where can I eat better
> food than this?" That was that house Negro. In those days he was
> called a "house nigger." And that's what we call him today,
> because we've still got some house niggers running around here.

This can be seen in present-day terms, not only in the guise of "black Republicans" who carry water for the system, but even for the so-called leadership that continues to talk about black people and "our" system and talking about what we should do "as Americans." Is there any wonder why those people from other parts of the world who have it in for this country and its racist history now include US as a part of the problem? With the white-run media promoting images of us has happy and satisfied, the people of the world who suffer have begun to hate us as much as they hate the white man. They now lump all "Americans" into the same mold and it's because of that "house nigger" mentality that the black people who get on television continue to display. As far as the world is concerned, "the friend of my enemy is my enemy."

Malcolm's description continues:

> This modern house Negro loves his master. He wants to live near
> him. He'll pay three times as much as the house is worth just to live
> near his master, and then brag about "I'm the only Negro out here."
> "I'm the only one on my job." "I'm the only one in this school."
> You're nothing but a house Negro …

I tell kids I talk to, even my own back in the day, that "college ain't for everybody." And I continue to speak and tell people that college is no guarantee of a job. I have an acquaintance who teaches at a community college and her job is to bullshit students into thinking that if they take classes and get a degree, they'll get a job. No guarantees, and no jobs in sight or being developed. Just the white man's word for it – and you know what the First Nation people said about his "word": the white man speaks with forked tongue.

The school's job is keeping the "field negroes in check," and this is the perfect lead-in to the following excerpt from Malcolm's speech:

> Just as the slavemaster of that day used Tom, the house Negro, to
> keep the field Negroes in check, the same old slavemaster today
> has Negroes who are nothing but modern Uncle Toms, 20th
> century Uncle Toms, to keep you and me in check, keep us under
> control, keep us passive and peaceful and nonviolent. That's Tom
> making you nonviolent …

Just like the "tom" I mentioned who talks to students about taking classes and that somehow that will get them jobs (she's a female so that would make her an "Aunt Jemima"), today's toms are geared toward pacification. And as I mentioned earlier, I can think of no bigger pacifier than today's ministers and preachers. Dr. Carter G. Woodson provides an ample overview as to why "keeping Negroes in check," as Malcolm alleged, is a major effect of the church:

> What the Negro church is, however, has been determined largely
> by what the white man has taught the race by precept and example.
> We must remember that the Negroes learned their religion from the
> early white Methodists and Baptists who evangelized the slaves
> and the poor whites when they were barred from proselytizing the
> aristocracy. The American white people themselves taught
> Negroes to specialize unduly in the "Praise the Lord," "Hallelujah"
> worship. In the West Indies among the Anglicans and among the

> Latin people Negroes do not show such emotionalism. They are
> cold and conservative (Woodson, 1933: p. 70).

So the key is to get black people emotionally involved so that the energy and spirit power can be channeled and aimed toward bullshit rather than constructive programs and activities. Woodson adds that,

> The American Negroes' ideals of morality, too, were borrowed
> from their owners. The Negroes could not be expected to raise a
> higher standard than their aristocratic governing class that teemed
> with sin and vice. This corrupt state of things did not easily pass
> away. The Negroes have never seen any striking examples among
> the whites to help them in matters of religion (Woodson, 1933: p.
> 71).

And to this day, the church and its jive-ass ministers (most of whom were "former" pimps, hustlers, con men, robbers or murderers who "found God while in prison) remain an important way to lock down black communities and keep the black masses "in check." This is what Malcolm referred to as learning to "suffer peacefully." Following is his analogy:

> It's like when you go to the dentist, and the man's going to take
> your tooth. You're going to fight him when he starts pulling. So he
> squirts some stuff in your jaw called novocaine, to make you think
> they're not doing anything to you. So you sit there and 'cause
> you've got all of that novocaine in your jaw, you suffer peacefully.
> Blood running all down your jaw, and you don't know what's
> happening. 'Cause someone has taught you to suffer -- peacefully.

This process of pacification is alive and well and apparent in nearly every American institution that has something to do with or interacts with black people. From the cops and the medical profession to lawyers, judges and the military, we are constantly being told we are "too emotional" and have to "chill out." Malcolm X put it this way:

> The white man does the same thing to you in the street, when he
> want [sic] to put knots on your head and take advantage of you and
> don't have to be afraid of your fighting back. To keep you from
> fighting back, he gets these old religious Uncle Toms to teach you
> and me, just like novocaine, suffer peacefully. Don't stop suffering
> -- just suffer peacefully. As Reverend Cleage pointed out, "Let
> your blood flow In the streets." This is a shame. And you know
> he's a Christian preacher. If it's a shame to him, you know what it
> is to me.

These are the answers in regard to today's black leadership, from top to bottom. So called "progressive" groups and individuals claiming to care about black people when all they really want to do is to teach us to – "suffer peacefully."

There are millions like that and I advanced a few decades back what I called "the theory of a thousand." In this theory I give big cities the benefit of having, at most, one thousand good bruthas and sistahs who believe in black liberation and African unity. A thousand. So New York, with all those African people – only a thousand who are worth a shit. And I've been to Dallas, Milwaukee, Chicago and Omaha and it's even worse because they are smaller in size. In Omaha, for example, that number can be counted on one hand. Dallas and Milwaukee are not much better.

This serves as an important fundamental foundation for understanding the "aunt Jemima", a term which will be defined in the following section. Everybody with black skin ain't black, and the increase of mulattoes and octoroos through interracial relationships is going to make identification even more difficult. There may be a few (such as Colin Kaepernick and Barack Obama), but the exceptions only further serve to prove the rule.

Now, let us move forward.

<u>DEFINITION OF TERMS</u>

Selling out. Most people in America, black and white, will write off the concept and counter with statements like, "everybody sells out at one time or another." My question is: do they? Really? Many people have different views of what selling out (and therefore being a "sell-out") actually means.

For instance, the Urban Dictionary simply defines selling out as, "One who betrays a cause for personal advancement." Wikipedia offers a longer definition of the concept of "selling out" as, " … a common idiomatic pejorative expression for the compromising of a person's integrity, morality, authenticity, or principles in exchange for personal gain, such as money. In terms of music or art, selling out is associated with attempts to tailor material to a mainstream or commercial audience; for example, a musician who alters his material to encompass a wider audience, and in turn generates greater revenue, may be labeled by fans who pre-date the change as a sellout." The more traditional Merriam-Webster Dictionary defines selling out as, "to betray one's cause or associates especially for personal gain." The Free Dictionary offers that to sell someone out is, "to betray someone; to reveal damaging information about someone."

What then, does this have to do with the term "Jemima" or "Aunt Jemima," and what does the term mean?

An article titled, "Aunt Jemima: It was Never About the Pancakes" by Sarah Doneghy appeared on the January, 2018 Black Excellence website. The following essay is being used to provide context for the behaviors, statements and attitudes of the selected African-American females that I highlight in this short book. This is not to paint a negative picture of these women, only a realistic one. We need to stop this sellout activity and for the most part black women have refrained from the kind of "uncle tomfoolery" that black males appear to have accepted as a way of life. But there are a few of these "sistahs" who are worthy of exposing and analyzing and that is what I'm going to do.

But first, some context.

The essay begins with the expected general truisms:

> It is nearly impossible to have grown up in America and not be familiar with Aunt Jemima. However, when thinking of Aunt Jemima, people often associate a person to the name not the pancakes. Before Aunt Jemima came to be an American icon, an initial interest needed to be established. This is the story of the woman who became a food, that became a product, which became one of the most recognizable figures in history: Aunt Jemima. (Doneghy, 2018)

In simpler terms it is a story about the white racist exploitation of black people after establishing a slave system where they worked these black people from "can't see in the morning until can't see at night." It is a story of the commodification of human beings who are, in a capitalist setting, viewed either as tangible assets or crippling liabilities.

Moving on:

> Aunt Jemima was first introduced as a character **in a minstrel show** – an American form of entertainment developed in the late 19th century. Each show consisted of comic skits, variety acts, dancing, and music. The shows were **performed by white people in blackface for the purpose of playing the roles of black people.** Minstrel shows portrayed black people as **dimwitted, lazy, easily frightened, chronically idle, superstitious, happy-go-lucky buffoons**. (Doneghy, 2018 – emphasis added)

So in other words, Aunt Jemima's image was conceived in a racist, negative portrayal of black folks. Those minstrel shows were the white man's way of degrading African people. To them it was "entertainment" in the way that watching blacks form "prayer vigils" and "protests" against the racism that has always been there is also a barrel of laughs. The concept of blacks as lazy, easily frightened, and the rest remains behind although it has been fine-tuned. But the concept of the "buffoon" is alive and well and some of the black women highlighted in this book make that point amazingly clear with their comments and actions.

At any rate,

> The inspiration for Aunt Jemima came specifically from the song "Old Aunt Jemima" written by a black performer named Billy Kersands in 1875. It was a staple of the minstrel circuit. **The song was based on a song sung by slave hands**. "Old Aunt Jemima" was performed by men in blackface. One of the men depicted Aunt Jemima – a Slave Mammy of the Plantation South. (Doneghy, 2018)

The author of the article didn't see fit to share the specific lyrics, but I do. And here they are, at least most of them:

> The monkey dressed in soldier clothes,"
> Old Aunt Jemima, oh! oh! oh!
> Went out in the woods for to drill some crows,
> Old Aunt Jemima, oh! oh! oh!
> The jay bird hung on the swinging limb,
> Old Aunt Jemima, oh! oh! oh!
> I up with a stone and hit him on the shin,
> Old Aunt Jemima, oh! oh! oh!
> Oh, Carline, oh, Carline,
> Can't you dance the bee line,
> Old Aunt Jemima, oh! oh! oh! "Oh!oh!oh!"
> The bullfrog married the tadpole's sister,
> Old Aunt Jemima, oh! oh! oh!
> He smacked his lips and then he kissed her,
> Old Aunt Jemima, oh! oh! oh!
> She says if you love me as I love you,
> Old Aunt Jemima, oh! oh! oh!
> No knife can cut our love in two,

The author's interpretation of the lyrics is what is provided as can be seen in the following excerpt:

> The lyrics tell of the promise to be set free yet remaining a slave forever. "My old missus promise me . . .When she died she-d set me free . . . She lived so long her head got bald . . . She swore she would not die at all . . ."While the lyrics depicted a reality, Aunt Jemima did not. There was a big difference between the stage Mammy and the actual female household slave. In fact, many argue that the Slave Mammy that became

the stereotype never actually existed. Well-known New York blogger, Julian Abagond had this to say:

"The Mammy pictured female household slaves as: fat, middle-aged, dark-skinned, undesirable . . . happy to serve whites, always smiling . . . The ugly truth is that they were: thin . . . young . . . **light-skinned, a daughter of rape; desirable to white men and therefore raped, utterly powerless, extremely unhappy . . .**" (Doneghy, 2018 – emphasis added)

And it is this latter part that is continually ignored in the history books and on film. These women who were "chosen" to work in the house were beauties, and the white man could rape them whenever he wanted. In fact, this is still taking place today. I know one light-skinned, green-eyed sister whose mother was finer than Dorothy Dandridge. And she cleaned houses. Now what do you think happened behind the closed doors in racist Omaha, Nebraska? The young sistah is still in denial even though she's light skinned and one of her children is an albino. It is clear what took place as there are no photos of her father in the house while she lies and claims that her father is "blue black."

What does that have to do with Aunt Jemima? Some of the sistahs that I analyze in this book fit that mold (Stacey Dash, Condoleeza Rice). And some that I didn't mention also do: Halle Berry, Vanessa Williams and others. They are light and bright and the white man is attracted to them. In fact these two women are now married to white men. The point is the Aunt Jemima people knew what they were doing: they didn't want white men getting boners at the kitchen table by staring at a box with some light skinned black beauty on it. So they came up with an image that they felt was both laughable – and abominable.

Moving right along:

The Mammy was created by white Southerners to redeem the relationship between black women and white men within slave society. Slave owners sexually exploited and abused their female slaves. Catherine Clinton's book *The Plantation Mistress: Woman's World in the Old South*, notes that "**Mammy was made to appear unattractive so no white man could want her over his white wife** therefore 'proving' that white men did not find black women sexually desirable." She was also proof that **black women were happy as slaves.** The Mammy helped put to rest any worries white people may have had around her, or women who looked like her. (Doneghy, 2018 – emphasis added)

A white man's creation. He knew what he liked and what he didn't like. And he continued to sneak "out back" and rape the enslaved black women whenever he felt like it, which helped him perpetuate the myth of "sacred white womanhood," which meant his wife was too pure and chaste to use for sexual purposes (except childbearing). He had it all figured out and was the only one on the plantation with what Kovel (1970) referred to as "free sexual choice". Kovel's symbolic matrix shows that everybody's sexual partner was under the white man's control and was limited to when he determined sex would take place. He was the only one who could have sex with white women, black women and, truth be told, even black men.

Another key is where Doneghy makes reference to the myth that "black women were happy as slaves." The myth of the contented slave is nothing to be scoffed at. In his book In 1845 *the* Narrative of the Life of Frederick Douglass, an American Slave, and Written by Himself, the following observed by the National Endowment for the Humanities.

> One myth that Southern slave owners and proponents perpetuated was **that of the slave happily singing from dawn to dusk** as he or she worked in the fields, prepared meals in the kitchen, or maintained the upkeep of the plantation. In his Narrative—particularly chapters 1 and 2— **Douglass quickly distinguishes the myth from the reality**. He uses incidents of cruelty that he witnessed along with songs of the slaves themselves—spirituals—to emphasize this distinction. (National Endowment for the Humanities, 2014).

Today when a Bureau of Prisons inspection takes place, these same slave-driver mentality havin' peckerwoods are warned when the inspector will arrive. Then they "arrange" things to make it look like the inmates are "happy." This is what the lie about slavery is supposed to do: take the guilt off the minds of today's white folks and make it appear as if enslavement was some kind of "favor" and that we swam over here looking forjobs. The Jemima of today is worse than the mere image of the one of yesteryear. An image is one thing, but those were good sistahs who never snitched. Today you have fat black bitches acting like the very buffoons of the minstrel days: for instance, Sheryl Underwood, Oprah Winfrey, Theresa Merritt (who played Eloise "Mama Curtis" on "That's My Mama"), the late Shirley Hemphill (who played Shirley Wilson on "What's Happenin'!), and the on-again, off-again "relevant" Jemima, Esther Rolle (who played Florida James on "Good Times") and the list goes on and on.

When you read a black history text or any information on enslavement, do you read about any black women selling out the race? No. It's always some black traitor or snitch who is male. And that's the point I'm making about that "happy slave" bullshit. TODAY is the time of the happy darkey and they are all around us, men and women. From pro athletes, celebrities, runway models, talk show hosts and TV stars to coons masquerading as "comedians," they permeate our culture.

What barely existed during the times of actual enslavement appears to be approaching a near majority today in 2018.

More background on Aunt Jemima is necessary:

> Aunt Jemima's pancake mix began in 1889 when two speculators, Chris Rutt and Charles Underwood, bought a flour mill. Together they developed the idea of a self-rising flour that only needed water. Initially, it was called 'Self-Rising Pancake Flour' … Rutt decided to use the name and the image of Aunt Jemima to promote his new pancake mix. However, Rutt and Underwood were unable to make the product a success and in 1890 they sold the business to the Davis Milling Company. (Doneghy, 2018)

How Rutt arrived at the decision to use the name and image of Aunt Jemima is beyond me. But one thing is for sure: it stuck. Black people felt it was some kind of compliment for "a negro woman" to be pictured on a box and white people felt comfortable because this female "coon" was literally serving them:

> **The Davis Milling Company developed an advertising plan to use a real person to portray Aunt Jemima.** The woman they found was Nancy Green. **Nancy Green was born a slave** in Kentucky in 1834 … In 1863 the Emancipation Proclamation set slaves free and Green moved to Chicago after the Civil War. There she worked for the Walker family as a domestic servant. **It was the Walkers who brought Green to the Davis Milling Company to audition for Aunt Jemima.** She was 56 at the time. Nancy Green debuted as Aunt Jemima at the 1893 World's Exposition in Chicago. (Doneghy, 2018 – emphasis added)

So peckerwoods brought this sistah in to audition to be the image of Aunt Jemima. How fitting. She was born in slavery so she was already programmed to be subservient to white folks and then she worked for white folks as a servant. A more fitting thrall could never be found.

Like an organ grinder's monkey, Ms. Green went to work "coonin'" as Aunt Jemima:

> The Davis Milling Company constructed the world's largest flour barrel to grab people's attention. Then they put Nancy Green on display (much like the flour) and gave her an act. She dressed as Aunt Jemima, sang songs, cooked pancakes, **and told romanticized stories about the Old South – a happy place for blacks and whites alike**, now accessible only by nostalgia, or by buying Aunt Jemima's pancake recipe. (Doneghy, 2018 – emphasis added)

So she was a professional liar. Dressing up like a coon and parading around like a retarded circus monkey is one thing, but claiming that slavery in the Old South was a happy place? She was committing blasphemy against her ancestors and was degrading black people. Just like the ones today – Omarosa Manigault, Condoleeezz Rice, Ezola Foster, and on a lesser level under the guise of progressive thinkers, Maxine Waters, Sheila Jackson Lee, Eddie Bernice Johnson – do in the name of political "equality." They continue their romanticized stories about better days ahead, vote and we'll be free and other bullshit that they sell to the gullible (and goony) black masses.

And as a result, when it came to Aunt Jemima,

> **Green was a huge success**. Her booth attracted so many people that special policemen were assigned to keep the crowds moving. The Davis Milling Company received over 50,000 orders, and **the fair officials awarded Green a medal and certificate for her showmanship**. After the Expo, Green signed **a lifetime contract with the company and traveled on promotional tours across the country**. By 1910 more than 120 million Aunt Jemima breakfasts were being served annually, roughly equal to the population of the country. **Green as Aunt Jemima was so successful that in 1914 the company renamed itself, 'The Aunt Jemima Mills Company.'** (Doneghy, 2018)

This book is about present day African-American female sellouts. But in order to understand this, we can compare and contrast what today's women do and say with what Ms. Green represented to the white man. I will site five (5) reasons in the comparison.

First off, in both cases, white boys made money by manipulating the antics and actions of a black woman. She fit the mold and model of what they wanted to present. The fact that they had "auditions" shows that there were more than a few black women who were willing to go through this degradation ceremony in exchange for money. That is a form of prostitution even though actual sex may not have taken place. So one might say that the embryonic beginnings of the "legend" of Aunt Jemima also included that of a prostitute

Secondly, she was awarded for what she did in the name of the state fair. The state fair at the Chicago Exposition was a major deal. It was truly a global event and lasted from May 1 through October 30th. During that time the Fair drew 27,300,000 visitors – that's twenty-seven MILLION people. So when Ms. Green received that award, she became a global sensation and that was just the beginning.

Third, she was given a lifetime contract with the company. The company was so impacted that it renamed itself "The Aunt Jemima Mills Company." Since when did a peckerwood corporation ever name itself after a black man or woman? They tend to steal ideas from blacks and place THEIR names on the business, but this was truly an unreported first. That lifetime contract was also probably a first, and although she probably only received chump change, she nevertheless turned her buffoonery into a virtual industry. The likes of Mantan Moreland, Stepin Fetchit, Willie Best, Eddie "Rochester" Anderson would follow suit. The formula was simple: make an ass out of yourself and engage in various stereotypical acts and you can get paid – for a long time!

This is important because the "lifetime contract" follows the buffoonish action and evidence of willing tomfoolery. Today's celebrities who have sold out have proven their loyalty to their white "master." None of them – including Oprah, Kathy Hughes, Beyonce Knowles – none of them would have lasted as long as they have without bowing at the feet of the peckerwood.

Fourth, she traveled on promotional tours for the company, thereby perpetuating the happy darkie myth and more likely than not embarrassing the hell out of black men and women along the way. But that lifetime contract was only "signed" by her, but it was written by THEM. And there were plenty other fat black women who could and would replace her if she dared to offer any kind of amendment to that contract. So she was a "slave" of a different kind – trapped and obligated to entertain her "master" at the expense of her own dignity.

Fifth and finally, her image persists so that future generations of black people can view what she did as an action that led to "success." And it's going on to this day. Later you will see that Gladys Knight surrendered her dignity to pose as the model for the "new" Aunt Jemima. A New York Times editorial titled, "Aunt Jemima Gets a Makeover" offered even more context when the news was announced in October of 1994,

> Mammy trademarks were hot. **Luzianne coffee, Fun to Wash soap, Aunt Dinah molasses: grinning, girthy black women were everywhere, selling everything.** As the cultural historian Patricia Turner writes in "Ceramic Uncles & Celluloid Mammies": **"Implicit in each rendition was the notion that these thick-waisted black women were happy with their lot, honored to spend their days and nights caring for white benefactors."** (New York Times, 1994 – emphasis added)

Today with these liberals and progressives boasting about a "post-racial America' under the belief that racism has subsided, that is because they don't understand how deep racism runs in American roots. America was conceived in racism with the relocation and genocidal attacks against First Nation people. The laws were written to degrade and deny people of color: the Alien Enemies Act of 1798, The Indian Removal Act of 1830, the Dred Scott Decision of 1857, the

Chinese Exclusion Act of 1882, and others, including Plessy v. Ferguson where racial segregation was made the formal law of the land. Conceived in racism and today it continues on as if it is "revisiting"; that fact is, racism never left and neither did selling out and its twin cousin, uncle tomfoolery.

White racism, arrogance and cultural imperialism explain the acceptance of the Aunt Jemima image. From generation to generation, the sales of pancake mix and the imagery that was selected became a model for the universal "coon."

Getting back to the Doneghy (2018) piece,

> The Davis Milling Company's marketing plan was brilliant. They delivered their customers something they had always wanted but could never have: **a 'real life Mammy'.** Along with the pancake mix, pamphlets were given out telling Aunt Jemima's 'life story'. According to the pamphlet, **she had been the house slave of Colonel Higbee, whose plantation was known across the South for its delicious pancakes.** After the war the Davis Milling Company, who had heard of the pancakes, **paid Aunt Jemima in gold to share with them her secret recipe.** That was the kind of **feel-good story people** wanted to hold onto. And with the pamphlet and Aunt Jemima's famous pancake mix, they could. (Doneghy, 2018 – emphasis added)

Let's get something straight: that sistah never saw any "gold" in her life. If she got paid anything, it was some chump change that amounted to little more than minimum wage.

Moreover, like some spoiled, racist children, they have to be pacified and told what they want to hear no matter how absurd – just like these right wing muthafuckas today who follow Trump and listen to his lie after lie and gobble them up as facts. The white race is not going to change because there is no reason for it to do so. With so much money being made with lies, bullshit, trinkets and other trivia, what are a few protests, a couple of prayer vigils and some liberal newspaper editorials? Why change when the money keeps rolling in no matter how fucked up you are?

Feel good stories. They feed them to their children by way of Black Pete, Little Red Robin Hood, Cinderella and Rapunzel while they subsequently poison children of color with Little Black Sambo, Ten Little Indians and the Frito Bandito. Feel good about your colorlessness as you live in your gated community, protected by your trigger happy cops and repressive legislation while people of color starve and your government finds like mad to keep brown people from coming into the country. Under such conditions, sellouts are not hard to come by.

Ads for Aunt Jemima got larger and larger. Ladies Home Journal and other major publications continued to run ads:

> The full-page color advertisements ran regularly in *Ladies' Home Journal*, *Good Housekeeping*, and *The Saturday Evening Post* and told tales of the leisure and splendor of the Plantation South. Aunt Jemima Pancake Mix, a labor-saving product, **was marketed with comparisons to a time and place when some American white women had the ultimate labor-saving device: a slave.** A line from a 1927 ad read: "Make them with Aunt Jemima Pancake Flour, and your family will ask where you got your wonderful Southern Cook." Or, just another way to say, "Your family will ask where you purchased a Slave Mammy such as this." **Slavery, and moreover, the fantasy of having slaves, was still the main attraction of the Aunt Jemima brand**. (Doneghy, 2018 – emphasis added)

The need for a slave, a mammy or some kind of "colored servant" continues. Women of color continue to clean the homes of these white people, and almost all of the yardmen and landscapers at Latinos. The "boys" who clean the pool, at least in California, are Asian or Puerto Rican. And the stigmatized list goes on and on.

Aunt Jemima never died; like Bebe's Kids she "just multiplied. For instance,

> **No one portrayed Aunt Jemima for ten years following the death of Nancy Green in 1923. Then in 1933, the Quaker Oats Company (which had acquired the company in 1926) hired Anna Robinson to play Aunt Jemima at the Chicago World's Fair**. At 350 pounds, she was much heavier than Green and she was darker in complexion. **The Quaker Oats Company loved her look** and she was sent to New York to pose for pictures. **An entire campaign was designed around Robinson as Aunt Jemima and her association with celebrities**. She had personal appearances and was photographed at some of the most famous places **making pancakes for Hollywood royalty, radio personalities, and Broadway stars.** The advertisements derived from those photography sessions "ranked among the highest read of their time" (Doneghy, 2018)

Throwbacks to the days of yore – then and this trip down memory lane continues to this day. Look at the TV programming; brand new channels featuring programs from the years when white folks had black people afraid and under control. Entire networks that boast of you not having to hear words like "word up," holla" and "booty call." Other stations that feature that colorless relaxing shows like "Andy Griffith," "Green Acres," "The Jack Benny Show," "Happy Days," "The Brady Bunch" and so many others. Evoking those memories of days when neighborhoods didn't have any niggas in 'em.

Aunt Jemima was their crowning glory depicting control and the justification that slavery didn't have to be cruel. It just had to BE.

Making Ms. Robinson believe she was a celebrity was the key to pushing those pancakes:

> Ironically, out of all the celebrities she posed with, none were more famous than Robinson herself. But Robinson wasn't famous for being their peer; she was famous for being Aunt Jemima, their slave. Having celebrities pose with Robinson brought **the Aunt Jemima brand** more sales and success than ever before. People have always wanted what celebrities have. Be it a designer dress, a car, or the ultimate status symbol: **a Mammy**. (Doneghy, 2018 – emphasis added)

The "brand" is the new term of young rappers and athletes. Don't these coons know that "branding" is what white boys did to their livestock? Don't they know that to "brand" something is to own it.

And then the "brand" became a part of popular culture:

> In the first half of the 1900's the Mammy was increasingly popular and was featured in a multitude of films, radio programs, and television shows. But no Mammy was more popular than Aunt Jemima. The 1934 movie *Imitation of Life* told the story of a Mammy, Aunt Delilah, who inherited a pancake recipe. **She gave the valuable recipe to Miss Bea, her boss who successfully marketed the recipe** ('Imitation of Life'). (Doneghy, 2018 – emphasis added)

Giving up inventions to white people has a long history in this country. These white people took credit and then turned around and patented or trademarked a plethora of black inventions. Among them, with their inventors, are: The shoemaking machine (Jan Matzelinger), the stoplight and the gas mask (Garrett Morris), the blood bank (Charles Drew), Otis Boylain (IBM computer) and the home security system (Marie Von Brittan Brown) – to name but a few.

The public relations campaign continued into the area of merchandising including dolls, bowls and salt and pepper shakers in her likeness (Doneghy, 2018). And then came the transition:

> …Throughout the 1960s, the Quaker Oats Company lightened Aunt Jemima's skin and made her look thinner in print images. In 1968, the company replaced her bandana with a headband, trimmed her waistline, and gave her a more youthful image. They removed the Southern Plantation settings and she no longer had a speaking role. If this was the Quaker Oats Company's attempt to present Aunt Jemima as a less racist figure, they failed. **By making her lighter, thinner, and younger, along with taking her off of the plantation and muting her voice, Aunt Jemima represented a house slave more than she ever had before**. (Doneghy, 2018)

Remember earlier when we talked about the beautiful "house negro" that the white man raped as she worked as a servant? The pancake mix had come done a 180-degree turnaround from making Aunt Jemima "undesirable" in appearance to make her actually quite alluring, the latter image being what the white man preyed upon during enslavement. The change was beginning to take shape, slowly but surely:

> Local chapters of the NAACP began pressuring schools and fair organizers not to invite Aunt Jemima to appear. In 1967 the Quaker Oats Company canceled its television campaign and in 1970 they removed Aunt Jemima's name from the Disneyland restaurant. (Doneghy, 2018)

The 1960s ushered in many changes that were spearheaded by the Black Power and civil rights movements. The Jemimas of today have evidently forgotten about or never learned about either of these. It was clear that the image was beginning to get on people's nerves, so much to the point that,

> **In 1989, after activists reportedly threw Quaker Oats into Lake Michigan and threatened boycotts in protest of the minstrel-inspired image, the company modified Aunt Jemima's likeness once again**. The Quaker Oats Company claimed that the change was to "celebrate the 100 year anniversary of the icon." **Aunt Jemima's headband was removed and replaced with dark curly hair**. She was also given **pearl earrings.** The company said it **was repositioning the brand icon as a "black, working, grandmother"** – words that have been used since the days of the minstrel show to **describe the Mammy**. Despite the 'makeover' Aunt Jemima **continued to be the black, obedient, female domestic whose only pleasure was to serve you.** (Doneghy, 2018 – emphasis added)

White people may alter their tactics but the strategy and vision remain the same. Let's look at the previous excerpt the point to the racist miscues and logical errors inherent in what Quaker Oats attempted to do.

To begin with, it took an act of social confrontation to get them to do the right thing. But then again, this is America and white people usually have to be forced to treat people of color as human beings. Fearing profit loss, those in power reacted to pacify the masses and place a band aid on the problem. This has long been a white tactic and because most Americans are so lazy and lulled into being patriotic, they continue to fall for the okey-doke. Any action by the oppressor is viewed as a sign of "progress" and then the protestors roll over and head back to their wage-slave lives.

Secondly, the cover story about the change being about an anniversary instead of the truth: they realized that the image of the "coon" had outlived its usefulness. They did not do away with the coon image; they simply placed a cosmetic disguise over the coon's façade. The black woman remained a "mammy" and a "maid" in the lives of most because the image had been emblazoned into the minds of the American public. So much so that they began to cut back in placing Aunt Jemima's picture on their products.

Third, the likeness was changed, the headband removed and now she had black curly hair. So what? What was that old saying that former vice-presidential candidate Sarah Palin harped on? "You can put lipstick on a pig and it's still a pig." (She was evidence of that). But the fact is even today, with all these black b beauties parading around television and movie studios, they remain viewed in the "likeness" of what their skin color represents: niggers. And in far too many instances (see the chapter on "Cast of Clowns")

Fourth, what's up with the pearl earrings? It can only mean that the branders were attempting to make a statement that Jemima was better off than most because she quietly served and was no real threat. She saved her hard-earned money and spent it on such trivial bullshit as earrings. This is typical programmed activity by the oppressor, known as "conspicuous consumption." That is where broke-ass niggas spend their money on fancy clothes, jewelry, and the like so that they can claim a status among their fellow low-income neighbors.

Fifth, the "black working grandmother" image was the same as the previous one. Who do you think was working in those homes in many cases. After enslavement ended, who do you think continued to work in white people's homes as a part of a long-time tradition? The woman I mention in my book, the light skinned, green-eyed beauty who wants to be so "black" and "community oriented" had a mother that was a real beauty. In Omaha, Nebraska that translates to mean if you work as someone's servant or in their home, the male of that household is going to get a look and act on it. Rape is common in these situations and the birth can easily be blamed on any black man because, after all, the bearer of the child is very light-skinned. It's being done all over the community in almost every city of major size.

Sixth, the importance of keeping the image of the "black, obedient, female domestic, with emphasis on obedience. Black servants in more contemporary times could get away with a few jokes or wise cracks but still had to know their place. They include "Beulah," "Benson", the wisecracking maid Florence of "The Jeffersons, and a host of others in movies. And don't forget Butterfly McQueen's youthful house worker line in "Gone With the Wind" when she made it clear, "I don't know nothin' 'bout birthin' no babies!"

And with the white man calling the shots, the image issue got worse even as he worked to "improve it:"

> In 1993, the Quaker Oats Company debuted a series of television ads for the pancake mix **featuring the singer Gladys Knight as a spokeswoman and using Aunt Jemima's face only sparingly.** They had the black, southern, Gladys Knight singing, smiling, and serving her 'grandkids'. There was no need for the picture when they had the real thing. It was a page right out of the Davis Milling Company's book. (Doneghy, 2018)

Up to that point Gladys Knight had been a powerful image in music and although her personal life involved some bad luck and poor mate selections, she was solid. Then she made the decision to become the face for Aunt Jemima. She did a commercial for Aunt Jemima syrup and sang the ditty, "If you want more flavor you can just stop lookin'/With Aunt Jemima – now you're cookin'."

Another sellout that has the white man laughing all the way to the bank. What a segue into the next section of our book. Hopefully you can see that the original "Jemima" was a slap in the face of black people, and it was one that black people for the most part, readily *accepted*.

SELLING OUT: BACKGROUND/HISTORY

In a society that is probably number one in the world in inducements and temptations, to not be a sellout is difficult. We can try but on some level we are made to be so dependent on even the most basic of needs that it is difficult to determine. When I use the term "sellout" I am talking about the selling out of views and values – the way Omarosa Manigault did to skin and grin (and probably screw) her way up the ladder, using her beauty and charisma to back one of the most racist men to ever serve as president and then turn right around later after being canned and claim that she was "tricked." More on that elsewhere in th is book.

According to Boyce Watkins, a man that I believe has been a sellout for a long period of time, an operational definition – one that he should be well aware of and acquainted with – is in order.

> What does it mean to be a sellout? Most of us grew up on this term, but I would be willing to bet that most of us don't know what the word actually means. Back in the 1980s, the term "sellout" applied to someone who was all too quick to give up his blackness in exchange for

a seat at the white man's table. It could also relate to someone willing to
do nearly anything to earn a buck. (Wakins, 2010).

In the last sentence Watkins just described himself. And that is what I am
talking about with these sistahs. They are not con artists, per se, but they do have
white people believing that they are "black" in terms of awareness when in reality
all they have is black skin. Even a broken clock can be right twice a day and that is
why I accept Dr. Maulana Karenga's 1967 definition of blackness when he writes,
"We say blackness is three things: color, culture and consciousness." This makes
sense to me because if blackness was just skin color, white folks with tans and
middle eastern would be deemed black. Which neither group is.

My point is that black celebrities become famous because white people
deem them as some kind of "representatives" or "models" that the masses of black
people should emulate and admire. One brutha, Michael Harriot, on a website
called "The Root" made some telling points that link con artists, fast talkers and
these sellouts to what I am writing about. Specifically pointing to Dr. Boyce
Watkins and his so-called "Black Business School," Harriott wrote:

> There are thousands of people who make a career out of this particular
> brand of **charismatic grifting.** Some of them are life coaches. Some of
> them are pastors. Some of them are "financial experts." The problem
> with Boyce Watkins, however, is that he lied. He misled his faithful to
> believe they were buying a product for, by and about black wealth, and it
> turns out that he was selling medicine to black people that turned out to
> be Kool-Aid.(Harriot, 2018)

What does this have to do with black female "Jemimahs"? They pawn off
their opinions as facts and dupe thousands of people into believing that they
actually "earned" what they have. The women I have selected are not beauties by
any stretch of the imagination. But one can listen to and watch their activities and
come to the conclusion that something took place "behind closed doors" – known
as "networking" or "a connection" to them – that was not above board and most
likely linked to selling out, the casting couch or a combination of the two.
Continuing:

> Obviously, being a sellout means that you've sold something. But
> that's not an entirely accurate definition, since we all sell
> something at some point. Most of us have been in situations where
> we wanted to take a stand on an issue, **but simply decided to
> choose our battles in order to protect our opportunities**. That
> doesn't necessarily make you weak, but there is a thin line between
> selling something and selling out completely. (Wakins, 2010 –
> emphasis added).

The majority of black people in this country have sold out, in my view. I have attended school with and worked with them. I have studied our history and its leadership. I have watched virtual morons who have black skin rise to high visibility in politics, society and educational standing. There is no way they would be there if they hadn't sold out and made a pact with the devil.

Watkins writes, "So, perhaps the term "sellout" means selling something of tremendous value in exchange for greater opportunity or financial prosperity. Can we agree on this definition? Good, now lets' get to the nitty-gritty. (Wakins, 2010). You see, the thing that is of "tremendous value" is your blackness. That is what the white man wants and needs. He cannot have skin color so he approximates himself with it, transforms the mind of the "colored" person and implies that everyone is white mentally and psychologically, just "different" when it comes to hue. That is why he considers it a compliment when he uses the term "color blind." What he is saying is that he doesn't see race because everybody is just alike – just like HIM. They may have different skin tones but everyone is accepting of white values, culture, norms, folkways and beliefs.

This is what is of tremendous value in my argument. And that which is offered up "in exchange for greater opportunity or financial prosperity" is where the problem lies. You give up what you are in exchange for fake inclusion in a system that has always hated your guts. In fact, that is one of the new buzz words of racist America: "inclusion." Add to it the terms "community engagement," "diversity," and "multiculturalism", and you have a promise that is given but never kept. So starved for humanity are black people that they have often questioned their own humanity. And white folks were the reason. And now these same people come forward seeking black allegiance in exchange for trinkets and other trivia.

Watkins, a charlatan along the same lines as Dr. Umar Johnson, explains that, "There was a time when an athlete, politician or celebrity was ridiculed for selling his/her soul for money. While we've always needed money to survive, there was always a set of standards and expectations to ensure that the individual didn't compromise his integrity during his climb up the ladder of power and success. We expected that a commitment to the community would certainly supersede almost anything else."(Wakins, 2010).

No there wasn't such a time. There was a time when black people who were conscious pointed fingers at blacks who sold out, but "ridicule"? No. Even while criticizing these blacks we nevertheless accepted them when they came back into the fold after seeing the error of their ways. People like Vanessa Williams and even the duplicitous Omarosa Manigault.

In the age of mass production, social media and the like, people like Boyce Watkins and Umar Johnson are on the intellectual end of the sellout scale. And their opinions are spewn forth to idiot millennials who spend far too much time on UTube and the trash that these kind of self-appointed "leaders" dole out.

For instance, Boyce claims,

> The 1980s changed all that. Great individuals like Harry Edwards
> (who led the Olympic Protest of 1968) toned down his message
> and began making gobs of cash from corporate America. Rather
> than having athletes like Muhammad Ali and Jim Brown, who took
> a stand on important social issues, we got men like **Tiger Woods
> and Michael Jordan, apolitical corporate puppets who take
> almost no public position on any important cause.** (Wakins,
> 2010 – emphasis added).

That is not what Dr. Harry Edwards did. Dr. Edwards actually flipped the script on peckerwoods and made them live up to their claims of wanting to have "fairness" on college campuses. He then became a consultant and got more black kids onto campus and stood up for black college athletes. If you read Edwards' *The Struggle That Must Be*, *Revolt of the Black Athlete* or **Black Students**, you will not read the words of a sellout, but of someone who has made a difference in his own way, walking the walk and talking the talk. In other words, the polar opposite of Boyce Watkins.

Then Watkins points to Muhammad Ali and Jim Brown as two athletes who took a stand. Yeah – back THEN when society was taking one. But don't forget that Ali was marched around the world to endorse the boycott of the 1980 Olympics. And don't forget that Jim Brown, even now, is selling out with his Amer-I-Can Program which is really nothing more than his making promises that he can't keep. Remember the sellout definition: something of tremendous value. In this case, the athletic AND political stands these men took. Now, they've gone back on it and with Ali dead, he is remembered more for being an "American icon" than for the man who stood up against the draft. And Jim Brown is just outright confused.

The evolution of selling out is one that is a lure used to entice the black masses into following in the footsteps of "coons." Just like Boyce Watkins makes promises of a "black business school" and offers little more than a community college course or two, and just like Dr. Umar Johnson proposes an "academy for black boys" – if you donate two million dollars – the end result of both of these is to funnel more blacks into the system or at least give the ILLUSION that they have a chance to get into the system – just like Affirmative Action did, remember?

Finally, Watkins has the unmitigated gall to write, "we got men like Tiger Woods and Michael Jordan, apolitical corporate puppets who take almost no public position on any important cause." Tell me: what public position on what "importance cause" are they supposed to take? Neither of them has credibility that goes beyond their respective sports, and both are married and chasing behind white women. They know what they are and because they couldn't take the heat from an audience about those choices, they stay out of the limelight. Woods has admitted that he's some kind of mixed breed, a self-defined, "Caucablasian," and Michael Jordan has ALWAYS been a sellout, even during his collegiate years.

Boyce needs to get his history and his economic facts straight. Or is he just lashing out at these two millionaire athletes because they wouldn't make a donation to his bullshit business school?

Moving right along, Watkins adds the following:

> **Selling out has become en vogue, and the trend is only going to continue**. We've decided that Bob Johnson having a billion dollars is more important than the fact that he nearly ruined an entire generation of young people in order to earn it. This is a sad day for our country and an especially sad time for black America. **In our quest to obtain what we want, we became all too quick to throw away everything that we need.** (Wakins, 2010 – emphasis added).

It seems to me that Dr. Boyce Watkins is writing about himself. How did Bob Johnson ruin an entire generation of young people? If he's talking about that Black Entertainment Television station, he should do his research. Just because black people show a police-dog like loyalty to something doesn't make it valid. I can say the same thing about Kathy Hughes and TVOne. They have stations and make money, but the relevance of their programming hails back to productions from the days when we didn't have stations, only the movies. They show classic black movies but they also show trash, mimicking what they see on white channels. How can you "ruin" an entire generation when you offered them nothing in the first place?

What does this have to do with black women selling out? Everything. Black women are the most successful element of our race. Black women in America are graduating from college and high school at a higher rate, starting businesses on their own and raising families as the white man arrests (mass incarceration) and guns down black men in the streets. And her strength is the "tremendous asset," along with her skin color, that the white man is targeting. Think back to the information provided about black female housekeepers and the rapes committed by white man. Well she's being economically raped once again and this time she doesn't appear to be putting up very much resistance.

JEMIMA'S ASSEMBLE!: A FORM OF SELF-HATE?

I often wondered as I see these individuals appear on talk shows, perform on stage or in some other televised or cinematic sphere, "is the paycheck waved from back stage so that culprit can see it or is there a refusal to automatically deposit it until the degrading act or statement is made"? One has to wonder to what extent these women will go to express an opinion to defend a position that makes them appear to be utter sellouts and indeed, "Aunt Jemimas?

Brennan (2003) provides us with important general insights when he writes,

> Now and throughout history, pejorative language has played a
> major role in the longstanding victimization of women … It [his
> study] concludes with observations about how this pernicious anti-
> female lexicon of derogation is part and parcel of a pervasive
> seamless shroud of anti-life rhetoric called upon to rationalize
> violence against other victims (born and unborn) in contemporary
> society and in times past.

In other words, are phrases, terms and words that paint a negative and insulting picture of women actually setting them up to be abused? Since what was just written is true, then we have to magnify and expand it when it comes to its application to black women. Black women have always been "thingified" just as the black male has been "beastified." It is therefore important to understand the English language and the symbols that we men have used to "thingify" females, and as a black man, I'm concerned about and committed to exploring this subject as it relates to the sisters. I am also concerned about how, in recent times, black men and women appear to have adapted this phraseology and applied it to themselves.

I would venture to say that 99% of black men in this country have referred to any woman as a "bitch" during their lifetime and that 98.9% still do, on occasion. It may be behind her back, but it's the attitude that counts, which means that we still feel that way about her, especially when she makes us angry. It's like the old joke teaches us: "A whore is a woman who will screw anybody; a bitch is a woman who will screw anybody – *but you.*" In *The Language of Oppression* (1974), Haig Bosmajian concluded:

> While the language of racial and ethnic oppression is often blatant
> and relatively easy to identify, the language of sexism is more
> subtle and pervasive. Our everyday speech reflects the

> "superiority" of the male and the "inferiority" of the female,
> resulting in a master-subject relationship. The language of sexism
> relegates the woman to the status of children, servants, and idiots,
> to being the "second sex" and to virtual invisibility . . . . *The
> language of sexism remains with us and exerts an influence on the
> male's attitudes towards and control over women and the women's
> attitudes towards themselves* (emphasis added).

The strained relations between black men and black women are, in my opinion, *the worst that exist between any racial grouping on this planet.* As a result, it might be added that our language (we do hail from an oral tradition) can also be the most coarse, hurtful, degrading and outright evil. Of course, the Anglo has enough power, money and connections to be able to hide his problems and besides that, he lives in a faraway suburb where the police will also cover up his domestic problems.

As black folk our issues, on the other hand, are in the "metro section" of every newspaper and on the 6:00pm news for all to see. Be that as it may, we all know that what I am writing is true: as a child when I told my friends that my mother and father were married and lived in the same house, most of them were shocked. And that was more than 50 years ago. And since its worse now, I think you have an idea that I know what I'm talking about.

This is the kind of "intimate alienation" that paves the way for the sister to be a target of extermination and to be an on-going victim of endangerment. Of course we need her – but in times of anger, frustration or hate, these are far too often the words that come out of our mouths after entering our minds. She may say it too, but when she says it, we have to admit that in far too many cases, she's right. After all, she can be broke and bothered on her own! Seriously though, an old friend of mine once shared these words with me: "If she ain't helpin' ya, she's hurtin' ya." This may seem trite and tragic – but I think it's true.

If you're not helping someone, then what else could you be doing but hurting them? Maybe it's not by design or on purpose, or maybe it's just because you are doing nothing physically or emotionally, but if it's not helping, knowing the plight that most black women are in, then in my book, it's hurtin.' In other words, why are you there? What do you do? Stand around and wait for an opportunity to leech? To beg? If you are not helping her in some way, then your mere presence is hurting her because you are wasting valuable skin and air with your existence.

Black men and women are in a strange situation when it comes to mate selection in America. For the most part, we are the darkest of all the people of color and as such, we stand out the most. What we do and what we like and enjoy seems to always be under surveillance. The manner in which we "woo and court" the female of our race has been studied, imitated and in many circles, admired. We black men are "cool," what some people would refer to as both suave and debonair. We have style and we are natural born talkers. Everybody admires that and black women are no exception.

White women are attracted to what we represent and the mythology that surrounds us. When they greet us they might shake our hand and smile, but their eyes are on our crotches. Most of them who are old enough want to know "if it's true," meaning, "do black men have huge dicks"? Many, especially those on high school and college campuses, are more than willing to find out.

The essential problem, as I see it, is that we don't control or own anything and in America, being cool and debonair and sexy oftentimes is not enough. Perhaps at one time during our history here, it was acceptable in certain circles. Immediately following slavery or immediately upon arriving in the North, black women had a different set of standards and the sexual mores of America were a lot different, more reserve and conservative – confined to certain spaces and certain places. But the more we were exposed to the Anglo, the more we interacted with white folks, and more we bought into the idea of supposedly being "free," the more freakish we became. Just like them. And this statement, in and of itself, goes a long way toward explaining our gradual alienation from black women and our own black families.

Self-hatred need not be visibly manifested, but many believe it is there and I believe so as well. Black women with dyed extensions in their hair, slathering on orange make-up, black kids shooting down each other in the streets. But I have written extensively on our history as a people and what I find is love, pride and unity, especially during the migration from the Deep South to the North (read my book, *Exodus!: Race, Migration and the Quest For a Better Life in Urban America*, available at Amazon.com. One article from Yolanda Olu of the *Gary Crusader* newspaper put it another way:

> Ironically, the condition of Black people and the self-hatred that is evident partially comes from a lack of **real education**. Blacks have been constantly force-fed the white version of history, and because of this, many Blacks have no clue about the truth of the Black past. It is hard for Blacks who tell non-traditional stories about Black history to be published and have their material used in public schools. It does happen here or there, but most elementary and secondary school students will probably never be exposed to the likes of the recently deceased Nigerian scholar, Dr. Catherine Obianuju Acholonu who wrote a series of scholarly texts demonstrating that there was a thriving civilization of Black people long before the creation of Adam. Also, Dr. Chancellor Williams, Dr. Ivan Van Sertima, and other pioneers have made significant contributions to knowledge of our past. (Olu, 2017)

Admittedly, I didn't know about the previous reference to Dr. Acholonu and I am a Black scholar and expert on the subject. Be that as it may, the low sense of self that prompts many of us to do the things way do may be motivated by money. But on the front end the lack of knowing who we are goes back to the previous section of this book on the sell out and how others are willing to purchase our tremendous gifts – gifts that we, due to our ignorance, may not be aware of or even appreciate.

As the article from the Crusader aptly asserted, "Ultimately, the Black condition will not improve until there is an understanding of the power and glory embedded in real Black history. This must come from research. The information is out there. A luta continua. (Gary Crusader, 2017). Until that time we seem to live to adore others while hating ourselves and seeking fortune, fame and so-called success "by any means necessary."

Parmer (1998), in her study titled, "Characteristics of Preferred Partners: Variations between African American Men and Women," examined the interaction of gender and education as influences on mate selection characteristics for 55 male and 111 female African American college students at a historically Black college/university. Students, age 17 to 38, were asked to rate 22 mate selection characteristics according to their importance in selecting a partner.

Although her population sample was obviously very limited, there is some information that is important for us to understand regarding this sample and her conclusions. For one thing, she found that the sisters who were upper class persons indicated that they knew about the "marriage squeeze" and the findings may show that they are willing to overlook or accept the money issues , compromise them, "perhaps settling for more primary needs such as love and emotional closeness in relationships" (Parmer, 1998). Personality scores were equally important for the men and the women.

But when it came to looks, black men were the ones that showed the same signs as the brothers on the street would show. As Parmer put it:

That African American men favored Physical Characteristics
(good health, chastity, good sex, good looks, same race, athletic,
sociability, and good cook) more than women did in this sample is
consistent with previous studies … Although men consistently
hold traditional physical mate-selection values, cultural differences
are believed to exist for African American men based on physical
characteristics such as good looks. Although physical
attractiveness was not explored in this study, the topic deserves
further study given that limited information is available about what
specific factors are important to African Americans …

And what are those factors, you may ask? We already know:

> Historically, members of the African American community have
> demonstrated concern for physical attractiveness associated with
> hair texture, skin color, body build, and facial features … Men
> have placed a greater value on White aesthetic values in regard to
> the notion of physical attractiveness … However, **since the "Black
> is Beautiful" movement of the 1960s and the 1970s, African
> Americans who value White standards of physical
> attractiveness are likely to be perceived as lacking a Black
> consciousness …** Although often unspoken, physical
> attractiveness continues to be important as a standard of beauty
> (Parmer, 1998 – emphasis added).

We know where this is leading: light skin, straight hair and Caucasian features. The sisters, they stick with us and do what they have to do with their features to get our attention. But as black men, we are petty and we are shallow. The process of selecting a partner is a universal phenomenon prevalent in nearly all societies. Questions concerning heterosexual preferred partner characteristics in the social science and family literature have been raised for several decades.

Some of the questions that we black men and women have to ask ourselves, maybe during some of those shouting matches that we refer to as "male-female relationship seminars," are questions like: How do men and women choose mates? What characteristics are important in the selection process? Do these characteristics differ by age, education, or ethnicity? One of the factors driving interest in mate selection is the significance of marriage in society, given the link to families and children. And even in that, the skin color of the child, which started during slavery, has been a subtle and not-so-subtle consideration. Black women knew that a light skinned child might stand a better chance in a racist society than a dark skinned child.

It would be a little satisfying to think that black men going after white women was our way of trying to save future children as well; that maybe if they were light they'd be better off. But we know better. Black men, for the most part, don't give a damn about the future of the black community. The on-going propaganda in the movies from blacks and whites telling us that "getting out of the ghetto" is the only way to go, has given us a view of the black community as only being a place rife with negativity. This goes way back to 1967; remember when Lou Rawls crooned "Dead End Street"? It went like this:

> I was born in a city the called the Windy City
> And they called it the Windy City because of the Hawk

The hawk. The all mighty Hawk
Mr. Wind
Takes care of plenty business around winter time
The place that I lived in
Was on a street that a
Happened to be one of the dead-end streets
Where there was nothing to block
The wind, the elements
Nothing to buffer them for me to
Keep them from knocking my pad down, you know
I mean really socking it to me
When the boiler would bust and the heat was gone
I would have to get fully dressed before I could go the bed
Cause I couldn't put on my goulashes cause they had buckles on them
And my folks didn't play that
They said "don't you tear up my bed clothes with some goulashes on"
But I was fortunate
As soon as I was big enough to get a job save enough money
To get a ticket to catch anything
I split
I said one day I'm going to return
And I'm going to straighten it all out
And I'm about ready to go back now
So I thought I'd tell ya about it

They say this is a big rich town
But I live in the poorest part
I know I'm on a dead-end street
In a city without a heart
I learned to fight before I was six
The only way I could get along
But when you're raised on a dead-end street
You've got to be tough and strong
Now all the guys I know are getting in trouble
That's how its always been
When the odds are all against you
How can you win, yeah, yeah, yeah

I'm going to push my way out of here
Even though I can't say when
But I'm going to get off of this dead-end street
And I ain't never going to come back again
Never
No, no, no

I'm going to push my way out of here

Even though I can't say when
But I'm going to get off of this dead-end street
And I ain't going to never come back again
No, no, no
I ain't going to come back to this city street no more

No - Cause I'm going to get me a job
I'm going to save my dough
Get away from here
I ain't going to come back no more
I'm tired of a dead-end street
I want to get out in the world and learn something
I'm tired of breaking my back
I want to start using my mind

Malcolm X taught us that you can't hate the root of a tree and not hate the tree itself. You can't hate Africa and our African features and not hate the people that have those features. That includes yourself. And if you're surrounded by many people who look like you do, confined to an area of the city because of racial segregation, redlining, steering and the like, then you have a recipe for what could be called "collective hate." And as a result the "escape the ghetto" (which you hear prospective college and professional athletes talking about all the time) becomes priority number one.

While the black men in Parmer's study emphasized good looks, other college aged students do not. They could be lying, of course, but even if they were, it means that they knew that caring for someone because they "look good" is scandalizing. Evidently black men either don't care what other people think or they're too naïve or ignorant to know. This was the way it is now, and even as far back as 1945:

> Hill's (1945) study conducted with college students at the University of Wisconsin was one of the earliest studies of mate selection in the social sciences. Hill asked students to select desirable attributes in a mate from a list of 18 characteristics. Students considered the most important characteristics to be dependable character, emotional stability, maturity, and pleasing disposition. When considering gender differences, women placed a higher value on ambition and industriousness in preferred partners whereas, in contrast, men placed more emphasis on having a mate who was a good cook and housekeeper. Although not ranked high on either list, good looks were more important for men than for women, whereas having a mate with good financial prospects was more important for women than for men.

There was a black study conducted at about the same time, in 1949, also regarding mate selection. This one took place on another black college campus, in North Carolina. The Himes study,

> … was administered to 130 male and female students using a two-part questionnaire that contained 27 factors. Both groups ranked mutual attraction as the most important factor of the top six characteristics. Men ranked self-control as second and sociability as fourth followed by economic security, sex appeal, and being considerate.

My how the times have changed! Of course mutual attraction would be first at a time when people cared about people that cared about them. But today, the women seem to be more concerned about what a man can do, "ain't no romance without finance" and other business-related variables. I'm not saying its necessarily wrong – it's just different. Men ranked self-control fairly high – and that was at a time when both men and women actually had some! Moving on to the sisters:

> Women selected attractive disposition, neatness and refinement, and good health as their top-valued characteristics. Himes concluded that the six top-ranked factors indicated a "deep concern with marital compatibility and harmonious personal relations with prospective mates" (p. 208). The least valued factors were ambition for social status, desire for children, similar education, religion, politics, and hair texture. Factors ranked as relatively unimportant in the Himes study were skin color, height, weight, social status, economic status, educational level, and age.

So in 1949 – 60 years ago – skin color and hair texture were no big deal for us. We may have been segregated, but we loved each other and looked for good qualities and thought about marriage. Look at the movies that try to re-capture those ideals, movies like "Lackawanna Blues," "Devil in a Blue Dress," and "The Cotton Club." I, for one, came in on the tail end of seeing black men opening doors for black women, calling older black women "ma'am" and so on. A black man that had a good job and was in a position to take care of a family was just as big a catch for a sister as the good looking, well-dressed brother. Probably even moreso. Doesn't seem that way today with the male-female ratio being as skewed as it is.

Some can attempt to "intellectualize" what is taking place is they choose to. For instance, Parma (1998) offers the following to explain both the skewed male-female ratio and the non-availability of black men:

An examination of current statistics may explain how experiences with racism and oppression have impacted the institution of marriage, as more eligible African American men are disenfranchised through negative experiences with the justice and educational systems. For example, in the United States, African American men are disproportionately represented in correctional institutions. This finding may reflect the fact that enrollment of African American males in elementary and secondary special education classes has increased and enrollment in higher education has declined … Lack of education, and the subsequent disenfranchisement are likely to decrease African American men's availability as potential mates.

And then comes the clincher: "The extent to which the African American family is able to survive poverty and achieve a measure of stability may rest with the educational attainment of African American men and women … The hope for strong, productive, and unified Black families of the future rests, to a great extent, with college students who must serve as models. Poor relations between Black college students, however, seriously threaten this group's contribution to the building of strong Black families."

Poor relations? I've been on many college campuses and I don't see poor relations between black males and coeds. What I see are "alienated arrangements conducted in private and on the sly. I see sisters doing the homework of these black men and some of them cutting classes and leaving to head either to the dorm room or to the apartment down the street. But thing about it is no one is talking about a real relationship or getting married. It's more like girl-swapping and man-swapping than anything that could be construed as real or rockstrong.

That is why I say that it is ridiculous to reply on college students for anything that has to do with the black family – that is unless the sister or the black man already has children and in that case, going to school might give them another option as far as employability.

Might.

And now the sister is starting to see the light, as it were. Many sell out, others turn to lesbianism, and a few opt for abstinence. But this book concentrates on the former "strategy," and now I would like to address some of the people that I have placed in the category of sellouts or, more specifically, "clowns" for the Caucasian.

THE CAST OF CLOWNS

Diana Ross

While many will argue that interracial dating and marriage are not signs of "selling out," I have to say that when one of the people is white, it most certainly is. People of color can intermarry and there's no major problem with me. But when that white man and woman tie the knot of matrimony, I hail back to the days when they were tying knots in lynch ropes and placing those ropes around the necks of black men and women. And as Malcolm taught long ago, "Of all our studies, history is best qualified to reward our research.

She may have been born in Detroit, but I don't see her as being OF Detroit. She just always struck me as an opportunistic bitch, Berry Gordy's former concubine, and a talented singer who didn't want to share the stage with the other members of The Supremes.

According to her bio, she was raised in a Baptist church and sang in the choir. But some of the biggest whores I ever bedded were the daughters of ministers or "sang in the choir." The choir was nothing but their cover for the lascivious acts they got away with behind mama and daddy's backs.

I go back to a 1973 Rolling Stone article about Diana titled "Diana Ross Goes From Riches to Rags: 'You Have to, Like, Glide …'" . And I will quote extensively from it and retrospectively analyze what it says. Remember that the article I am about to quote from is 45 years old, and the fact that Ms. Ross changed very little in terms of her uncle tomfoolery proves the true tenacity and trait of a Jemima.

And now, the article, the evidence – and the indictment:

> Diana Ross is going out of her mind. She just threw a glass of champagne in somebody's face, and now it's the bathroom scene in *Lady Sings the Blues*, and she's running amuck with a razor. Billy Dee Williams won't give her back her works and she's raving for a fix – snarling like a rabid bitch, teeth and nails and then she gets a cut-throat razor and goes for the throat and she means it. When they got through somebody asked Billy Dee if he thought Diana Ross could act. (Thomas, 1973)

That was not acting. I always saw Diana as some ghetto star, a street corner slut that Berry Gordy immediately spotted and decided to put on the corner. She comes across like somebody who knew she had talent, but also was always willing to do whatever it took to get it, and WITH whomever it took to get it. She was raised in a black community in Detroit, got exposed to Berry Gordy and Motown, and from there started meeting powerful white men – most of whom she probably screwed. At any rate, she saw that she fit the model of white man's version of beauty: boney, no tits, flat ass and eyes bulging out of her head. Not quite the standards that bruthas envision when they're thinking up their concept of "thickness."

But she sells an entirely different image to the white media and to those who want to see her as some kind of "rags to riches" story. For instance, the Rolling Stone reporter wrote the following:

> Here was this little slinky, not long out of the Supremes; and it's common knowledge the **Supremes were a consummate corporate invention, with Diana Ross in her ravishing wigs and dazzling shimmer and gloss, working the most amazing pair of livid red lips in America over a faceful of blinding white teeth,** animating and insinuating her 103 pounds of lean sheen – she's exquisite, polished till she shines. But the girl never acted in her life except for a couple of dumb skits on Johnny Carson, **and here she is with the audacity to impersonate the most beloved jazz martyr of all time**. There were a lot of people outraged. Diana got a lot of spiteful letters, **a lot of them from righteous old black jazz veterans.** (Thomas, 1973 l- emphasis added)

Why didn't those "righteous old black jazz veterans" inform Ross and the others that Billie Holiday was a dyke? Why didn't they do more than just mention the drug addiction, and where does Billy Dee's role fit in. Holiday, like Ma Rainey, Alberta Hunter, Ethel Waters and even Bessie Smith. They might have messed around with men but that was a front: these sistahs were dykes pure and simple. And so was Billie Holiday.

Furthermore, the article lists the Supremes as a "consummate corporate invention," which they were. They were shined up and taught manners. They paraded into white clubs and so on and with that Motown sound, won over millions of white listeners. Berry Gordy taught them how to be Jemimas of the highest order. But even after Diana left the Supremes, mostly because of ego, she continued to tom and kiss ass and that's how she landed that movie role that is the subject of this 1973 article.

Continuing:

> And tight up against her, here's Billy Dee Williams, coming off a big break in *Brian's Song* on TV, a hot new black leading man with ten or twelve years in the theater under his belt – a seasoned actor – so he had his doubts about her, too. And then early on in the shooting they come to the bathroom scene and Diana Ross throws this fit and Billy Dee had to fight for his life. I don't know, says Billy Dee, I don't know if she can play Billie Holiday – she *is* Billie Holiday. And Williams has got scars to prove it.(Thomas, 1973)

That "big break" in Brian's song showed the world that Williams could also be a tom. After all, he was playing the role of Gale Sayers, a bootlicker from Omaha, Nebraska who, like other Omaha athletes who turned professional (Bob Boozer, Bob Gibson, Ron Boone, Michael McGee) turned their backs on black people and never looked back. Sayers remained a tom long after his football days and although injury cut his career short, he wrote a book that showed how subservient he was in life. The title of his book was I Am Third. What he meant is that god was first, his friends and family are second, and he comes in third. The perfect formula for an uncle tom – and the subject of a movie to influence (one-way) integration.

I remember when it was aired. They showed this peckerwood Brian Piccolo playing running back and Sayers beat him out. But they became friends, and I am talking about the white man's version of interracial friendship. That means that they feel free to call you "nigger." And that's just what Piccolo did. And when he died from cancer, Sayers was right there kissing his ass and giving that speech that will go down in history. Mike Puma of ESPN documented the situation as Sayers, who had won the rushing title, appeared for his award at a ceremony in New York. Here is what that uncle tom said:

> "He has the heart of a giant and that rare form of courage that allows him to kid himself and his opponent -- cancer," Sayers told the audience. "He has the mental attitude that **makes me proud to have a friend who spells out the word 'courage' 24 hours a day of his life**. . . . I love Brian Piccolo, and I'd like all of you to love him, too. **Tonight, when you hit your knees, please ask God to love him."** (Puma, 1971 – emphasis added)

The movie that was made was called "Brian's Song." A third rate football player with a movie named after him, featuring a Hall of Fame running back that kisses his ass throughout the same flick. This movie catapulted Billy Dee Williams into the hearts of America, spreading that black-white integration friendship bullshit. And Billy Dee landed many a role after that, including the one of Lando Calrissian in "Star Wars."

I only add this information to show you how one tommish act can began another. Williams was a proven tom and Diana was as well. Put them together to earmark an important point and personality in black music history and you can distort that history will just enough bullshit to make that movie a hit. And there was the pimp to guide the Jemima "prostitute":

> Berry Gordy was there. It's his picture, he put in close to four million dollars of Motown money, **and Diana Ross is his most treasured**

> **possession,** so he stayed close to the production. **And when Billy Dee said that, Berry dug it right away.** You've seen the ads by now, just the slim bejewelled wrist clutching an old RKO mike, a handcuff dangling like a manacle, and in classy bold type on top it says: DIANA ROSS **IS** BILLIE HOLIDAY. (Thomas, 1973 – emphasis added)

Two uncle toms, the first one who is Berry Gordy claiming that Diana was his "possession" (pimp mentality) and the other one falling for the promotion of that pimp, teamed up on someone who was more than happy and willing to prostitute herself for fame, and the 1972 movie was a runaway hit. But it did a disservice to Billie Holiday despite the sound track. Adding Richard Pryor as piano man was a good public relations move, but totally irrelevant to the real life of Holiday or Bobby Tucker, who was the real "piano man." He wasn't beaten to death by some thugs – he died of a heart attack in 2008 – some 36 years after the movie hit the screens.

> Ralph Gleason goes along with that, and John Hammond, and a lot of those other respected old hepcats who should know, because they were there. **They saw Billie Holiday come painfully apart, stitch by stitch, and along the way, because she couldn't help it, she sang jazz better than anybody had ever heard before.** She broke all the rules – changed the whole idea of the singer in the band to where she was no longer just another sideman stuck back behind the clarinet player and taking 16 bars of swift vocal. **She became the star of the show. Everybody from Ella Fitzgerald on down has been trying to catch up with her ever since.** (Thomas, 1973 – emphasis added)

Respected old "hepcats"? This writer is a revisionist. These white boys sat back and copped dope for Billie to continue getting high. And when she was high she was at her best. The white boys knew what she was up to and kept hit hidden. That's what these "hep cats" did to her. She broke all the rules of right, and did so because she was a lesbian and an addict. Diana only played the dope user part of Holiday's life. And that part about Ella Fitzgerald trying to catch up: they caught up, alright. You see what the other women were about in their private lives. I can't say the same thing about Ella, but her third husband was a white man named Thor Larsen.

So much for the Jemima influence and the complicity of the uncle toms who inspire and motivate them.

> Billie Holiday sang with the best bands there were, Teddy Wilson and Benny Goodman and Count Basie, all of them, and she was the first to sing as zingingly as they played. She brought a high radiance and

<blockquote>
sophistication into those steamy little Harlem cellars and took it all downtown to the plushest nitespots and finally into the sacred hush of Carnegie Hall. She hid nothing. **All her devotees knew she was banged out on stuff up there, they knew where she went when she left the bandstand in between numbers and came back with a faraway gleam in her eyes and made every song she sang into a stylized personal confession of hurt pride and carnal knowledge**. For those that knew and adored her, she remains the immaculate and tragic aristocrat of jazz, the saddest story of them all. (Thomas, 1973 – emphasis added)
</blockquote>

What did I tell you. The article refers to them as "devotees" but the fact is they knew she was going backstage for a "hit." She was fucked up by the time she got on stage, high as a kite. And this is the point that Diana drove home because I believe that boney bitch was a junkie herself at one time.

The rest of the article is the writer showing off his command of flowery language and descriptive uses of the Diana Ross situation. I left out the bullshit to get to the point that establishes the Jemima tradition. For instance, where it is written that,

<blockquote>
… Diana Ross' achievement is not so much in bringing Billie Holiday back from the dead for a couple of hours in the dark; she has sought and found a Billie Holiday who never lived – beyond all the blues. "I believe that if we had stuck straight to what we had in the book, we would've had a documentary about a lady that was just one tragedy after another. **I read between the lines and I tried to find that other side of Billie Holiday that wasn't in the book, that's not on the back of album covers.** I tried to find the person that Billie Holiday was at home, that very few people knew about." (Thomas, 1973)
</blockquote>

The article says that Diana "sought and found a Billie Holiday who never lived …" Then it wasn't about Billie Holiday! Diana couldn't cut it and therefore the producers, writers and directors said, "Fuck it," let's just make a movie and tell people that it's "sort of" like the life of Billie Holiday. They'll buy it." And buy it they did. Peckerwoods, working with uncle toms, butchered what Billie Holiday was about and marched out this boney, bug-eyed prostitute who would do anything for fame and glory. That's why they omitted the lesbian part – had they included that the gay community, quiet as it was back then, would have nevertheless been up in arms. Don't forget a large number of those Jewish Hollywood movie moguls are gay.

The fluff piece in Rolling Stone claims,

> **But Berry Gordy believes in making people happy**. Not just because
> he's moved zillions of Motown 45s that way, but because he's a happy
> man, and he truly believes as an article of faith that what the world needs
> now is love – it's his *philosophy*. That's why he got Michel Legrand to
> write a heartstruck love theme for the picture. (Thomas, 1973) (Thomas,
> 1973)

Making people happy? He believes in making money, and he peddles just as many songs about grief and bitterness as he did about so-called happiness. And a lot of those pity party, woe-is-me jams were crooned by none other than Diana. For instance "Love Child," "I'm Living in Shame," "Last Time I Saw Him," "Good Morning Heartache," "Reach Out and Touch," "Touch Me in the Morning" – do these sound like "happy songs" to you? Like Aretha, Gladys Knight and a slew of black female singers, they sung about depression and grief. They belted out lyrics written by men and in the process, they degraded themselves. And black people ate it up.

The Supremes were good but Diana was the star. According to the article and Berry Gordy,

> **The girls had been singing a little bit here and there, and on the
> block they met Smokey Robinson, and it was he that first introduced
> them to Berry.** The Primettes they were called, because back then about
> 1963 there was a brief period when brother and sister groups were very
> popular, and Motown had a new act called the Primes at the time. **The
> Primes changed their name to the Temptations, and the Primettes
> were left a little in the lurch, so they became the Supremes**. More or
> less on the spur of the moment, in 1964, the girls had "Where Did Our
> Love Go" and it was a smash. **"We did have a little school. For
> choreography. And we had a lady who taught the girls how to talk
> and act and sit nicely. . . ."** (Thomas, 1973 – emphasis added)

You see how it works. Smokey just so happens to "meet" these girls "on the block." On the "ho stroll" would be more like it. Smokey was probably out there hounding for pussy behind Claudine's back and came across these three cuties who told them they wanted to be stars. He had green eyes and light skin and of course he probably cut a deal. But the main thing is that he introduced them to a man with a pimp mentality, a man who took them under his wing, gave them an "identity" and had a woman teach them how to kiss ass and act as white as possible. They call it etiquette classes.

Check out the following:

> You can picture it, some stern old dowager in an enormous hat and too
> many bracelets putting these foxy little starlets through their paces –

Diana is walking around the room with a book on her head. She slips both legs demurely to one side as she sits for that kind of question-mark symmetry of posture. "How many times must I tell you, when a lady mounts a grand piano, she does not climb, Miss Ross. She *glides!*" Whatever it was, the Motown charm school took the kinks out, and the Supremes came out just right, three little kittens with a lot of droll feline moves and long sharp nails, svelte, slinky and a little bit naughty, singing stuff like *Are you just a breathtaking first night soul-shaking one night love-making next day heart-breaking guy* . . . (Thomas, 1973 – emphasis original)

Charm school. Transforming street girls into "ladies." But Diana had game and she saw right away that if she gave away enough ass and batted those lovely eyes at the right person, she could get whatever she wanted. How do you think they went from "The Supremes" to "Diana Ross and the Supremes"?

The Temptations were producing hits and so was Stevie Wonder. But the Jemima had her sets sight on being *numero uno,*

… because right from the start Diana was very quick to catch on and she learned fast. She'd sit there and watch what all the other acts did, some particular two-step reverse kick-and-swivel grandstand maneuver the Temptations might have, the way Stevie Wonder kind of half swallowed a key rhyme, **any little winning trick at all–then she'd get up there in front and steal their thunder.** Pretty soon she was getting down in her silver fishnets and going "A little bit softer now . . . a little bit louder now . . ." "She stole everybody's act," says Berry. **"When they came on, they looked ridiculous. They had to change their act every day. They all hated her."** (Thomas, 1973 – emphasis added)

She was a divider, a selfish egotist and an opportunist from the get-go. You see what Gordy just said about her: she was stealing from other groups and incorporating it into her own "style." In doing so that put the pressure on the other acts to revamp their own presentations. This is what Jemimas do: they disrupt in order to gain attention for themselves. That is what the women named in this book, from Candace Owens, Stacey Dash and Sheryl Underwood to Condoleezza Rice, Whoopi Goldberg and Omarosa Manigault do – they curry favor with men of power, usually men of another race, turn their backs on their own people, and then head out on their own hoping for individual glorification.

In the case of Motown and Diana's activities, "They came to BG and complained bitterly, and he straightened her out. But by then the Supremes had five hits in a row, and they were moving up in the Revue, right behind Smokey. They never did close the show, though" (Thomas, 1973) Berry didn't straighten anybody out. He was an expert at the bureaucratic style. He pulled her to the side, probably took her to a hotel, laid in bed with her and told her to slow down a little bit because "the hits will be coming." Then he went back and told the complainers that he "straightened her out." With all the backstabbing and sellout behavior that she continues to exhibit even today in 2018, does it seem that this Jemima was ever "straightened out"?

You see, as the racist reference in the article points out, "Berry Gordy and Diana were raised in the same part of **darkest Detroit**; they both remember the Shakers running the block – they were the local cut-and-rape street gang, and their chicks were called the Shakerettes. Billie Holiday was across town, at the Flame Showbar, and Berry used to go there all the time." (Thomas, 1973 – emphasis added). So they were both street wise and transformed it into something that was marketable. Gordy had a pimp mentality and Diana had a prostitute orientation: they were a perfect symbiotic match.

Read carefully the following excerpt because the writer's racism shines through and so does the histrionic behavior of Diana Ross:

> When she first quit the Supremes, she got lonely – she used to go and watch them a lot. She'd always been the one in the middle and she had long ago stepped out front of the other two – there was that sudden switch she pulled one night on a television special called *TCB* with the Supremes and the Temptations, where they just flashed a series of shots of **Diana enraged and unbound**, her Afro humming with untold combustible voltage, each pose **more sultry and menacing** than the last, every one a snapshot of terrifying and **almost deadly Mau Mau beauty**–and then she was revealed in a single soft spot, in a shimmer of pristine silver, singing "Someday/there'll be a place for us." But there was comfort in the Supremes, and some people thought she was taking a chance shedding her cover. She came out with "Ain't No Mountain High Enough." (Thomas, 1973 – emphasis added)

What was just described is the behavior of a paranoid schizophrenic, someone who is a "shape shifter." She's a Jemima and is therefore an expert at flipping her allegiances and moon walking over to the highest bidder. The writer is describing her in such a way that she sounds far more dramatic than she is; she's just someone who doesn't give a damn about anyone but herself. And in the process of chasing that "gold ring" (read; closest white man), she will do what has to be done. I'm surprised she didn't raise up her dress and show her panties to the world!

The article continues:

> She's not so easy to push around any more either. One time in Las Vegas she saw Sinatra's show, and a few bars into "My Way" something was a little off, so Frank just said "OK! Hold it!" and he gave the band a little venom and then he started again from the top. **If Diana doesn't like the way her show is going, she's likely to flare up the same way one of these nights. BG says she can get real bitchy about it.** (Thomas, 1973)

This bitch ain't NEVER been "easy to push around." Any time it took place it was part of a scam, a plan to front like she was "boney and defenseless." Other than that, Diana was the kind of woman who would scratch your eyes out if you pissed her off. That scene with the straight razor that you saw in "Lady Sings the Blues" – that was the REAL Diana! Even the previous excerpt makes the statement that, "If Diana doesn't like the way her show is going, she's likely to flare up the same way one of these nights. BG says she can get real bitchy about it."

This was in 1973 when Diana was 28 – that means that today in 2018 this Jemima has reached the ripe old age of 73:

> Diana's 28 now, **married to a PR man called Bob Silberstein**, the mother of two kids, one 15 months and another, Tracee Joy, born a few weeks ago. It's been a couple of years now since she outgrew the Supremes and became Diana Ross full-time. And now she's a movie star as well, and there are precious few of those left, and none who are as well-bred for the role as Diana. (Thomas, 1973)

So she marries ANOTHER white man, and this time she landed herself a Jew. And a powerful one at that. Here is a snippet on how they "hooked up":

> In the 1970s, **he managed Diana Ross**, the Rolling Stones' Ronnie Wood,[5][7], Billy Preston and Chaka Khan whom he discovered while managing Rufus. **Silberstein was born into a wealthy family of Jewish garment manufacturers in Elberon, New Jersey** … He graduated from West Virginia University and tried teaching. Silberstein was married to Diana Ross from 1971 to 1977.[5] They have two biological children together: Tracee Ellis Ross, and Chudney Ross.[6] He also raised Ross' eldest child Rhonda Ross Kendrick, **whose biological father is Motown founder Berry Gordy.** (Wikipedia, 2018 – emphasis added)

Look at the spin this obviously white writer puts on the kind of two-faced bitch Ross is and downplays her "Jemima-ism":

> She is living proof that **stars who really shine are not born, they're professionally made.** After all, down in the ghetto in Detroit with six kids in the family and holes in the walls where the rain came in and

> roaches everywhere and Dad working two jobs at the garage – **a pretty little fox like Diana could've been a hooker, like Billie Holiday.**"I could've been, that's true. The girls that I did see that were prostitutes were beautiful ladies. They looked good. We kind of knew what they were doing but not really. They were nice people. **It was a profession, you know. It would've been easy for me.** (Thomas, 1973 – emphasis added)

Three points from the previous passage shows that the writer knows that Diana is a prostitute and furthermore that she almost admits it.

First, the claim by the writer that stars are not born but are professionally made. That is bullshit. If you have no talent then there is nothing to "make". Stars have natural talent and professional shylocks like her husband and others (and Berry Gordy) come along and pimp that talent, market it, roll it and control it. All "professionals" do is exploit that which they view as being marketable

Secondly, the writer describes Diana's lousy living conditions and then adds that, "a pretty little fox like Diana could've been a hooker, like Billie Holiday." Can you see how he's made the connection? Using terms like "pretty little fox," the kind of slang that a street playa would use. She had all the makings of a hooker, the location of a hooker and the attitude of a hooker. This leads to my third point.

He quotes Diana as saying, "It was a profession, you know. It would've been easy for me." If she saw all that then she went after it. It is only now, with the benefit of retrospect, that she tries to make it sound that as a poor child with no money, and with men walking by drooling over her, she simply shook her head "no" and looked the other way. Bullshit! She's all but confessed about how good the prostitutes looked and how nice they were. You know they gave her advice, a tip here and a tip there. And since she's a prostitute now that she's famous, you KNOW she must have been one when she was poor. Did she or did she not make a song called "I'm Living in Shame"?

The article continues:

> **Because it's difficult to figure out ways to get out of what the white man calls the ghetto. Either black people end up being the best in sports, or else it's show business.** You know, we all got rhythm. Or some of the girls **make their money to drive around in Cadillacs and have beautiful clothes by being prostitutes, selling their bodies**. I knew a lot of pimps. It's a possibility if I had've got strung out over one of these guys it could've been me. If I had fallen in love. . . ." (Thomas, 1973 – emphasis added)

What she said in that first sentence is all the most reason for her to take her boney ass out on that ho stroll. Getting out of the ghetto is one explanation that uncle toms and Jemimas use to rationalize their selling out. Look back to those lyrics to Lou Rawls' "Dead End Street" that I shared with you earlier. And once again she's focused on the nice cars and clothes that prostitutes have. Diana Ross knows full well what she was and what she still is: a gold-digging Jemima, with some talent, who will do what it takes to live as "white" and away from black people, as possible.

Diamond and Silk (Lynette Hardaway and Rochelle Richardson)

You may not have heard of them and if you haven't, you ain't missed much. With the likes of Paris Denard and other negro conservatives kissing Trump's ass, these two women may have been lost in the shuffle (no pun intended). But they are mentioned here because their views qualify them for what can only be referred to as "the Hall of Shame."

Known as Diamond and Silk (Lynette Hardaway and Rochelle Richardson, respectively, they were raised to be bullshit artists because they had role models. According to one source, "Hardaway and Richardson are the daughters of **husband and wife televangelists** … currently affiliated with Jericho Deliverance Temple church in Raeford, North Carolina … During a 2016 interview with *Newsweek*, they were "reluctant" to give their ages but stated they are "old enough to vote".(Wikipedia, 2018). Bullshit artists with something to hide – just like their parents. Peddling that Christian bullshit to gullible black people just like the two sisters, Diamond and Silk, peddle that conservative Trump line to anyone dumb enough to accept it.

Who are these women, you may ask. In a nutshell,

> Lynnette Hardaway and Rochelle Richardson, popularly known
> as Diamond and Silk, are American live-stream video bloggers, social
> media personalities and political activists. They are known for their
> commentary in support of United States President Donald Trump.
> (Wikipedia, 2018) .

Two overweight women who choose names that are the opposite of what their looks remind you of when you see them. They start off small, as most bloggers do, and then figure out a way to get some major attention. I will share with you how these Jemimas puled that off.

First, the usual bold-faced lies:

> The duo received media attention during the 2016 campaign and again in
> April 2018 when they reported that Facebook had notified them they
> were "unsafe to the community", and when they accused Facebook of
> blocking and censoring their Facebook page. There is no evidence that

Facebook blocked or censored Diamond and Silk's Facebook page. In
April 2018, Republican members of Congress brought up the duo's
censorship claims at Mark Zuckerberg's testimony before U.S. Congress.
(Wikipedia, 2018).

Since the Republicans have a history of lying, what these two skanks were
able to do was right up the right wing alley. So now they had a little fame from
white men (the target of all Jemimas) and they were on their way.

These bitches were insane from jump Street. They reacted to Trump the way
someone with a white mindset would react – and that is how Jemimas think. Note
fhe following:

> Formerly Democrats … their switch to the Republican Party occurred
> when they saw Trump announce his candidacy on television. **According
> to Hardaway, "When he announced and we heard everything that
> he stood for, it was on and poppin', and we've been on the Trump
> train ever since."** … They came to wider prominence in 2015 as
> supporters of then-presidential candidate Donald Trump after posting a
> video **criticizing former Fox News host Megyn Kelly for asking what
> they considered irrelevant questions during the first Republican
> presidential debate .**(Wikipedia, 2018 – emphasis added)

Of course they were "formerly Democrats" in the same way that these
Jemimas – all of the ones that I have covered in this book – were "formerly black"
before they turned into some kind of "Afro-Saxons" (as Nathan Hare would call
them). These coons switched because that is where the money is at and Obama
could not run for office again. So these opportunistic negroes made their move.

Now they say that when they heard Trump outline "everything he stood for,"
they were on the "Trump train." These bitches were out to get paid and get on
television no matter what the cost. In America, negative publicity is still publicity,
and with their look – two fat women with attitudes – they would be able to provide
plenty of "comic relief" to the political scene, and provide it they did.

By questioning the blond and racist Megyn Kelly, they again showed the
Republicans that they would attack anyone who attacked Trump. Like the true
lapdogs that they apparently hope to be, Diamond and Silk were a part of the "cast
of clowns" that the Republican Party had lined up as representing black folks: Paris
Denard, Omarosa Manigault, Ben Carson, and a few others. But these Jemimas
combined street lingo with political commitment and were able to finagle
appearances on some major television programs.

> Although **officially unaffiliated with the Trump campaign**, they urged
> support for Trump via **social media efforts and rallies and traveled to**

> **three states for the campaign …** The duo first joined Donald Trump as the "Stump for Trump Girls" on stage at his Raleigh, North Carolina, rally on December 4, 2015 … They later warmed up the crowd at the Trump rally on January 2, 2016, in Biloxi, Mississippi … They initiated a "Ditch and Switch" campaign to encourage Democrats to register as Republicans … and created a website explaining to voters which states had closed primaries and when the deadlines were for changing party affiliations .(Wikipedia, 2018 – emphasis added)

These "toms" were putting in work! Trump doesn't claim them. They don't have any kind of executive clearances. They're just two fat black bitches who work for chump change and appeared on stage as Trump was campaigning in front of lily white, racist audiences with few if any blacks in sight. For instance,

> On November 2, 2016, Diamond and Silk appeared with Lara Trump, wife of Eric Trump, in Winston-Salem, North Carolina, on behalf of the Trump campaign … **They were paid $1,274.94 for field consulting work by the Trump campaign …** They regularly appear on Fox News shows including *Hannity*, *Fox News Sunday*, *Watters' World*, and *The Ingraham Angle*, and Fox & Friends … as well as ABC's *Nightline* … **Hardaway is notably more talkative, while Richardson often just expresses agreement … .**(Wikipedia, 2018 – emphasis added)

Bums performing "stunts for bumps" like two crack head bitches willing to perform any sex act for a hit off the pipe (which is also known as "the glass dick"). They were where they had to be, and that small amount mentioned that they were paid was probably pulled out of Eric Trump's wallet. These women were the laughing stock. And that explains their "regular appearances on the TV shows mentioned above.

Both can't be talkative. But as it is with all good comedy teams, one has the charisma and the other is the stooge. Martin and Dean featured Deano while Jerry made an ass out of himself; Abbott and Costello featured Costello, but it was Abbott who was the brains of the outfit; Laurel and Hardy were together 28 years and Oliver Hardy was the logical one who made an ass out of his hilarious sidekick, Stan Laurel. And now we have Diamond and Star.

But it is their views on race and related issues that shows that these Jemimas are on the same level as Whoopi Goldberg was the time she showed "understanding" for Ted Danson's blackface appearance at the Friar's Club roast. These women don't necessary go full bore to the right, but their stands on issues show an abysmal ignorance of what is going on racially and politically in this country. As Wikipedia (2018) explains their "racial views,"

> Following the controversial Unite the Right rally held in Charlottesville,
> Virginia, on August 11 and 12, 2017, Hardaway and Richardson,
> appearing on *Fox & Friends*, were critical of both the far-right and far-
> left groups taking part in the event. Hardaway criticized Neo-
> Nazi groups and the Ku Klux Klan for "spewing hate and ... creating
> violence" declaring "all of them should be condemned and denounced.
> Period". In the same interview, she also said she does not "... like Black
> Lives Matter and Antifa." They further noted that they feel statues
> of Civil War Confederate soldiers should be kept in museums
> .(Wikipedia, 2018)

I am in agreement that those civil war statues should not be torn down, but my reasons are different. I want them to remain so that future generations of white and black people can see the racist assholes who were responsible for murdering off First Nation people, enslaving black people, and making life hell on earth for the rest of this nation. But as for that other shit, these women merely stated the obvious, which was more than what Trump would do. But they made it appear like there was "problems on both sides" in the same way Trump did.

> Hardaway and Richardson, in December 2017, expressed support
> for Omarosa Manigault Newman following her controversial firing
> as White House liaison and assistant, faulting the treatment of her by
> African Americans and the media generally: "What I find appalling, to
> my brothers and sisters [is] how you ... can laugh at, pick at, gloat at
> somebody because they either left the White House or you listened to a
> salacious story that Miss Piggy went around, running around telling
> everybody." (Wikipedia, 2018).

With Omarosa in the White House, Diamond and Silk probably figured that they had a way to get next to Trump. But they found out that he doesn't like any black people, male or female, and after getting rid of Omarosa he called her a "dog." That's his way of calling her a "bitch," since a female dog is a bitch. He also referred to black NFL players as "sons of bitches" so what does that make their mothers? And yet Diamond and Silk stood silent until another member of the "Jemima Clique," Omarosa, got canned in shame. Then they call Sarah Huckabee Sanders, Trump's spokesman and flunky, "Miss Piggy", as if name calling is going to do anything but piss off their master all that much more.

And,

> In the same live-stream, they criticized *Good Morning
> America* anchor Robin Roberts for saying, "Bye, Felicia" to Newman
> during a segment on the ABC show which aired on December 14, 2017
> … Addressing Roberts' remarks, Hardaway said, "How is it that you

want the community to come up and then when a sister is sitting at the
table, 'Well, she didn't represent us'? Are you crazy?: .(Wikipedia, 2018)

And don't get me wrong: Robin Roberts and her CBS counterpart Gail King are two more Jemimas that skin and grin and scratch when don't nothin' itch. These Jewish men who run these stations know what they're doing and they don't respect any women of color. Les Moonves is married to Julie Chen, this Asian woman who as TWO shows on CBS ("The Talk" and "Big Brother") and he still fucked around behind her back. NBC offers their own version, Hoda Kotb, and she and Kathy Lee Gifford sit around babbling with one trying to "out-white" the other. ABC has bisexual (my opinion) coon Michael Strayhan.

So all the major stations (Fox totally belongs to Trump and all the hosts kiss his ass and don't need or want any black input) know the value of the Jemima and Diamond and Star are simply trying to get their piece of the rock. But I first suggest that they each drop about 50 pounds, put down the mayonnaise sandwiches, and engage in some serious study before getting on the air wasting valuable time and teleprompter space exposing their ignorance.

Diamond and Silk lied on Facebook and continue to take chump change to attend events. To sum up, note the following:

> Artist and activist Bree Newsome has described Hardaway and
> Richardson as "a modern-day minstrel show" and stated in an interview
> that the pair's presentation relies on "stereotypical images of black
> women". Columbia University professor Keith Boykin argued that if the
> pair, "the way they speak, the way they talk and act and behave, were
> saying anything that was contradictory to Trump, the Trump supporters
> who defend them would be the first to attack them." Boykin argued that
> conservatives give attention to Hardaway and Richardson because they
> "only want to listen to the people who reaffirm their narrow, limited
> vision of what blackness is all about and how black people should
> perceive white people and specifically how they should perceive Donald
> Trump." .(Wikipedia, 2018)

The saying in the street is "you gotta bring ass to get ass." That means if you're going to bring it, then you better have your shit together. These two Jemimas do not. When you're a Jemima, you don't have to be concerned or worry about what black people think of you; your job is to curry favor and kiss the ass of the system. And that is what Diamond and Silk and the rest of the women in this book do.

GERALDINE ALEXIS: 'THE WHITE MAN'S PURPOSE'

I am not a Christian nor do I subscribe to the tenets of any organized religion. But I do know this. When a person of Geraldine Alexis' misinformed ilk uses her low self-esteem and unconscious self hate to promote religious beliefs based on a "dream" she had, this is the epitome of religious blasphemy!

You may or may not believe that a Jemima like this exists but I met her and couldn't believe what I read in her book or what I saw with my eyes. This brown-skinned black woman, complete with false green colored contact lenses, was actually a counselor in the Omaha Public Schools. I sat on a panel with her and destroyed her in front of an audience, letting them know that if they were wondering why their children were faring so poorly in school, a lot of it had to do with the counseling they were receiving and that woman right there – I pointed down the dais – is one such counselor.

The audience, which was fifty percent black, deserved to know what I had learned. And I told them. Many of them gasped. But they should not have been shocked. Omaha has long been a bastion of racism and segregation. In fact, the school district spend in excess of $300,000 after the 1954 desegregation decision fighting desegregation. All the way up to 1976 when they finally caved to legal and social pressure.

A beautiful black woman with an alluring name who doesn't know her ass from a hole in the ground, and could well have some mental problems. Following is my analysis of her book, the idea and contents for which came to her from a dream she had. She told me this to my face. Now, I'm gonna tell YOU and analyze the words of this creature feature paragraph by paragraph. I'll warn you: I have been "somewhat critical" of this particular Jemima.

My analysis begins:

THE BOOK: APPEARANCE AND BACK COVER STATEMENT

Like the author, this book proves that all that glitters ain't good and even the more literal cliché, "don't judge a book by its cover" even rings true in this case.

The book is impressive looking enough; an eye catching cover with the full title, "White Man's Purpose: A Revelation From God," emblazoned across the top. In the center of the cover, in green print, we find the quote, " … I have come to have a love and appreciation for their purpose."

This is a quote from the author, obviously a victim of Anglophilia, because the "they" of which she speaks are – that's right, white folks! Ms. Alexis loves white folks and she admits it. If this isn't the perfect description of a "house nigga," then I don't know what is. Malcolm X, in his "Message to the Grass Roots," provides a description that still applies to this very day. In part, the following is what Bro. Malcolm had to say about these kinds of Uncle Toms:

> To understand this, you have to go back to what the young brother
> here referred to as the house Negro and the field Negro back
> during slavery. There were two kinds of slaves, the house Negro
> and the field Negro. The house Negroes - they lived in the house
> with master, they dressed pretty good, they ate good because they
> ate his food- what he left. They lived in the attic or the basement,
> but still they lived near the master; and they loved the master more
> than the master loved himself. They would give their life to save
> the master's house - quicker than the master would. If the master
> said, "We got a good house here," the house Negro would say,
> "Yeah, we got a good house here." Whenever the master said "we,"
> he said "we." That's how you can tell a house Negro.

And Malcolm, during this 1964 speech, concluded that, "we've still got some house negroes running around here. And as you will see, as I break down this woman's book point-by-point, Geraldine Alexis is one of 'em! Why would God send a black woman a "revelation" that the white man is supposed to lead all other races? If Ms. Alexis is hearing voices, they're certainly not the voices of God – but probably just one more symptom of a serious mental disorder!

But incredibly, there's more.
In addition to mis-identification and association with the oppressor, there is an even more central flaw in the book: she loves these white folks for all the wrong reasons! In my analysis, I will dissect, point-by-point, Ms. Alexis' inaccurate views of white history, black history, black culture and, for that matter, the meaning of life, in general!

The publishing company, based in Kearney, Nebraska, clearly ripped this woman off. Hopefully, they will read these words, claim that the words are libelous and take me to court. It will be at that time that the entire state will witness how I prove the backwardness of this publishing company, the sick "I love whitey" contents of the book, and one more point: the possibility that this company took advantage of a woman who, clearly, is out of her fuckin' mind!

Just like "it's not nice to fool Mother Nature," it is equally wrong to take advantage of the mentally retarded. This is not name-calling: as we go through this book you will be so amazed that you will have to laugh to keep from crying. If a white man wrote a book like this, the civil rights "Negroes" and even the most conservative of Uncle Toms would be on the publisher and the author like white on rice (no pun intended). It is beliefs like this, uttered by a "tom" named George W. Althouse (owner of a beauty supply company in the black community) that won Senator Ernie Chambers his seat in the legislature. All Ernie had to do was expose what Althouse said to a room full of white men and then run on his own merits. Ernie dusted Althouse in the election and hasn't been defeated since.

What did Althouse say?

Chambers said an Althouse statement compelled him to enter the race. Althouse reportedly received a standing ovation from other state senators after a speech in which he criticized Chambers for his stridency and called for black and white Americans to work together. ***"If it was God's plan that the white man was to be in command, then there's nothing we can do about it,"*** Althouse, a black, was quoted in the World-Herald. "So let's all join up and work together. Sooner or later we'll all sit around a table and talk out our grievances, and then we can all say 'God Bless America'." (Omaha World Herald, 1995: 1A—emphasis added).

This thing about "God's plan" and these white boys being in command – this is the thrust of Ms. Alexis' book!

The eye-appealing and slick cover is about the only redeeming qualities of this book – a book that, by the way, is only 73 pages long. But don't be fooled: it's double-spaced all the way through, and that includes quotes from the bible that are indented AND double-spaced. So these publishers drug the book out, expanded it and charged her for it. By doing so, they probably helped her meet the page minimum.

So before I analyzed the book, I typed the entire thing. It only took about 4 hours (including breaks). My single-spaced, 14-font version came to a grand total of 33 pages. This is about half the length of one of my shorter research papers. But here is the clincher: I have taught at the largest universities in this state, and if this "book" was handed in to me as an essay or a research paper in one of my undergraduate classes, I would give that person an "F"! Why?

Poor grammar, poor syntax, inaccurate punctuation and misspellings are rampant. The ideas are jumbled and there is no thesis statement. The paper lacks any semblance of documentation, other than out of context quotes from the Bible and the references that ARE used are shallow, superficial and lacking in scholarship. Her primary source, ***The Open Bible***, is a watered-down childish primer version of the actual book. She lists three sources on her bibliography page.

Want some more laughs? Check this out: she's selling this book for $25.00! Can you believe it? ***Seventy-three pages of bullshit for $25.00!*** And that doesn't include the five bucks that you're supposed to include for tax and postage! Holy Jesus, Holy Jesus! What noivz! And where do you send that money order? Check this out: "Chosen Publishing"! Now the actual publishing company is listed as "Morris Publishing" out of Kearney, Nebraska. She really thinks she's "chosen"? Maybe she was chosen by the Ex-Lax Company, because that's the reaction you get once you read this book: it makes you want to shit!

Now, the back page of the book, which lists her reasons for writing the book as well as her credentials. Let's start with her "credentials," first. Here is what is says:

> ***Geraldine Alexis, MS, LMHP*** is called to do the work of an evangelist, is an entrepreneurial Licensed Mental Health Practitioner, as well as school counselor. She visits incarcerated males to teach the word of God couple with life skills. Evangelist Alexis has earned both her teaching and counseling degrees from the University of Nebraska at Omaha. She studied religion/ministry at Grace University in Nebraska and Newport University located in California. She is presently matriculating at Creighton University (emphasis original)

Called to do the work of an evangelist? Called by whom? If that is the case and she is called by God, then shouldn't she be committed enough to at least learn how to write? And spell? Shouldn't she know that the name is "Psalms" and not "Psalm" as she writes throughout her book? Shouldn't she be considerate enough to research her topic before spewing forth half-truths and lunatic fringe opinions in the name of "salvation"? And finally, isn't this what all of these hallelujah huckers, male and female, tend to say when they're asked of their authority. "I was called" or "I was summoned"?

This woman teaches public school children and counsels them. Can you now see why the Omaha Public Schools are in a downward spiral? This woman, who clearly has visions and hears voices, has an office where she is supposed to help our future generations. Maybe that's why the school dropout rate is so high: the kids meet with her one time, hear what she has to say, and are so confused and dizzy from her goony concepts that they just say, "fuck it, I want home schooling"!

She talks about all the white folks that she's been around and it is as if she's bragging about it. But in her credentials she writes that she studied religion/ministry at Grace University – perhaps the whitest school in the entire Midwest. If you study religion under white folks, invariably God will become equated with being white and being male. And this is what Ms. Alexis implies throughout her book: God and the white man are buddies and the white man is the only one who can set the world straight. You'll see what I mean when you check out some of her "messages" that lie ahead.

Now, her own words, stating what the book is about and what her mission is. You will find both purposes equally goony:

> Psalm (sic) 92:5 reads, O Lord, how great are thy works! And thy thoughts are very deep. Hence, as you partake of the revelation God has imparted into my spirit, do this with a spiritual heart, mind and ear.

Hold it! How is a woman who claims to be so involved with her religion and so aware of God, who claims that she talks to God and vice-versa, going to incorrectly spell "Psalms" and then not even put the excerpts she is using in quotation marks?

Then she has the gall to claim that we (the readers) are partaking of the revelation God imparted to her spirit. Is that what it was – or could it have been gas? Who knows? All I know is that the only "revelation" that I could see manifested was how this book revealed how ignorant and out of step with social reality Ms. Alexis really is!

The self-praising back page statement continues:

> "Not only did He make us individually, but He made us as collective racial groups, as well. God allowed for his creation of groups of people to comprise distinct colors. Therefore, there are no 'oops' colors. God made each race for a particular purpose. When each race embraces its purpose this world will be a better place to live in."

I deal with the "God made all groups" concept later in this analysis. But for now let me address her claim that, "when each race embraces its purpose this world will be a better place to live in."

This sounds really nice, doesn't it? But it's a line straight out of the Wizard of Oz. You see, in Ms. Alexis' sick world, each group has a "place" – as opposed to a role. And the "place" for the white man, as she says throughout this book, is on top. Yeah. He was ordained by God to lead everybody else, according to Alexis. And do you know who else had this very same idea? Every pseudo-scientific racist that ever put on a science laboratory coat; from Herodotus, Peter Camper, Carleton Coon and Joseph De Gobineau and Van Eyrie to Malthus. And today's white supremacist groups, all had the same belief. Somehow, despite being robbed when it comes to morals, skin color and dick size, the white man is supposed to save "de po' nigrahs." Oh, and one more person had the same belief in black inferiority that meant whites would have to lead: a white boy by the name of Charles Manson. ***Remember him??!!***

Despite her love of white men, Alexis nonetheless claims that her role in all this is purely spiritual. But even her own misguided words betray her, as she writes:

> The intent of this book ought to promote the reader from religiosity to ***spirituality,*** from a pseudo-lifestyle into a ***lifestyle of truth***, as well as, out of bondage into ***freedom***

realizing the premise (sic) of the American way (emphasis original).

Somebody told this woman she had "the truth." This sounds an awful lot like the rhetoric of that bullshit artist, Les Beauchamp. But I'll deal with him elsewhere in this book (and I'll make sure he gets a copy, too). At any rate, how can this woman believe that what she is writing is somehow "divinely inspired" or based on some revelation. Now, don't get me wrong: I do believe that this woman hears voices – but it ain't the voice of God! It's probably some officer from an inter-galactic mental ward putting out an all points bulletin!

That takes care of that. Now, a message to the publisher.

A WORD TO THE PUBLISHER

Morris Publishing of Kearney, Nebraska should be sued for what they did to Ms. Alexis. Sure, she went the "vanity press' route and paid to have them print her book. She had to. Any credible publisher would have read the first couple of pages, turned to a few of the back pages, put the book down, got up from his chair and then puked all over the fuckin' desk!

Furthermore, Ms. Alexis went to Morris Publishing in good faith and signed contracts after (presumably) reading the large and small print. But this becomes a matter, not of law, but of an ethical obligation by the printing company. They put that woman out there to make an utter ass out of herself because the book is not intellectually representative of Ms. Alexis' strong beliefs in religion or anything else. Even though I disagree with everything she writes, as a member of the media I know that she at least deserves the right to be ***fairly represented.***

Morris Publishing gave her back some proofs to go over. I saw them. If the original draft of the book was error-filled in the first place, how can they expect this "rookie" to be able to correct her own mistakes? Ms. Alexis told me that she had one man look it over for her, but I get the distinct impression that he was looking more at her face and figure than he was the book. She got duped by whoever this guy was, and then just decided to "go to press." What a major mistake. She submitted a laughable piece of bullshit to some white boys in Kearney and they photocopies and gave it back to her as a "proof." Desperate to get published, she handed it right back to them. And this "book," The White Man's Purpose: A Revelation From God, is what the public will now judge Ms. Alexis by.

Ms. Alexis deserves better. Her ideas were already stupid enough in their own right. She was already going to catch hell from anyone with an IQ over 20! But Morris Publishing compounded the problem, adding insult to injury, by printing this book, double-spaced, and not editing for typographical errors, syntax, punctuation or grammar. Even if the borderline insanity that the book represents DID get accepted by the mainstream, she would then have to address the poor manner in which her ideas were presented.

The profit motive is why landlords charge blacks more, why banks stay away from investing in black communities, why stores move out of the ghetto and so on. I therefore do not expect these publishers to be any different. But here's what THEY ought to expect: that somebody with a fully developed brain (unlike their client) would come along, see this book, and automatically ask, 'who in the hell published this shit'? And when the writer is a black woman, the question is, 'what did these white boys do to this sister?' They took the money, pure and simple. And that's all they cared about. Now she's stuck with a legacy similar to that of Ichabod Crane, and they're generating interest off of the check they deposited.

I don't expect white boys to do anything except be white. And as Karenga (1967) wrote long ago, white doesn't just represent a color, "it represents a mentality that's anti-black." That is why I am not holding them responsible for Ms. Alexis' quasi-illiterate presentation of her ideas. But here is what I charge them with: self-aggrandizement. They saw the title and read the content; it praised the white race, praise that is totally undeserved. But the white man has never been above taking credit for that which he did not do. Look at his history. So they went ahead and let this black woman put her head directly onto the chopping block and, in printing this sick crap, they pulled the rope that bought the guillotine crashing down on her future.

At one point I got the address to Morris Publishing from Ms. Alexis and emailed them for information. After all, I figured that if they were going to print simplistic bullshit like that which is found in her book, then they would be totally flabbergasted with my high-quality manuscripts – of which I have more than fifty. As one of the top editors in this State, I was summoned by Ms. Alexis through a mutual friend, to "check out" her book. I never charged her anything because I am always glad to help another black person get their ideas out in the public eye. We sat down at the McDonald's on 40th and Farnam and she babbled while I drank my tea and read through the draft sent back by Morris Publishing.

I literally gagged. I turned to this gorgeous woman and told her to her face: "This is a piece of shit – don't do it!" After all, I was confronted with a choice: leave the book alone and allow my people to be humiliated by the rantings of this lovely lunatic – and pave the way for them to publish MY work, or say to hell with the publishing, and do the right thing by exposing the flaws in the book and also laying responsibility at the feet of some peckerwood publishers who benefited four-fold: they got paid for their work, they did very little work, they got their name all over the book as the company responsible for publishing the book and finally, they now have a "minority publication" that they can boast about to potential customers. I chose the latter.

I don't care what the small print on the contract says. Ms. Alexis is the mother of a child and a member of the black community (despite the fact that she doesn't live in it or care about it). She doesn't deserve to be ridiculed by presenting a book that is the literary version of "Laugh-In." She paid her money and has a right to a product that is representative of the educator and counselor that she claims and seeks to be. For Morris Publishing to "bum rush" this book into publications format, box it up and mail it to Ms. Alexis is tantamount to sending a time bomb to someone and then bragging about the fact that "well, at least it didn't blow up right away." No matter where the person is or when the bomb goes off, *you are still a murderer.* THAT is the point.

For over 30 years I have been fighting on behalf of black people and others who would be taken advantage of by white folks. And for 30 yeas, I've been winning. As soon as I am finished wiping the vomit off of my shirt after having read Ms. Alexis' book, I am going to contact the **Kearney Hub** newspaper and whatever publishing association Morris Publishing is a member of, and take them to task for what they did to this poor sister. As has always been my mantra: "whatever you do to my people, I'm gonna do to yours."

She is about to get her comeuppance right now, in this analysis. Morris Publishing – yours is comin'.

TABLE OF CONTENTS: OVERVIEW

Nowhere on earth will you find a 73-page "book" that is divided into five chapters – double-spaced chapters at that! And yet, here it is. The Chapters, and their titles are as follows: "Chapter 1: God's Children"; Chapter 2: Our Purpose in Life; Chapter 3: White Mans' Purpose; Chapter 4: White Man's Purpose In Relation to Minorities and Chapter 5: Conclusion.

Each chapter has titles for its sub-chapters, which makes for even more amazement and laughs when you read each one. But I see why that would benefit Morris Publishing – sub-headings take up more space and the book can be expanded and made to appear larger than it really is. Of course, the more pages, more they charge.

As it relates to this particular book, n most cases the title of the sub-chapter has nothing to do with the content of that chapter. What did she do – steal titles from episodes of "Bonanza" or "Miami Vice"? Moreover, with the reading of each sub-chapter, you are experiencing what the Chinese referred to as "death by a thousand cuts." Little by little, you become more confused with what she is trying to say, more insulted by the lack of time taken to use correct grammar, and all the more closer to wanting to pluck out each one of your fuckin' pubic hairs, one by one – to EASE the pain inflicted by this poorly written tome.

One thing is for sure: after reading this article, perhaps this area should more accurately be called, "Table of COONtents."

PREFACE:

Sis. Alexis is a strong black woman. But somewhere down the line, she fell off a skyscraper and hit her head very hard on some concrete. This is the only way to explain such gooniness – major head trauma! Now, let's look at her journey into whiteness and how she explains it. She begins what seems like another version of the "Never-ending story," by writing,

> While growing up, I oftentimes found myself in the company of the white race. Sometimes of my own free will, others (sic) times out of obedience to God. I was born and raised in Omaha, Nebraska and am (sic) a product of North Omaha. North Omaha is the section of Omaha where the majority of Blacks populate (sic). I began to launch (sic) out into the white community by attending schools in West Omaha (highly populated by whites). Although desegregation via busing was big at that time, most schools I attended, in West Omaha, were predominantly white despite efforts to diversify school population (p. 1).

She offers nothing that makes her life unique. All of us have found ourselves in the company of the white race. The question is, what was the quality or caliber of those interactions? Were you there cleaning the house, fixing the car, or at poolside chatting with the homeowners? Were you debating them on race issues or trying to raise their pitiable consciousness, or were you sitting idly by while they cracked one stale nigga joke after another? In her attempt at an explanation, Ms. Alexis fuzzies it up by saying that sometimes she was in the white presence of her own free will and other times out of obedience to God.

This is important to remember because as you read on, this woman makes it appear as if the white man is God's chosen representative here on earth and that somehow, all life revolves around the white race. If God is all-knowing and at all places all the time, then of what relevance could being in the white man's presence serve? We were in his presence during slavery, but look at what kind of relationship THAT involved! So as a reason for her hanging out with white folks, she wants us to believe God told her to do it. Somebody – call 911!

She was born in Omaha and claims to be a product of North Omaha. She explains that North Omaha was predominantly black, but doesn't explain how it got that way (later in the book she does, and it's the lousiest reason every concocted). She claims she "launched" into the white community by going to school around white folks. But these are general statements. Did she date white boys? Was she in love with them? Did she have a "hankering" for them? What is it about this woman that makes her view being in the company of peckerwoods something "special"? We will try to unravel this web of deceit as we move deeper into Ms. Alexis' world, a place I refer to as "goony-goo-goo land."

The preface continues:

> After high school graduation and working several years, I
> matriculated at (sic) the University of Nebraska at Omaha where
> I was outnumbered racially and found myself, once again, in
> classrooms of predominantly whites. Although I yearned to be
> with my own racial kind, this began to be a trend in my life for
> many years to come (pp. 1-2).

Why did she yearn to be with her own "racial kind"? Why didn't she explain this? Because she's lying. Her emphasis is on all the white folks she was around and she's making it appear as if all this whiteness was fulfillment of prophecy. If she wanted to be around her "own kind," she easily could have been. She's related to damn near everybody in Omaha, including this family of fine sisters, the Cottons. All she has to do is walk into any place where there are guys and she'll be the center of attention. Everybody knows the Cotton family. So what was holding her back?

Furthermore, elsewhere in this book she claims that God didn't create different colors so that there would be distinctions. To her, we are all the same. Well if that's the case, what does she mean by her "own kind"? According to her logic, peckerwoods ARE her own kind, as are the Japanese, the American Indian and the Latino!

But let's look closer at this "own kind" comment. A partial explanation might lie in the following passage:

> Being of the black race, I applied for, what I thought to be, a position for
> a minority internship. This was a program offered to minority college
> students pursuing a bachelor's degree in teaching to give them "hands-
> on" experience in the school setting coupled with other opportunities.
> This educational endeavor was offered by the Omaha Public Schools.
> Although I did receive an educational opportunity to gain "hands-on"
> experience in a school setting, I later discovered that I had erroneously
> applied for a program with the Westside Community School District

> (located in West Omaha) as opposed to the Omaha Public Schools,
> which are located throughout the areas of Omaha (sic) (p. 2).

So far we have someone who claims she wants to be around her own people but, gosh darn it, she just keeps on popping up in places dominated by white folks. For shame! Now, after reminding us (and herself) that she is a member of the black race, she decides NOT to become active in the Urban League Guild, NOT to become a member of the Council of Negro Women, NOT to become active in the black student organization at UNO. She is invisible when the community is standing up to police brutality and other forms of racism. Is Alexis anywhere to be found? No. Being black, she sees a chance to apply for a MINORITY internship! We're not good enough to associate with, but by golly we're sure good enough to exploit when the end result is an internship that will do what? Put you in classrooms *with even MORE peckerwoods!*

Now here is a woman who wants to be an educator, someone who wants to teach others. But she's so loony, she applies for a position in the wrong district! Or did she? I don't think it was an accident. Her love of white people clearly should have had her looking out for what DISTRICT she was going to apply to! And everybody knows, ain't no niggas in the Westside School District. They don't even have black house pets!

So OPS, which has more than 40 schools she could have applied to is somehow overlooked and she ends up at a district only a fraction the size of OPS, and it just so happens to also be lily-white? In 1980, OPS was 25% black; in 2004 it is 58% black. She was somewhere in between in terms of interacting with black students. But instead what does she do? She opts for Westside, where there aren't even any black counselors or principals? Do you REALLY think this was some kind of quirk?

Now, playing the role of Rosa Parks or a female Medgar Evers, she claims to be *the first* to get accepted into a program that she applied for by accident. Is this really a bragging point? At any rate, she posits,

> I was the first Black, and I believe the only Black to be selected to
> participate in that program. Once again, I found myself away from the
> racial group of people and culture I was accustomed to. My interactions
> were generally with those who were very different in style, character,
> values and so forth than myself, the white race (pp. 2-3).

She didn't "find herself" in that situation – she planned it and, as a result, there was no element of surprise. Ms. Alexis is manipulating situations by acting as if her situation and conditions are coincidental or quirks. And as a result, her interactions with white folks represented a dream come true. And that is the bottom line that Ms. Alexis won't come clean about: she LOVES white people and in hanging with them so long, she has acquired what psychiatrist Roderick W. Pugh once referred to as "adaptive inferiority." She loves white folks at the expense of her own race. As we burrow deeper and deeper into the chuckhole that is Ms. Alexis' life, you will see what she REALLY believes in. And it ain't us!

When she finally has to deal with blackness, it is a sorrowful situation, as she gives birth to a handicapped child:

> If this was not enough, prior to graduating from college, I conceived a child that suffers from many deformities. She is a two time liver transplant (sic) coupled with kidney problems, heart problems, lymphoma diagnosis, pneumonia, and the list continues. This was very unusual because I am a descendant of a large intermediate (sic) family and a very large extended family, as well. Out of all the people in our family, no one has ever had a child with defects. Hence, the maladies my child faces, yet today, has caused me to interact more intensely with the white race. I began to suspect at this point that my being around white individuals most of my waking hours was not a coincidence, yet, God's providence (p. 3).

Why is there no mention of the father? Why is there no mention of the relationship that led to the impregnation? On some level, this kind of information would have to deal with blackness. So she avoids it. But when she comes up for some air, we have a woman who takes the fact that she has a special needs child and does what? Links it to a situation where now, she can write about even MORE white folks that she interacts with! Of what relevance is that? The priority should be the child, not how many peckerwoods it takes to screw in a light bulb!

What is an intermediate family? Does she mean nuclear family? And if her family is so large, then what stopped her from hanging out with them on a regular basis? And so what if nobody in her family had ever had a child with defects – would this be another reason she would use to stay away from her family and, instead, hang out with crackers?

Now comes a total breakdown in logic. Ms. Alexis assumes that because she has a special needs child, this mandates that she associate more with white people. Omaha is full of doctors from the Middle East, China and beyond -- ***medical professionals of color.*** Ms. Alexis WANTS to be around white people and that is why she is hiding out in northwest Omaha and avoiding her own family. If she knew her history, she would know that it was the white boy who bought disease to this country in the first place! But instead, being the Anglophile that she is, her conclusion is, "Hmmmmm, maybe my being around white folks means that this is what GOD wants."

This is blasphemy. Why would God want a woman with a vulnerable child to associate even more with a race of beings that HATE black people? That's like having an 11-year-old daughter and then moving in with R. Kelly! That doesn't jibe, does it?

God seems to get the blame for everything she does. And in each case, it has something to do with kissing up to more white folks. Ms. Alexis is a Jemima and doesn't want to admit it. So, when in doubt, blame it on a superior being! Yeah, that makes a lot of sense. Check it out:

> Oh, it does not stop there. Being a child of God, He placed upon my heart to fellowship at Trinity Interdenominational Church which is mostly white. I have been in membership with this church for three years. Although I did not understand why the Lord would separate me from my family and friends and send me away to Trinity located in West Omaha, I obeyed (p. 4).

For those of you who don't hail from Omaha, Trinity Interdenominational Church is a suburban church full of pious peckerwoods who promote segregation during the week, then fill up the collection plate on Sunday. This white boy named Les Beauchamp, who is known for these cheesy television commercials with special themes, leads the church. I don't want to get ahead of myself because I deal with Beauchamp later in this book. Let it suffice to say at this juncture that God didn't place anything on this woman's heart.

There are 458 churches in Omaha and 116 of them are black, and many are much closer to her house than Trinity is. So she's got no excuse and she is committing blasphemy, yet again, by laying this bullshit at the feet of God. SHE made the decision to attend Trinity because when it comes to white churches, Trinity is the whitest of them all. The people at Trinity Church would make the Stepford Wives look like the Parkers!

She further denigrates the Supreme Being when she says that God is responsible for separating her from her family and friends and "sending her" away to this cracker church. How loony can one person be? She's a counselor in the public school system – shouldn't she know something about accepting responsibility for one's own actions? If she talks to God so much, why didn't she ask HIM why she was being sent into a den of her enemies? The fact is, she loves white people and she wants to *use* them. She is a beautiful black woman who knows she's sexy and dresses the part. There is no way those white boys, including Beauchamp, haven't noticed. You do the math.

She says she obeyed the Lord. How can we believe that when she didn't obey the rule that, "Thou shalt not take the name of the lord thy God in vain; for the Lord will not hold him guiltless that taketh his name in vain" (Exodus 20:7). This is what Ms. Alexis ought to remembering and obeying.

And yet with each passing paragraph, Ms. Alexis shows that she is as irresponsible as her book is cruddy. See for yourself:

> I would continually cry out to the Lord for some sort of revelation as to why I am constantly in the presence of the white race. The kicker was that God had me interacting with the high status white race who looked upon their own race that was of a lower status, than they, with disgust. Thus you can only imagine the thoughts they held for me. I would have to dialogue with doctors, lawyers, business owners, and so forth. I would literally cry! Oftentimes asking myself, why me? (p. 4).

She's crying out for the Lord and she's seeking a sign or a revelation as to why she's around all these peckerwoods. All she has to do is get up off her perfectly sculptured ass and walk the fuck out! That's all she's got to do. Instead, she sits around moaning about why she loves a colorless race so much, and then, when she finally goes over the deep end, she will use a book to try to justify her utter fascination with and love for those white folks.

She refers to white folks as a "high status race." High status compared to whom? Black folks? And how did they get that status? They stole it and then created an empire on the backs of the racial groups that Ms. Alexis apparently hates! That 'high status' race of people who are so misguided that they have to use force on countries that are smaller than they are, rape innocent women and screw little boys in the butt in the name of their religion. Oh, THOSE white folks? But then again, understanding Ms. Alexis' mindset, maybe compared to her warped views and background, these white boys ARE high status!

She knows that even white boys cannot get along with their own race, and she knows that based upon that fact alone, they must think even LESS of her. But she also knows that the white man has never been able to stare at a pair of 36" breasts (or any man, for that matter) and look the other way! She might be inferior but she ain't THAT inferior!

Ms. Alexis sounds like a frustrated call girl. She sounds like she is for sale. She defines white men based upon their occupations, not based upon anything that they have done in the area of morals or service. What relevance, for instance, do business owners have to this whole case? No doubt she meets them at Trinity Church and they see her and approach her (or vice-versa). She knows them as more than just passing acquaintances, and she enjoys it. Why would she cry because she has to dialogue with doctors, lawyers, business owners and so forth? Haggling over price, perhaps?

Unfortunately, there's more:

> Then the turning point surfaced, (sic) I had to attend two summer classes at Creighton University, where I am presently matriculating. One of the classes was a multicultural class that discussed different racial groups. However, somehow we skimmed pass (sic) the section that would enlighten me about the race that I have had so much interaction with, the white race (p. 5).

The class is one that deals with multiculturalism. This is already watered down enough. But not for Ms. Alexis. She wants to study the apple of her eye, the white man! Studying Asians, Native Americans, Blacks and Latinos is not enough. These bullshit type courses, which skim over the surface of even these few groups, have the nerve to add information on gays, the handicapped, and left-handed quarterbacks. But no, she takes a class on multiculturalism and while everybody else is there (mandated by OPS rules and regulations) that this course be taken so that whites can learn more about kids of color, she sits her black ass in the classroom dreaming about Troy Donahue and Harrison Ford!

Now she's really mad as she writes, "I was furious that more information and discussion was not shared about these individuals. I was the only Black student in this class, and the other class, as well. This is when I went to the Lord in deep prayer (p. 5). And what did she pray for? See for yourself:

> I began with, "Lord, I know this is not a coincidence that I have been among this race of people for the majority of my life. I have had very little time with my own race of people. Please, reveal unto me what you are trying to teach me through these encounters." This is when God revealed the **white man's purpose** to my spirit (p. 5—emphasis original).

Of course it was not a coincidence. It was all a reality because of actions that Ms. Alexis took – but didn't want to assume responsibility for. She was a sellout, obsessed with white folks, and didn't know how to handle the obsession. Realizing she was sick, she didn't bother to turn to that extended family or all of those fine-ass female cousins of hers – she instead, puts the blame on God and paints herself as some kind of unwitting victim.

So she prayed and God revealed to her the white man's purpose? Why would God do that? If God truly knew the white man's purpose, then he would also have to know that it is a purpose that is rooted in evil. So why doesn't God strike down the white man, instead of steering some fine ass sister his way? The fact is, God didn't have anything to do with the choices that Ms. Alexis has made, is making or will make. She's got major issues, and at the root of all of them is her tendency toward hypocrisy.

At this point there is good news and bad news. The good news is that this is the end of the preface. The bad news is that we still have 68 more pages to go!

Chapter 1: God's Children

The question is: if we're all God's children, then why does Alexis prefer the company of the very race that is giving her people so much hell and headache? On the following pages you will find statements that border on the insane; as if this woman has been living in a cavern for most of her life. Let us begin with our analysis.

He Created Us All

> You have heard the song: Jesus Loves the Little Children, all the children of the world. Why would He not? God made us all. Can anyone give me a legitimate explanation as to why God would not love each and everyone (sic) of His creatures? Despite popular opinions as to how particular groups of individuals came into being, God did, in fact, make each and every one of us in this world. The Bible says that we are fearfully and wonderfully made. That means out of billions of people in the world there is no duplicate of you … (p. 6).

With these general truisms out of the way, here is what I want you to remember: later in this book Ms. Alexis has a "chitlin' flashback" and claims that black people were here first and that all other races of man came from that group. At another point she buys into the Bible-based Adam was first and Eve came from his rib. The fact is, Ms. Alexis doesn't know the front door of the asylum from the basement door. She's just writing and writing and the more she does, the bigger of an ass she makes of herself.

Ready for another contradiction? Check out the following one:

> In other words, God knows each of us personally. He knows the number of hairs on our head, as well as, (sic) our every thought and deed. Isn't it awesome the way God has organized and landscaped the earth with trees, plants, flowers, rocks, oceans, mountains, stars, a sun, moon, sky, and so forth so beautifully with color? Well, as so far as the human race is concerned, he took as much effort to arrange. Adam, the first man with a head, arms, legs eyes, thighs, hands, fingers, feet, toes, skin, and so forth, and yes, with color (pp. 6-7).

If God is the master "arranger" – as she claims that he is – then why is she trying to undo what she claims he has created? Why is she, in her case, asking him "why" she is continually in the presence of white folks? That is not her place: ***"Hers is not to question why, Hers is but to do – or die!"*** Again, we see where she subscribes to the Adam's rib theory – but don't worry; before the end of the book she'll be advancing different reasons for the origin of man.

The most over-used Bible quote (other than John 3:16) follows, as Alexis flaunts her alleged religion and her so-called "religious background:"

> Then God said, "Let Us (sic) make man in Our (sic) image, according to our likeness; and let them rule over the fish of the sea and over the birds of the sky and over the cattle and over all the earth, and over every creeping that that creeps on the earth" (Genesis 1:26).

Sis. Alexis must have the Sesame Street version of the Bible. First of all, she boldfaces everything, I guess in an attempt to give God props the way the Bible does. But it's tacky because the transition from her words to the words from the Bible is non-existent. It's called a segue, sister – a segue!!! And this thing about "let them rule" is actually, "let them have dominion." She uses capital letters where there should be none, and if I'm not mistaken, "according to our likeness" should be "after our likeness." I was raised in the Baptist Church and I've read the Bible three times. Check it for yourself.

The sub-chapter concludes with the following Bible reference: "And the Lord God fashioned into a woman the rib which He had taken from the man, and brought her to the man (Genesis 2:22).

This passage is bullshit. Any book or religion that is created by a man always finds a way to degrade the woman, some way to make her feel like less than she is. Like Ms. Alexis, for instance. If you accept this, you will laugh at jokes like the following one:"*Why did God give women sex organs? " ANSWER: So that men would talk to 'em. "*If you find that funny, you're an asshole.

No woman who is in her right mind can believe that she was created to serve a man, just as no black is going to serve a peckerwood – the way Ms. Alexis wants us to. More on this elsewhere in this spine-tingling analysis.

No Oops Individuals/Races

This chapter begins with the same integrationist bullshit that permeates much of what Ms. Alexis has to say on the issue of race. For instance, make due note of the following excerpt:

> Not only did He make us all individually, but He made us as
> collective racial groups, as well. God allowed for His creation of
> groups of people to comprise distinct colors. Therefore, there are
> no "oops" colors. God made each race for a particular purpose.
> When each race embraces its purpose this world will be a better
> place to live in (p. 8).

Now later in her book, this confused public schools counselor claims that the human race originated in Africa. She claimed that "the Black race is the first race of the earth making them the mother of all races." Now which one is it?

So if the black man is the original man, and man is made in the image of God – as she stated earlier – then that means God must be black. That means that God couldn't have "assigned" Ms. Alexis to go to the white church or hang out with white folks. That wouldn't make sense. So it seems as if Ms. Alexis is lying in order to justify her pro-white behavior, does it not?

Furthermore, if there are no "oops" colors, then why does she think whitey is getting the leadership nod for God? She says the white man was ordained by God to lead. IF that is the case, it must be based on color, right? And if that is the case, then that means God DOES favor one race over another. Ms. Alexis should make up her mind and stop allowing white racists to do it for her.

Continuing:

> The term "oops" pertains to a mistake. You have heard the phrase,
> "He/she was an 'oops' baby." I beg to differ with such a statement in that
> God is the maker of life. Therefore, whether it is an individual or a
> collective racial group of individuals, they all were created by God.
> Guess what? God makes no mistakes. So, when it comes to critiquing
> who and what color God has created His people to be, the person who
> does the critique may find him/herself critiquing the Almighty God, our
> creator (p. 9).

Isn't that exactly what she is doing – critiquing God? Who is she to blame God for the fact that she is surrounded by white folks? And then, to further compound her audacity, she lies on god and claims that she was informed by the Lord that the white man was supposed to LEAD everybody else. In other words, the Lord said that the white man was superior to everyone else! If lying on God and implying that he plays "race favorites" is not a biting critique, then I don't know what is!

Next, another in a long line of ill-timed Biblical quotes: "Before I formed you in the womb I knew you, And before you were born I consecrated you; I have appointed you a prophet to the nations" (Jeremiah 1:5). This one is followed up with the following:

My frame was not hidden from Thee, When I was made in secret, And skillfully wrought in the depths of the earth.

Thane eyes have seen my unformed substance; And in Thy (sic) book they were all written, The days that were ordained for me, When as yet there was not one of them (Psalms 139: 15&16).

Now here is how the two verses above are SUPPOSED to read:

My substance was not hid from thee, when I was made in secret, **and** curiously wrought in the lowest parts of the earth. Thine eyes did see my substance, yet being unperfect; and in thy book all my members were written, which in continuance were fashioned, when as yet there was none of them (emphasis original).

Ms. Alexis has a responsibility to study before she picks up a pen exposing her ignorance. She has to understand what the Bible says before she attempts to quote from it. She also has to understand the context in which it was written. The Bible she is quoting from is some popular culture, dumbed-down version, and it misconstrues the essence of the actual passages. This only adds to the nuttiness and confusion that Ms. Alexis was already born with!

Moving on:

True story, (sic) I remember teaching a fifth grade class of predominantly white students. Predominantly in this sense was 99%. We were engaging in a social studies lesson. One of the white male students asked if he lived in a ghetto. We all are fully aware of the awry (sic) definition used for ghetto, in present day America. Today, a ghetto is characterized as being an underdeveloped area for a low social economic class. In other words, this label is associated with being a Black thing. However, in the past times it was not defined in this manner (pp. 10-11).

To begin with, I have found in dealing with human beings that those who begin their sentences with "This is the honest to God truth," "I swear it's the truth" or as Ms. Alexis does, "True story" – they are all liars. They preface their comments this way because they know, better than anyone else, that they are lacking in credibility. If this was not the case, why bother to make the statement; most people will believe you and assume you have no reason to lie. But you give yourself away when you begin by telling people, "true story" because you know, while they may not, that you're getting ready to tell an unadulterated lie.

The lie begins when she's teaching this class of 99% black students social studies. She says one of the white male students asked if he lived in a ghetto.

Who's he? Was the kid asking if he, himself, lived in a ghetto? Because if he was asking that, he was probably making fun of her and she, being the fool that she apparently is, didn't catch it. So she took an insult and tried to turn it into a lesson plan. As you will see, she fucked it up.

She says that a ghetto is an underdeveloped area for a low socioeconomic class. White people might live in low-income areas, but they don't' call them ghettos, and neither do urban planners – which I happen to be. Instead of her using the chalkboard and showing how racist America is, instead of referring to the classic book American Apartheid and showing how segregated white folks have made things, she denies that the ghetto is a "black thing." What she should have done is drawn a chart on the board and showed how the American Indian is confined to the reservation, the Latino to el barrio, and that Chinatowns and Japan towns have the highest population densities – in some places 280 people per square mile – than any other enclave in the nation. Then, she could have shown that blacks are confined to ghettos, places where city services are inferior to other parts of the city.

Instead, she takes the word ghetto as a personal attack and denies that it is not a place where black people live. It is not a label – it is a fact. Black people are "ghettoized." But she doesn't understand this because her definition and perception of what a ghetto is as warped and distorted as that "revelation" she received from God. So now she makes the issue worse and mis-educated students who are already racist, at the same time. She explains her own ignorance in the following way:

> So, I used this question as an opportunity to enlighten these students with the truth, as well as, the prejudices and racist beliefs upheld and attributed to certain racial ethnic groups. Oh and by the way, racial groups who are loved by God and created for a purpose, as well. I proceeded to answer his question by using the series of questions that were listed within our social studies text which were the following:
>
> ♦ Are most of the people where you live of the same race?
> ♦ Do most of the people in your area embrace the same culture?
> ♦ Are most of the people where you live of the same economic status?
> ♦
>
> In the process of enlightening students with "the truth," Ms. Alexis does just the opposite; she makes something up on the spot, because she is not bright enough to know about anything beyond her own limited world. People who go around talking about "the truth" have issues in most cases – she's not exception.

Before answering the question about the ghetto, she refers these white kids to a racist answer found in their ethnocentric textbook. For what purpose? To provide a bullshit definition of what a ghetto is, that's why. Just because people in your community are of the same race as you are, just because most of you share the same sick culture, and the same socioeconomic status – this does not make it a ghetto. Why? Because there are other factors that go into creating a ghetto, and once of those factors is external control. Suburbs provide their own goods and services.

But wait: I'm not finished schooling you yet. But Alexis has more simplistic answers and explanations:

> If you can answer yes to each of these questions, the you live in
> what is known as the original meaning of ghetto which is a group
> of people of the same race, culture, and economic status living in
> a given area within a city. Ghettos were prevalent in the United
> States, years ago (p. 12).

How foolish this woman is! Let me explain to you what a ghetto is, and why the dictionary definition that she gave is piecemeal and pitifully perverted.

Ghettos originated in Germany, and they were places where Jews were forced to live. It was a large fenced in place and they could only venture out to work and had a curfew. If they were caught outside, they were subject to severe punishment. That is the origin of the ghetto – not here in America. So Ms. Alexis lied to her students. But it gets worse as she continues her journey into the world of insanity:

> Each time a racial group immigrated into the United States, they
> would gravitate to their own racial kind for survival reasons thus
> forming a ghetto. So, in the original sense of the word, this white
> male does live in what modern-day America erroneously ascribes
> solely to Blacks, the ghetto (p. 12).

This woman is distorted history in much the same way she has distorted her own personal reality. Let me show you how.

She says ghettos were formed because immigrants gravitate to their own kind. Perhaps Ms. Alexis is not familiar with the hatred that these white immigrants received from their own race when they arrived at Ellis Island. They went to where they were "steered." The first group set the tone and all others of "their kind" followed suit. It had nothing to do with choice; they were segregated and lived in squalor and dirt – because city services, including garbage pickup, were denied to them. Ms. Alexis should read more and talk less.

She writes that the concept of "ghetto" does not fit these new immigrants and yet, it does. They were denied and forced to live in squalid conditions, doubling up in one-room dives with white boys collecting high rents. They had curfews and were arrested for minor infractions. That is ghetto living, and that is what blacks face today. Since that time, these same white ethnics who were dogged out by the American white boy have joined ranks with him and turned their hatred – not only their former white oppressors – but on the newly arriving black people, who came North from the South looking for jobs.

Then there are the facts. But here is the moral lesson: a black woman in a classroom of whites, with the opportunity to teach valuable racial lessons. And she screws it up. In doing so, she provides evidence that there are black teachers who can't cut the mustard because, after all, she is one of them. Instead of bringing in someone with expertise, or going home that night to study the issue before discussing it on the following day, she tries to wing it and, in doing so, makes an ass out of herself and trivializes the importance of "the truth."

The name of this sub-chapter is "No Oops Individuals/Races." But there is one big "oops," or so it seems to me. And that is this: allowing this mentally unstable self-hater to counsel children in the Omaha Public Schools. That is the biggest "oops" of all.

His Focus Is On the Heart

Let's get one thing straight: the heart doesn't do anything but pump blood. It has nothing to do with emotions of love, jealousy or those kinds of pangs. People need to stop lying about that shit: "I love you with all of my heart." What they should be saying is, "I love you with all of my MIND." That would make more sense. God's focus is on the soul, a spiritual essence that cannot be defined or seen. Now with that correction out of the way, let's see what the black version of Jessica Simpson has to say this time around.

She writes,

> Although God purposefully made racial groups, God does not particularly take note of color. This is true in that within each group of races lie a multitude of colors. All blacks are not the color black, but rather a hew (sic) of colors ranging from black to an undertone white. By the same token, all Whites are not the color white, but tones of white, red, and brown. The same description is true with other racial groups (pp. 12-13).

A woman who teaches the fifth grade who doesn't know the difference between "hew" (to chop, as in to chop wood) and "hue" (a shade or color). This is why the public schools in Omaha are going to hell in a hand basket: morons in front of the classroom who are just literate enough to be able to graduate with a teaching certificate and now, with the union behind them, almost impossible to get rid of.

What is the purpose of these lies about white not being about tone color. White folks designated themselves as white on their own. Then, they designated people like Ms. Alexis "non-white," a slap in the face since the prefix "non" means "the absence of." So if you're non-white, you're "less than" white, meaning that you're less than human. This skin hue crap is irrelevant, because blackness is not just color; it's "color, culture and consciousness" (Karenga, 1967). And white is not like the color, but a way of life and an attitude. The Omaha Public Schools need to order a case of Weekly Reader's and send them to Ms. Alexis' house – she needs a refresher course in spelling, writing, social studies, math, government and evidently, genetics!

This concept of God being "colorblind" is stupid. Check out what Ms. Alexis says about it:

> Thus, when God sees His children of His creation, He does not home in on color. One reason God does not take note of color is because He looks within an individual to his/her heart. The last color I have known the heart to be is red. The heart is the determining factor as to how God views an individual, not the individual's skin color (p. 13).

Race is linked to culture. To not see color is to deny each racial grouping its uniqueness and beauty. Ms. Alexis is lying, once again. She doesn't have a clue how God views race, because she gets her information from a white racist – Rev. Les Beauchamp. He is a fraud and a charlatan; a frustrated Hollywood wannabe. He sells Ms. Alexis that colorblind bullshit because this is how white folks view race relations: pretend not to notice that someone is black or brown or yellow, and in that way you can get along with them. Translation: see them as tanned white folks and then any difference is easier to tolerate. Like master, like flunky.

Again, all the heart does is pump blood. Anyone who tells you that the heart is the basis of emotion and love is a liar. The heart is a metaphor for something much deeper. It's all about the mind, and if you're a racist, you hate people because of their skin color and their racial background. You don't hate them with your heart. She uses a Biblical quote in an attempt to prove that the heart carries some kind of emotional powers:

> But the Lord said to Samuel, "Do not look at his appearance or at the height of his stature, because I have rejected him; for God sees not as man sees, for man looks at the outward appearance, but the Lord looks at the heart (1 Samuel 16:7).

The heart is a metaphor. If you are kind, good and compassionate, that is not an expression of the heart, but of the mind. So the title of this sub-chapter, "The Focus is on the Heart" means really that the focus is on what kind of person you are and how you treat others. All the heart does is pump blood.

He Loves Us All

Continuing to quote Scripture (but apparently too confused to apply it in her own personal life), Ms. Alexis, one of the biggest Aunt Jemimas of all time, continues to act as if she and God have tea every afternoon at four o'clock sharp. Here we go:

> Hence, God loves us all. Whether we possess a black, white, red, yellow, or brown hew, (sic) makes no difference to God. God deals with attitudes, dispositions, and the like. Color is not an issue when it comes to whether or not an individual will receive the love of God. For,(sic) God loves us all (p. 14).

If God deals with attitudes and the like, when is he going to deal with all those lies that Ms. Alexis is telling on him? She blames him for everything, and takes no responsibility for her own situation. She moralizes, but appears to not give a damn about morals. Now, it's back to Bible quotes and more of her pontifications about what God does and does not want:

> For the Bible says, it is not what is on the outside of a person that destroys him/her, but rather what lies on the inside of a person that causes the most damage for others and oneself. God does not particularly care about how we look on the outside. He is concerned with the mattes of the heart. Yet, man in is minute understanding of God's creation continues to look to the outside of a person to determine his/her value or worth. Believe it or not, this type of calculation of human worthiness is exercised among those who attend church, as well (pp. 14-15).

If God doesn't care about how we look on the outside, then why should Ms. Alexis? And yet all she does is whine and whimper about all these white people she's surrounded by. So? She says that such judgments of looks are even exercised among those who attend church – as if those who attend church are not above sinning. Some of the biggest cockhounds, sluts, gamblers, alcoholics and wife-beaters can be found in the church on Sunday morning. Look at what was found in the Catholic church during the week of August 15th: Catholic priests, hundreds of them, guilty of dickin' little boys in the booty. And Nebraska is full of them, by they control Boys Town, Creighton University and the Catholic Charities, so all is kept quiet.

And like those Catholic priests, Ms. Alexis is also an example of someone who talks out of both sides of her mouth. She wants to write a book about God ordaining the white man to lead the world but then turns around and says God doesn't see skin color. Which one is it?

She concludes the chapter on the most often used and abused quote from the Bible, John 3:16:

> *"For God so loved the world, that He gave His only begotten Son, that whoever believe in Him should not perish, but have eternal life (John 3:16).*

God loves us. Okay great, we know that if you believe that kind of thing. The problem that should be posed to Ms. Alexis is, do YOU love YOUR self? And what did "God" do to make you so fucked up in the head?

The World Around Us

This woman spends page after page whining and crying about how she's had to struggle, how she was the only black in her classes and so on. Is she not only concerned about her own "self-worth"? But now, look at how she points the fingers at other people:

> The world around us is in a dire mess. More and more, an individual is living as he/she sees fit for his/her own self-worth. How many people do you encounter on a daily basis who are concerned for your self-worth? If you interact with anyone what even cares about your self-worth, it is an occasion that is few and far in between (sic). Since our cares/ concerns are rarely generated toward one another, this world has become turmoil (p. 16).

Her pontifications continue:

> This catastrophe has so enveloped our world that we think it is normal to live in this manner. We live within (sic) a dysfunctional world, countries, states, cities, communities, groups, families, as well as, live as a dysfunctional individual. In addition to these dysfunctions and unbeknownst to us, the purpose for our lives as racial ethnic groups and/or individuals just passes us by (p. 16).

A woman who lives her life as a hermit, only coming out to work, shop and ride around in her SUV, has no right to give advice on what is taking place around the world. Why? Because she is doing nothing that is going to make any impact, that's why. She's just another one of those people who whines and complains about the world being a "ball of confusion," but sits back and does nothing in her own way to make things better. In fact, she makes things worse as she sits down and writes a book giving all glory to the enemy of course race, the same man whose ancestors kidnapped us and enslaved our ancestors. She expects us to believe that God came to her and told her that the white man should lead the rest of the world.

How sick can you get?

To purge herself of guilt, she falls back on Bible quotes, as if this is somehow going to balance out the total lack of credibility that she displays when she talks about her "revelations." Following is another quote from the Bible:

> But realize this, that in the last days difficult times will come. For men will be lovers of self, lovers of money, boastful, arrogant, revilers, disobedient to parents, ungrateful, unholy, unloving, irreconcilable, malicious gossips, without self-control, brutal, haters of good, treacherous, reckless, conceited, lovers of pleasure rather than lovers of God; Holding a form of godliness, although they have denied its power; and avoid such men as these (2 Timothy 3:1-5).

That was the H.R. Pufnstuff version of that passage. Here is how it should have read for anyone with a decent vocabulary:

> This know also, that in the last days perilous times shall come. For men shall belovers of their own selves, covetous, boasters, proud,, blasphemers, disobedient to parents, unthankful, unholy, Without natural affection, truce-breakers, false accusers, incontinent, fierce, despisers of those that are good, Traitors, heady, high-minded, lovers of pleasures more than lovers of God; Having a form of godliness, but denying the per thereof: from such turn away.

See how more relevant and mature the passage sounds? Let's move on, as Ms. Alexis gives out free (and unsolicited) advice on "working" with each other and, of course, with God

<u>Work Together</u>

So now we have to deal with more sub-chapter headings. It seems to me that she wrote down a bunch of stuff and then tried to divide it up and give each "section" a title, or a name. In only a few cases do the sections actually reflect the title given them. But then, that's part for the course in a book that reflects the rantings of someone who sounds very much like a scatter-brained hillbilly.

We begin with more of her advice:

> God made all things to work together. He desires that all things
> be decent and in order. We find that all of His creation is
> obedient to His will except for us humans. If you take notice, the
> ocean, grass, trees, animals, and so forth obey God's commands.
> You can observe each of these God made (sic)
> elements/creatures submitting willfully to God's will for them by
> carrying out the daily functions God named for them to perform.
> Even the moon, sun, and stars carry out the directives of God,
> night and day (pp. 17-18).

The time spent showing concern for the fishes of the sea, the chipmunks in the trees or the ants cavorting in the grass could be better spent trying to find out if that tumor in her head is benign or malignant! Now that she's given the kingdom of thingdom its due props, let's see what she has to say about human beings (we know it can't be good):

> Yet, when it comes to human beings, we are all out of whack. God
> commands and we defy. God says be kind to enemies, we curse them.
> God says give, we take. Time does not allow me to speak of the acts of
> defiance we have brought upon the earth since we were realized (sic).
> For, the list goes on and on and on (p. 18).

So what? What is she going to do about it? And if she is so concerned about the defiance of man against the will of God, why did she choose, of her own free will, to join the most racist church in the entire city? A church that is elitist in its practices and that is led by a minister – Les Beauchamp – who is as crazy as a hyena on crack! It's easy to sit down and list what's wrong with the world; but the TRULY religious person, one that is committed to the welfare of his brothers and sisters – as I am – is the one who is working day and night to do something about these horrific conditions. What does she do? Nothing but complain and ride around in an over-priced SUV. Some contribution.

Moving on:

> God expects His children to work with Him. In doing so, this will
> display to the world that we are, in fact, the children of the living God.
> God has a set of principles he awaits his children to obey. I will give you

> one. One of God's principles is for His children to love everyone versus
> the world's principle to hate those different from you. His ways are not
> the ways of the world. When will we ever embrace and execute this
> ideology? (pp. 18-19).

It is Ms. Alexis who whines about wanting to be around her own "kind." So doesn't this contradict the statement above? She pretends she doesn't like being around white people all the time. Isn't that another contradiction? The problem is, or so it seems, is that Ms. Alexis is a hypocrite and a megalomaniac at the same time; she hates herself but loves to tell other people what to do. She claims she believes in God, and yet she blames God for her Anglophilia.

But here is the horrifying part: this woman teaches young children. She is in front of the classroom and not only that, she "counsels" them. How many minds has she warped with her brand of "evangelism"?

But it's not over:

> It seems the only way we will carry out the will of God is if we
> comprehend the outcome. Oh how we limit ourselves from attaining so
> many blessings because of this. This derives from our not understanding
> why God has asked us to do a thing. Therefore, we do not comply with
> what we are suppose (sic) to do. This ought not be. God has specifically
> said for us not to lean toward our own understanding, but rather we are
> to trust in Him. Hence, our lack of understanding ought not hinder our
> doing what God has predestined for us to do (p. 19).

Comprehend the outcome? How can you comprehend something that hasn't happened yet? This woman is out to lunch. She speaks in riddles, mixes those with general truisms and then adds a pinch of bullshit and to her, that's a "revelation"! She believes in predestination, but if that was the case, then why does she talk about people changing? If your future is predestined, that means that there's nothing you can do about changing it! Didn't she see the movie "Final Destination"?

I don't want to sound like a bully, but this woman has some serious mental issues. She's a schizophrenic, and I believe she might also be bipolar. Want proof? Check out the following statement:

> Even I had reservations in writing this book. Due to the very fact of my
> not knowing the purpose as to why this message was placed upon my
> heart to share with the world. This lack of understanding resulted in
> some hesitation on my part. However, I have learned early on in my
> walk with God that it is better to obey His voice than my own feelings or
> reservations (pp. 19-20).

A message was placed upon her heart to share with the world? What was that message: never lean too close to an open container of ammonia? Could it have been, when a boulder is about to fall on your head, move out of the way? Maybe it was, never put too big a piece into your crack pipe. I don't know. But I know this: God didn't put the evil that she's talking about on her heart. God didn't tell her to sell her soul to the cunning Les Beauchamp. She did all these things on her own and of her own free will. But what does she write? That she has walked with God. Maybe she was walking with Hannibal Lectre and got the two confused.

She writes that she hears God's voice. Do you know what they call people who lie and say they talked with God? Retards, that's what! She's hearing voices and claiming it's god when, in reality, it's probably the director of the mental hospital telling her that she's behind on her payments! What nerve!

What happens is that she takes what she reads from the Bible and gives it a literal translation. For instance, take the following quote from Proverbs, which she handily inserts on page 21:

> Trust in the Lord with all your heart, And do not lean on your own
> understanding.
> In all your ways acknowledge Him, And He will make your paths
> straight.
> Do not be wise in your own eyes; Fear the Lord and turn away from evil
> It will be healing to your body, And refreshment to your bones (Proverbs
> 3: 5-8).

The first part of the scripture that she quoted, "trust in the Lord with all your heart, and do not lean on your own understanding" – that is a not meant to be taken literally. It means believe in a higher spirit, and don't think you have all the answers. But weak-minded people take this to mean that they shouldn't think at all; and that's why they end up putting their hard-earned money into a collection plate after being fed a couple of hours of bullshit by some jive-ass "preacher" who just got through screwing one of his congregation members, drinking a pint of whiskey and burning up his lips on a red hot crack pipe.

In fact, all of those passages above are words that foster dependency. That is what religious books do; they are aimed to make you think in the abstract, about the future - to believe that "God will handle it." But if you don't get up off your ass and do something, God's not going to do a solo, because God works through YOU!

But instead of being proactive, she quotes passages that tell the reader,

"In all your ways acknowledge Him, and He will make your paths
straight. Do not be wise in your own eyes; Fear the Lord and turn

> *away from evil. It will be healing to your body, And refreshment to your bones."*

This is the kind of thing that makes people like Les Beauchamp, the white man who is head pastor at this black woman's suburban church, rich. Then he finds some weak-minded cutie like Geraldine Alexis and before you know it, she's thinking she hears God whispering in her ear when, in reality, its Beauchamp! "Put some money in the collection plate, put some money in the collection plate, (can I come over?), Put some money in the collection plate (that's a nice blouse), put some money in the collection plate." Subliminal bullshit – that's what it amounts to.

She's lied on God, she's hearing voices and she doesn't want to be around black folks. But she thinks she has enough credibility to give out advice – like the fable that follows:

> This reminds me of a story I read, in Our Daily Bread devotional, about an old man and his donkey. The old man and his donkey were traveling throughout many villages on their journey. When they came into the first village, the village people said that the old man looked so tired and that he should ride on the donkey to regain his strength. Therefore, the man hopped upon the donkey as they were leaving out of that particular village. When they came into the second village, the village people exclaimed that the old man was not very nice for riding the donkey, and that the man should walk. So, the old man climbed back down from the donkey as they were exiting the second village. When they came into the third village, the village people said that the donkey looked so tired and that he should be carried. The last time the old man and donkey were sited (sic) the old man was carrying the donkey (pp. 21-22).

This story is older than the men that Ms. Alexis probably dates! Of what use is this ancient parable? She explains it, thusly:

> The moral of this story is that there are too many voices in the world today. You have your mother, father, sister, brother, spouse, children, extended family, church family, friends, co-workers, enemies, and people you do not even know, as the old man encountered, speaking into your life. They will have you carrying heavy load, like a donkey, if you listen to all of their voices. Therefore, it is better to know and listen to the voice of God than any man (p. 22).

You see: if you let a nut talk long enough, eventually he'll indict himself. Now the moral is about listening to voices, right. Now isn't that what SHE is doing? Doesn't she claim that God is, indeed, "speaking into" her life? Then what does she conclude? She says it is better to listen to the voice of God than any man. But how does she know if it's God or not? What if it's Rich Little doing one of his impersonations? What if it's her mind playing tricks on her? There is no way she could know for sure, so what she does is ASSUME that it's God's voice she's hearing (that is, if she's really hearing any voices) so that people will listen to her. But the fact is, almost every single retard at your local mental institution will tell you that he (or she) has talked to God. Evidently, Ms. Alexis is no exception.

I guess the following quote is being shared as a way to "warn us" against worshipping false gods. Here it is:

> And Samuel said, "Has the Lord as much delight in burnt
> offerings and sacrifices as in obeying the voice of the Lord?
> Behold to obey is better than sacrifice. And to heed them the fat
> of rams.
>
> For rebellion is as iniquity and idolatry. Because you have
> rejected the word of the Lord, He has rejected you from being
> kind (1 Samuel, 15:22&23).

Obedience. These Christians fall for the okey-doke every single time. They'll obey "God" when it's handy, but most of them do worse shit than I ever thought about doing. The Christian religion has a lot of room for hypocrisy. That is why it is so attractive to scoundrels, pimps, prostitutes and thieves. That is a religion that tells these ne'er-do-wells that if they sin, it's okay; all they have to do is say they're sorry. The Catholic branch is even worse: all you have to do is say some "hail Mary's" and you're home free to fuck, freak and frolic for another year or two!

This religion is perfect for someone like Les Beauchamp, an effeminate wannabe "community leader." And don't you think for one minute that when he got a look at Alexis walking down that aisle to shake his hand, that he was thinking about not coveting his neighbor's wife or house or oxen – or that ass!

Ms. Alexis tells us that, "God speaks in many ways and uses many means to get a word to us. As you read this book, listen to what God is saying to you specifically. Yes, God speaks through books, as well. The Bible, the main book says He will use rocks to carry out a function that He has purposed us to do if, in fact, we refuse to comport" (p. 23).

Now, what she is implying above is that her shitty book somehow provides a mystical link between God and the reader. She is then convinced that God speaks through books. He does? What was God's message in the book, *A Clockwork*

Orange? That rape is good? Or how about the Divine One's message in the book, Harry Potter? That sorcery and wizardry are the way to get into the Kingdom of God? Nigga, please!

While acknowledging that the Bible is the main book (that's debatable –I think the Koran and Torah would have something to say about that), she adds that God will use rocks to carry out a function he has for us. Well, at least I know where God can get the rocks from: her head!!!

Now, another Bible quote:

> ***To him the doorkeeper opens, and the sheep hear his voice, and he calls his own sheep by name, and leads them out. When he puts forth all his own, he goes before them, and the sheep follow him because they know his voice.***
> ***And a stranger they simply will not follow, but will flee from him, because they do not know the voice of strangers (John 10: 3-5) (pp. 23-24).***

What in the hell does this mean? While you're trying to figure it out, let's move on to the next section, where the all-powerful Ms. Alexis teaches us how we all are, after all, "created for a purpose."

<u>Created for a Purpose</u>

Ms. Alexis is obsessed, and she really seems to care. (About WHAT, I have no idea!). She wants to be an evangelist, but she hasn't put in the work necessary to be an intelligent one. Instead, she babbles, paints herself into corners from which there is no escape, and then when all else fails, she can point her fingers at God!

Ms. Alexis explains that,

> We all were created for a purpose. Therefore, we are not mistakes. God had something in mind each time each of us were born. Yet, as opposed to us embracing this truth, we continue to tell some people that they are mistakes. Other races try to demean and treat some racial groups as if God did not know what He was doing when He made their race of people (p. 24).

Take notice how this woman is afraid to say "white folks." She is so intent on spreading the blame for racial prejudice around to everybody else, she can't concentrate on the source of it: whitey! She refers to white folks as "other races" when, in reality – despite their small numbers on a worldwide level -- they are the main practitioners and promoters of racial hatred!

Now notice above how she claims that these "other races" (whites) demean other people and that God created other races of people. And yet later in this book she claims that the black man was the original man and all races stemmed from there. Which one is it, Ms. Alexis? She is the guilty party in all this. Want more proof? Read on:

> How arrogant and pompous one must be to judge one of God's creations. Within the Bible, God asks, "Where were you at the beginning of time?" "Where were you at the world's conception?" If you answered correctly, you were not around. How then can those who were born tens of thousands of years after the beginning of item question the Almighty God's work? (p. 25).

Throughout this entire book, all this woman has been doing is "judging God's creations." She judges the white man – with a thumbs up, of course. She judges the people who demean, the people who lack understanding and so on. She even makes the judgment that racist Les Beauchamp is someone a special messenger of God. Yeah, he's "special alright" – as in "special Olympics!

It is Ms. Alexis who has called into question God's creations. She runs to white men for advice on how to deal with per problems, but when it comes to God, she questions why she is doing what she's doing. She arrives at the conclusion that she can "undo" what God has done, although in reality, God had nothing to do with this woman's actions. If she believes in predestination – as she apparently does – then she has to grasp the fact that she's a bootlicking Uncle Tom. Can I make it any simpler?

Her complicity in the white man's racist ways is made more evident in the following statement:

> Yet I have witnessed, children of God buy into this attitude of questioning why did God make this race or people? Or, it would be better to oppress, if not directly, then indirectly, this or that racial group. Such deviant behavior is an affront to God's purpose ultimately causing a disruption in almost each and every individual's life. The end result is dysfunction which is so prevalent in our world, today, as well as, a loss of purpose (p. 25).

Say what? The only racial group that is doing any "oppressing" is the white race. Why can't she come out and say it? I'll tell you why: because she is in love with them and doesn't want to offend. She is willing to call what they do "deviant behavior," but she hangs out, associates with, talks regularly with, trusts, adores and admires that race. That means that she aids and abets them in their crimes with her silence.

The claims the end result is dysfunction and a loss of purpose. Don't these two words sum up Ms. Alexis' problems perfectly? Based on her ideas, it is clear that she is mentally dysfunctional, is it not? And in terms of a loss of purpose, any time you associate yourself with the enemy of your own race, realizing that that enemy is anti-black and a segregationist, then you are truly lost. But she does have a purpose, and it is "the white man's purpose," which she is seeking to justify with this feces-laden book.

More self-revelation can be found in the lines of the following paragraph:

> Then the Lord answered Job out of the whirlwind and said,
> "Who is this that darkens counsel by words without knowledge.
> Now gird up your loins like a man, and I will ask you, and you
> instruct Me! Where were you when I laid the foundation of the
> earth! Tell Me, if you have understanding, Who sets its
> measurements, since you know? Or who stretched the line on it?
> On what were its bases sunk? Or who laid its cornerstone, When
> the morning stars sang together, And all the sons of God shouted
> for joy? "or who enclosed the sea with doors, when bursting
> forth, it went out from the womb; When I made a cloud its
> garment, And thick darkness its swaddling band, And I placed
> boundaries on it, and I set bolt and doors, And I said, "Thus far
> you shall come, but no further; And here shall your proud waves
> stop"? (Job 38: 1-11).

The reason I include these quotes from the Bible, as long and drawn out as they are, is that I might want to make reference to them for one of my future books. A second reason is because I want the reader to see how this woman leans on the Bible and yet violates the tenets of it at every turn. But then again, she's a self-appointed evangelist and, as I've said before, "show me an evangelist, and I'll show you a bullshit artist with a tambourine."

Let's move on to Chapter Two, where the black Roseanne Barr teaches us about our "purpose in life."

<u>Chapter 2: Our Purpose in Life</u>

Who does this woman speak for? You? Me? The white race? Who is the "our" in "our purpose in life"? Is she writing about all of humanity? But perhaps the real question is, what qualifies her to speak for anyone other than herself? The self-proclaimed pretension of power is ultimately self-defeating – as we will see on the pages that follow.

Ms. Alexis has issues – now that's a fact.

<u>We All Have Purpose</u>

Her language is blatantly patronizing. Writing as if she's the only person on earth with a brain, Ms. Alexis continues to lecture on issues of which she is ignorant. The following paragraph proves my point:

> As previously stated, each individual, as well as, racial group has a purpose to fulfill on earth. In the Bible, on the one hand, Pharaoh had the purpose of enslaving the Israelites. On the other hand, Moses had a purpose to fulfill which was to free the Israelites from slavery. These are two examples of individuals fulfilling their purposes that were predestined by God since their inception (p. 28).

Each racial group has a purpose? Isn't that somewhat insulting? A purpose according to whose plan? Ms. Alexis sounds as if she's writing a job description or something. This "everyone has a purpose" crap feeds right into her belief in predestination – all of reality is already set and we're just playing it out. That is such bullshit – it means that people can't change or alter their experiences or the conditions around them. It's the philosophy of losers who feel impotent or unable to bring about change, so they concoct some Grand Lie about how everything is going to take place anyway, so there's no need resisting.

Ms. Alexis' rants continue:

> Consequently, the Egyptians, one cultural group, under Pharaoh's rule were predestined to make life difficult for the Israelites. Whereas the Israelites, a different cultural group and followers of God, had a purpose to be brought out of slavery into the promise (sic) land predestined by God. These are two instances whereby racial groups came into the knowledge of and realized their purposes. To know, as well as, fulfill your poise as an individual and racial ethnic group and to shun other alternatives is a real plus! Therein lies a true sense of alignment with God (pp. 28-29).

The Egyptians were a "cultural group"? This sounds like some white historian's interpretation. The Egyptians were BLACK, meaning that they were African people. This attempt to "whitenize" and "Asianize" Egypt, or attribute the magnificent of the pyramids and the Sphinx to being created by some aliens visiting earth is so typical of white folks – and those who are obsessed with white folks.

Another tactic is to refer to the Jews as Israelites. The Israelites are not a "racial group" – they are peckerwoods with hooked noses, pure and simple. As Senator Ernie Chambers has stated, "if he's more racist than he's stingy, he's white; if he's more stingy than he is racist, he's a Jew."

Ms. Alexis writes that, "to fulfill your purpose as an individual and racial ethnic group and to shun other alternatives is a real plus! Therein lies a true sense of alignment with God." This is another contradiction. Why doesn't she fulfill her purpose as a black woman and stop kissing the pink asses of every white person she meets? Why doesn't she "shun other alternatives" and attend a church filled with black people, HER people?

Next comes another long Biblical quote:

> And David said to Solomon, "My son, I had intended to build a house to the name of the Lord my God. "But the word of the Lord came to me saying, 'you have shed much blood, and have waged great wars; you shall not build a house to My name, because you have shed so much blood on the earth before Me. 'Behold a son shall be born to you, who shall be a man of rest; and I will give him rest from all his enemies on every side; for his name shall be Solomon, and I will give peace and quiet to Israel in his days. 'He shall build a house for My name … (1 Chronicles 22: 7-10).

The only good thing about these long quotes is that in most of the book, it signals the end of a sub-chapter. Let us move on

Unique Talent

Our next trip through the large void that is Ms. Alexis' mind continues as she recalls,

> It was shared in a class that I participated in that a poll was taken of selected individuals. Through this poll, it was determined that each individual does something far better than 10,000 other individuals. Therefore, whatever God has ordained you to do, no other person within a 10,000 count can match your ability to fulfill your purpose. No matter how hard another tries, he/she cannot touch the unique talent God has afforded you and only you to execute in His master plan (pp. 30-31).

Who developed that so-called poll? It sounds like bullshit to me; either that, or she made it up. At any rate, I'd like to see the data set that was drawn from that established that "each individual does something far better than 10,000 other individuals."

This skewing of reality is then followed up with an outright lie when Ms. Alexis claims, "No matter how hard another tries, he/she cannot touch the unique talent God has afforded you and only you to execute in His master plan." That is so wrong. What "master plan"? And if it is to include everyone, why would unique talent be only given to one person, then a different unique talent to another person and so on and so forth? Again, she is LYING on God.

Ms. Alexis writes on:

> Then Jesse called Abinadab, and made him pass before Samuel,
> And he said, "Neither has the Lord chosen this one."
> Next Jesse made Shammah pass by. And he said, "either has the
> Lord chosen this one."
>
> Thus Jesse made seven of his sons pass before Samuel. But
> Samuel said to Jesse, "The Lord has not chosen these."
>
> And Samuel said to Jesse," Are these all the children?" And he
> said, "There remains yet the youngest, and behold, he is tending
> the sheep."
>
> Then Samuel said to Jesse, "Send and bring him; for we will not
> sit down until he comes here."
>
> So he sent and brought him in. Now he was ruddy, with beautiful
> eyes and a handsome appearance. And the Lord said, "Arise,
> anoint him; for this is he" (1 Samuel 16:8-12) (pp. 31-32).

In case Ms. Alexis doesn't know it, the chosen one above is not white. To be "ruddy" is to be "colored" in complexion. So even as she strives to justify her white master and the "revelation" of God, she offers us nothing of substance – and her opinion doesn't count for much.

Forfeited Blessing

She's already perverted reality across almost every other area of life that there is, from philosophy and history to religion and psychology. Now she seeks to take sports and use it to make her point. And, as can be expected, she screws that up as well.

She begins with the following statement:

> Yet, there is a way to miss your calling or transfer your purpose
> on earth (sic) to another individual. That way is by not being

> where you are suppose (sic) to be or doing what you are suppose
> (sic) to do. I heard a story about a basketball play called the
> "Alley Oop" performed and mastered by Michael Jordan and
> Scotty Pippin. This play is a masterful way to display how we as
> God's children can, in fact, lose out on our purpose I life, thus,
> forfeiting it to another (pp. 32-33).

How can you transfer your purpose on Earth to another individual? If it's your purpose, then isn't it yours and yours alone? And doesn't that mean that it's yours to either take advantage of or screw up? How can you transfer something designed for you – this "unique individual" as she puts it – to another person? It wouldn't fit, would it?

I think this woman has been brainwashed by one of those loony suburban ministers from Trinity Church. I think she's spending entirely too much time in the presence of Les Beauchamp. Anyone who would make the kinds of commercials that he makes, commercials that imply that he can help anyone "find God," has got to be a nut. And there is Ms. Alexis, walking right beside him all the way to the loony ward.

Now comes the sports analogy: the issue of the Alley-Oop pass, Michael Jordan and Scottie Pippen. What does that have to do with anything? Let us look at Ms. Alexis' own words:

> This is the analogy of the "Alley Oop" and how one can lose out
> on his/her blessing. The play is that Michael brings the ball down
> court. As he brings the ball down the court, he throws the ball
> close to the net where Scotty is supposed to be. The kicker is that
> Michael does not throw the ball to where Scotty is, but rather to
> where Scotty is supposed to be. If Scotty makes it to the point
> where Michael throws the ball, Scotty is then able to catch the
> ball and slam dunk the ball into the net and obtain a blessing.
> However, if Scotty does not get to where he is suppose to be to
> get the ball into the hoop, well you know the story (p. 33).

A dunk shot compared with a blessing? The combination described above is not the original nor is it the most effective duo involved with such a play. The fact is, Magic Johnson and Michael Cooper had perfected "The Coop-a-Loop" at about the same time as Jordan and Company were "occasionally" using the Alley Oop. The Coop-a-Loop was a staple play in the offensive arsenal of the Los Angeles Lakers. Just thought I'd mention that to show that Ms. Alexis' knowledge of professional basketball is as surface-oriented and superficial as her understanding of the Christian faith.

The concept of people knowing their "place" (instead of their "role") is something that the white man created to maintain his own position of privilege. He put his own white woman in her "place," which was up on a pedestal. And while he lofted her up high, he was raping black women, who also had a "place" – which was underneath HIM! It is clear that this is the position that Ms. Alexis has willingly assumed for herself: as the witless and willing thrall of the white boy.

Ms. Alexis continues:

> Hence, most of the time we miss out on the blessings or purpose God has ordained for us to own, because we are not where we are suppose to be. We miss out, because we are not doing the things we are suppose (sic) to do. We miss out, because we allow our will to be done as opposed to God, our creator (sic), will to be done (p. 34).

The will we have is God's will. We are God's functionaries here on Earth. As long as people like Beauchamp and Ms. Alexis keep trying to get us to look to the stars and believe that some goblin or goon from space is dictating what we must do, we are never going to progress as a people. Ms. Alexis has bought into the white man's bullshit and is now spending money out of her own pocket to promote his wicked culture and way of life. She is, in simple terms, doing the work of the Devil. And I'm not talking about some asshole with horns and a long tail. I'm talking about the biggest murderer, rapist, thief and child molester on the planet.

In conclusion, the poor soul provides another excerpt from the Bible:

> *Then Saul said to Samuel, "I have sinned, I have indeed*
> *transgressed the command of the Lord and your words,*
> *because I feared the people and listened to their voice.*
> *"Now therefore, please pardon my sin and return with me, that*
> *I may worship the Lord."*
> *But Samuel said to Saul, "I will not return with you; for you*
> *have rejected the word of the Lord, and the Lord has rejected*
> *you from being kind over Israel."*
> *And as Samuel turned to go, Saul seized the edge of his robe,*
> *and it tore.*
> *So Samuel said to him. "The Lord has torn the kingdom of*
> *Israel from you today, and has given it to your neighbor who is*
> *better than you.*
> *"And also the Glory of Israel will not lie or change His mind;*
> *for He is not a man that He should change His mind" (1*
> *Samuel 15: 24-29).*

Using Scripture in boldface throughout her book makes it no less blasphemous; in fact, that makes it more of a perversion. After all, as Exodus 20:7, one of the Ten Commandments, makes most clear, "Thou shalt not take the name of the Lord thy God in vain; for the Lord will not hold him guiltless that taketh his name in vain." Not only is Ms. Alexis a liar and a hypocrite, but also a blasphemer and sinner.

When Judgment Day gets here (yeah, right), man, is SHE gonna get it!

<u>Fingerprints</u>

This sub-chapter has an interesting name – and, it is perhaps appropriate. I am sure that before Ms. Alexis was checked into the Trinity Church Hospital for the Religiously Insane, she had to have her fingerprints put on the record books!

She is so convinced that everybody is unique and yet she doesn't allow for it as she pontificates about how we need to follow white folks simply because she says so. For instance, she writes,

> The sad thing about us losing out is that each of us has our very own unique purpose or blessing that is meant solely for us. We all are unique. It does not matter if you are a twin or triplet. It matters not if a person dresses like you, speaks like you, walks or talks as you do. You are a unique individual with a unique plan for your life. There is no other you. Case in point, this is determined by your very fingerprints. No two person's fingerprints are the same (p. 36).

If what she writes is true, and that indeed, each of us has our own very unique purpose or blessing, then why can't she let sleeping dogs lie and stay the fuck out of our business? Why does she sit down and write a book that seeks to deprive us of that uniqueness? She is writing and saying, "it's my way or the highway." She is not allowing for people to think for themselves; she is too busy trying to get all of those dumb enough to buy her book that her "revelation" means that we have to listen to what she says and then fall in step as we race to see who can kiss the white man's ass first.

Now I don't know if she thinks she's a messenger of God or what, but it sure sounds a lot like it when she shares the following quote from the Bible: "'For I know the plans that I have for you,' declares the Lord. 'Plans for welfare and not for calamity to give you a future and a hope" (Jeremiah 29:11).

Let's suppose the Lord actually said that – which, by the way, I sincerely doubt. If he has plans, then that means that whatever he dictates, we should do, right? Well then answer me this: why does Ms. Alexis feel she has the right to question God about her relationships with white folks? If God indeed, ordained it (which I doubt), then why doesn't she just accept it and keep her big mouth shut? You know why? Because this is all one big unadulterated crock of shit, that's why. Ms. Alexis is attempting to do to us what Les Beauchamp is doing to her – both figuratively and literally speaking.

From there, Ms. Alexis jumps back on the "me-first" bandwagon and in doing so, contradicts herself once again:

> Furthermore, that means that you have no competition when it comes to fulfilling your destiny. So many of us are stressed, not blessed, as well as, without rest due to our possessing a competing spirit. Who are you competing against? Yourself? God has commanded destinies to be realized on earth and has endowed each individual with the precise talents/skills to attain his/her own destiny. Thus, you are the only person for your particular lot in life. That destiny that God has predestined for you to reach has your *fingerprints* all over it. No one else's fingerprints will do (pp. 36-37—emphasis original).

This preceding paragraph is so rife with hypocrisy that Ms. Alexis should apply for membership in the Liar's Club! She talks about unique roles and unique destinies and yet she continues giving orders trying to get everyone to change and see things HER way. That is what Christians do: they tell you that you have to do things their way or you'll burn in hell. It is the only religion that does that! Doesn't that tell you something in and of itself? If we are like fingerprints, then why doesn't she leave us alone? Why does she write a book talking about "The White Man's Purpose," telling us this cracker is destined to lead the other races? If that were truly the case, wouldn't his own actions show this to be true? Of course they would. But do they?

He fails at almost everything he does except for making money and making war. His woman hates his guts and his kids can't stand him. On television – which he controls – he paints himself to be a buffoon and bungler and the butt of the rest of the family's jokes. He's hated the world over – as 911 proved – and he underestimates the rest of the world. He makes jokes about every other racial and cultural group, and he's so cursed that he can't even have children above zero population growth (the only place in the world where he's producing more than he's dying is in, of all places, Northern Ireland!). And this is the CLOWN that this so-called black woman wants us to follow? Better check the white man's ass – for HER fingerprints!

The following Scripture supposedly buttresses or supports her point of view and perspective:

> And we know that God causes all things to work together for good to
> those who love God, to those who are called according to His purpose.
> For whom He foreknew, He also predestined to become conformed to
> the image of His son, that He might be the first-born among many
> brethren;
>
> And whom He predestined, these He also called; and whom He called,
> these He also justified; and whom He justified, these He also glorified.
> What then shall we say to these things? If God is for us, who is against
> us? (pp. 37-38).

How can God be for us if Ms. Alexis claims he revealed to her that the white man was supposed to lead the rest of us? How can God be for us if, as Ms. Alexis claims, we are to follow the one person who has created a weapon powerful enough to destroy God's planet a thousand times over? Ms. Alexis has once again flip-flopped (sometimes, perhaps literally) so that she can curry favor with the white man. And she does the same thing in the following statement:

> Therefore, what is meant for you no one else can have unless you
> forfeit it by disobeying God. It is written in the word of God that God
> desires obedience better than sacrifice. There are many children of God
> who believe they do not have to submit to God's will., But rather, they
> can sacrifice to make up for their lack of obedience by paying tithes,
> working at the church, giving to the poor and so forth. Yet, to display
> that you truly love God is to obey Him. The Bible says that he knows
> the right thing to do yet does not do it; then to him it is sin (pp. 38-39).

Therefore, if you don't do what God says you forfeit your rights? What kind of free choice is that? If we are all unique then we all have unique ways of viewing reality. So then, if that is the case, why would we have to forfeit our rights to think as we want to think and act as we please? This totally counter poses what she's written earlier.

Secondly, she describes the white man's method of operation, as well as the "out" that most Christians, black and white, have as a part of their "belief system." She writes, that sacrifice doesn't cut it with God and that some people disobey God's commands but seek to make up for it by paying tithes, working at the church, and giving to the poor. What do you think the white man has been doing for the past several centuries?

While paying lip service to God, this peckerwood has made himself a god on earth. He sets up charities and social service agencies so that he can boast about how humane he is. He talks about how poor Jesus was, but then turns around and builds multi-million dollar super structure and calls them "places of worship." He pays tithes because he can afford to, but he doesn't give the ten percent; he just writes a check because, as his culture has taught him, "everybody has a price." As long as he can impress the greedy-ass pastor, the typical Christian figures he's got it made. Buy off the head man and you can win favor with the Supreme Being. Ask Les Beauchamp – his church as some of the richest and most racist business people in the entire city.

Closing out the sub-chapter, Ms. Alexis talks about people who disobey God embarking "on sins territory." This whole nation is sins territory, and her buddy, the white man, rules it. And yet she wants us to follow this man because she had a "revelation."

Is Ms. Alexis trying to convert people? If she is why didn't she give the book a different title? By using the book as an instruction manual on how to get "tight" with God, and by giving the book the title it has, Ms. Alexis is implying that God, and the white man, are one! The book should be called "God's Purpose," but that wouldn't move off the book shelves. So this minor league intellectual, knowing NOTHING about her history, decides to interject the controversial and taboo subject of "race" and now the book sounds like something that would interest the average person.

Finally, she writes,

> If the Lord has given you a directive and you know it is His voice, to engage in an alternative measure or turn a deaf ear to what thus saith the Lord is to embark upon sins territory. After you have completed reading this book, the question to ask yourself is are you signing by not complying with God's directives? If you have answered in the affirmative, then dovetail the former question with will you continue to sin? (p. 39).

Now I have some questions.

Will I continue to sin? Damn skippy. Will I try to control it or work toward improving my moral outlook? I'll do my best. Did this book have anything to do with my decision? No. Does Ms. Alexis need brain surgery? Hell yeah!!

<u>Destined Harmony</u>

Both the title and the content of this particular sub-chapter is an utter lie. There is no "destined harmony" for this world or its people. Once again it appears as if Ms. Alexis has fallen for the bullshit of the white Christians who have her looking to the sky for solutions and ultimate salvation. It simply ain't gonna happen without her turning her life around, getting her mind right and doing something to fight the oppressor, instead of kissing his ass.

She writes,

> The ultimate destiny for this world is harmony. Whether you or I participate in harmonizing this world or not, God's will, will be done. He is calling all individuals coupled with racial groups to ascertain, as well as, avail their purpose. In turn, we will reap God's favor.

How is the ultimate destiny harmony when, everywhere you look, you see war, pestilence, greed and corruption? Now there might be some harmony when mankind is eliminated, but that's the only kind of happiness I can foresee. As long as whitey is on the planet, his goal is to incrementally get more and more control of it. And he'd rather blow it up than share it.

But as far as interracial harmony? Don't count on it.

It is now time for the regularly featured irrelevant Biblical quote:

> … And I heard a loud voice from throne, saying "Behold the tabernacle of God is among men, and He shall dwell among them, and they shall be His people, and God Himself shall be among them,
>
> And He shall wipe away every tear from their eyes; and there shall no longer be any mourning, or crying, or pain, the first things have passed away.
> And He who sits on the throne said, "Behold I am making all things new." And He said, "Write: for these words are faithful and true .." (Revelation, 21: 1-5).

Again, she gives an incorrect Bible citation. The preceding quote are verses THREE through five of Revelations 21, not ONE through five! And this brings me to a point that must be made.

You can tell how much someone believes in something or cares about something by the amount of care that is reflected in the object of their attention and affection. If I love my children, I am going to care for them and love them as much as I can. That, in turn, will be reflected in how I treat them, how I assist them when they are in need, how I defend them against their enemies.

The same thing goes for the Bible and its teachings. If a person who claims to be an evangelist truly loves and cares for those teachings, then that will be reflected in how they behave, how they relate to people and how they represent themselves when it comes to "spreading the word." Look at the flawed thinking, the poor written presentation and the lousy interpretations that Ms. Alexis has offered up in the name of "loving God." Can we really believe her? Can we believe she's sincere when she consistently represents the Psalms as "Psalm"? Can we take her seriously when she cites the wrong verses as she did previously? No, we cannot. And this is a point to bear in mind as we struggle through the remainder of this incredibly sloppy piece of literature.

Continuing:

> He who overcomes shall inherit these things, and I will be his
> God and he will be My son. But for the cowardly and
> unbelieving and abominable and murders (sic) and immoral
> persons and sorcerers and idolaters and all liars, their part, will
> be in the lake that burns with fire and brimstone (Revelation 21:
> 7&8).

Well, it's pretty clear who the unbelieving and abominable folks are. I'm not saying that other racial groupings don't commit crimes. But come on, it should be pretty clear that this white boy is a pimple on the asshole of humanity, let's face it. He's such an asshole that every single category of HIS OWN LAWS that mandates capital punishment – he's committed himself, from kidnap and treason all the way to murder.

And not only is he a cold-hearted person, he's a coward on top of it. So that's the caliber of being that this sister, Geraldine Alexis, is hanging out with and craving the company of. Oh sure, her words say "no, no," but her body and mind say, "oui, oui, oui"!!!

As if she hasn't screwed up and blasphemed enough, now she wants to tell us "God's purpose for our lives." The next sub-chapter outlines her views in this critical area.

God's Purpose For Our Lives

Acting as if she was the "thirteenth discipline," the nerve and gall of this woman reaches its apex in this sub-chapter. Either she's plagiarizing these concepts, mimicking what she's heard Beauchamp mutter during one of his Tupperware Sermons, or she's so far gone that she truly believes she is "god-chosen."

For instance, on pages 41 and 42 she offers the following:

> The way each of us can play his/her part in orchestrating
> harmony is by finding purpose. To find God's purpose for your
> life, you must participate in self-monitoring which requires
> examining your ways against God's (pp. 41-42).

Has SHE examined HER ways? Has she bothered to sit down, take a look at herself and say, "Hey, maybe I'm a little bit too fucked up to be going around giving out religious advice to people?" Of course not. She gives advice to others that she thinks she is too good to apply to her own situation. Another example of hypocrisy.

The fact is, had she engaged in some kind of self-monitoring, she would have understood the need to study and prepare before writing a book that will be accessible to the entire public. And since she was writing about black people, it would make sense to think about how she was making the race look when she published a book that had so many mistakes in it. Her personal sloppiness was transferred to her book; her lack of concern about her race made most evident in her own words. And her defense of the enemy of our race, the elevation of that enemy to the level of "savior" is an insult to every single man and woman of color on the planet.

More advice from this woman is forthcoming:

> Discover your interests/talents/skills. Pay attention, on purpose, to
> whatever you do well. If you find that most people struggle to do
> something that comes with ease to you, then I would pay particular
> attention to that interest/talent/skill. This could possibly mean that you
> have embarked upon God's purpose for your life (p. 42).

What gives this woman the right to give out this advice to people? Where are her credentials? Her degrees from UNO qualify her to teach CHILDREN, not pontificate to ADULTS! This "I'm-Okay-You're-An-Asshole" psycho-babble is for the birds! She's talking to grown people who have a right to make their own decisions, but instead she goes off on a tangent – like the one in the following passage:

> As a school counselor, I oftentimes tell the students to watch for
> what peaks their interest. What seems to come as ease for them
> to perform. What skills do they display an abundance of
> confidence. For example, I remember when I was young. I talked
> and talked and I talked and I talked. My mom and dad used to b
> so upset with me, because they wanted me to be quiet. I was
> oftentimes scolded for talking, and was told that if I would say
> another word, then I would be sent to my room (p. 42).

What? A big, unstoppable mouth? Noooo. Not HER! She continues her rant:

> Well, little did my parents know that they were trying to deter a
> talent that God had endowed me with to fulfill my purpose. For, I
> now go into the youth centers to speak with those separated from
> society to let them know that God loves them. I speak daily with
> children, via my counseling profession, in regards to appropriate
> behavior, cognition, and emotions. I speak and listen daily, as a
> therapist, as individuals share their concerns, problems, and
> impasses. Hence, what God has gifted you with needs to be
> nurtured and brought into full fruition to fulfill His divine plan
> (p. 43).

She goes into youth centers and speaks? Oh my God, nooooo! Our youth already have enough problems without having some space-case come forward with rhetoric from the planet Zangor!

How can she speak about appropriate behavior when she has isolated herself from her family? How can she speak about emotions and cognition when she obviously has issues with her own parents? Does she not BLAME them for not being more supportive? That's what it sounds like to me! She blames God and she blames her parents. But what about the person who fathered her child? She never mentions him once, meaning that she also blames him, whoever he is.

"Menace to Society"

Ms. Alexis' ignorance is truly evident in this sub-chapter. Not only does she display an abysmal ignorance of humankind's relationship to nature, but she also lacks knowledge of how talents and skills are developed. Since I am highly blessed in both areas, I'll explain it so that you won't be misinformed by the ravings of a woman who obviously won a cough syrup drinking contest.

She claims that,

> One essential part of human beings (sic) existence is to aid (sic)
> towards the advancement of society. When God made us, he
> deposited talents(s) inside of us to bring about a positive change
> in society. Anything we do contrary to this is labeled as being a
> "menace to society." Therefore, those of us who do not use, in a
> constructive way, the talents which (sic) the Lord has deposited
> within our being has, in fact, become a possible danger to society
> (pp. 43-44).

She says that God made us to bring about a positive change to society. That is such a stupid statement. The fact is, those in power don't want change, so does that mean that if you don't succeed, God is going to kick your ass? Why hasn't be punished the people who work to prevent change from taking place? She tells another lie when she says that if we don't work toward this change, we are labeled as a "menace to society." Who labels us in such away? God? Or the white man? Neither.

Societies are built to support a lot of change. Therefore I don't know what Ms. Alexis is talking about. American society is resistant to change, which is why it took over fifty years for white folks to realize that separate but equal was inherently unequal. Most people accept the way things are and are apathetic. Therefore her claim of being labeled is a lie.

Her third lie is when she says that those of us who don't use the talents God gave us are a possible danger to society. How is that? Does she have evidence? Does it apply to everyone, or just to people of color? This white system has neglected, rejected and squandered talent for a century – where is their comeuppance? When is whitey going to get what he deserves? If we are to follow Ms. Alexis' distorted lead, he never will.

Moving on:

> Even when nature acts out of source (sic) or does not carry out
> the activity for which it was made, it then becomes a menace to
> society. For instance, when oceans and rivers jump the banks and
> flood parts of the earth as opposed to doing what God has made
> them to do, then it causes a disruption in the progress of society
> (p. 44).

She says that nature "acts out of source." What she means is "acts out of sorts." She doesn't care enough about her subject matter to correct stupid mistakes – another reason why she lacks credibility. But let's deal with the statement itself.

Can nature act out of sorts? I don't think so. Who is man to claim that nature is the deviant when tornados, hurricanes, floods and the like occur? It is the white man who is out of sorts. He is the one who wants to bore through redwood trees, dig tunnels through mountains, set up shop on a beach or a fault, or kick back in the desert or a valley. And then when nature does its natural thing, he calls nature the disaster. The disaster was the asshole who knew these things would happen but decided to "set up a home" anyway! It's like calling the shark on "Jaws" a killer; he wouldn't kill white folks if they'd stop swimming around in and "exploring" in his toilet stool! Whitey talks of "killer grizzlies" and the lion or the tiger. Keep your white ass off his turf trying to kill HIM and you won't have any problems.

This is the same thing that Ms. Alexis has apparently bought into. Nature doesn't "act out of sorts." And there is no way you can -- or should – punish nature for doing what comes naturally. But instead, she makes asinine statements like, "when oceans and rivers jump the banks and flood parts of the earth as opposed to doing what God has made them to do, then it causes a disruption in the progress of society." Say what??

Let me tell you something: the Native Americans worked with nature and got along just fine. These white people get off on trying to "control" nature and "harness" things. They want to play the role of God on Earth. That's why they end up getting their asses kicked. Every time there's a tornado, you read about at least one white man who got up on a roof, climbed his garage, sat up in a tree, with a camera, trying to tape it, or "get a closer look." Then, you read about that same white man getting scraped off the side of a mountain five miles away. What possess them to engage in such buffoonery? It's like the Last Poets once said, "the white man's got a God Complex."

Furthermore, what's the big deal even if the storms DID cause a disruption of society? The society is immoral anyway! If Ms. Alexis read the Bible as she claims she did, then she knows about the cities of sin, Sodom and Gomorrah. Look what God allegedly did to THEM? And what does the white "Christian" man do? He constructs Las Vegas (and Reno) and Atlantic City, two more dens of sin! He never learns and the reason why is because he is a non-believer! The only God that he's believing in is that God on the dollar bill!

Now, another important Scriptural reference (all emphases are original):

> *He established the earth upon its foundations, So that it will not totter forever and ever*
>
> *Thou didst cover it up with the deep as with a garment; The waters were standing above the mountains.*
>
> *At Thy rebuke they fled; At the sound of Thy thunder they hurried away.*
>
> *The mountains rose; the valleys sank down to the place which Thou didst establish for them.*
>
> Thou didst set a boundary that they may not pass over; That they may not return to cover the earth … (Psalms 104:5-35).

This passage proves my point! All was well until the white man came along and started trying to take over the world. And this is the man that this black woman wants US to follow?

She claims that,

> We, as humans, are very upset when there is a gale, tornado, and
> so forth, because this is when nature is not doing what it is
> suppose (sic) to do and is overriding the will of God. Thus,
> nature has become a menace for us all. Yet, it is very rare that
> nature does cause disharmony to society. However, we humans
> act out o a daily basis, if not more. So, why are we so upset when
> nature causes disharmony in society? Yet, we feel it is okay for
> humans to display, more than not. This is not okay. This brings
> us to the very heart of this book the ***white man's purpose*** (p.
> 46—emphasis original).

Nature isn't "overriding" the will of God – it is bringing that will into fruition, you nitwit! What does she think – the whole world is supposed to be like California all year around? Nature is no "menace for us all." This is what makes Ms. Alexis so twisted: she rejects nature, but the real "menace" – the white man – she wants to follow to the ends of the Earth. Is she a nutcase or what?

Finally, with the fodder out of the way, she gets to what is supposedly the whole point of this book: the white man's purpose. Let's check it out and see what this crazy woman is talking about.

Chapter 3: White Man's Purpose

As if we don't know what the purpose is, based on what we've seen here on American shores. But what SHE has in mind simply adds insult to injury. So let's see what we find when a black woman – a true Aunt Jemimia - takes the side of and gives support to a white man (maybe she's been betrayed by so many black men that she's given up on them). Maybe we should ask why she doesn't mention any of the fathers of her children, Hmmmm?

Lead in Love

This is where Ms. Alexis' self-hate and the hatred of her own race becomes most evident. Let us begin what constitutes an overdue psychological assessment of this very sick African-American female:

> Granted, certain people of the white race believe that they have
> worked hard with their hands to achieve superiority over other
> racial groups of this world. This belief is coupled with other
> races either being jealous of the white race or thinking they can

> complete with the white race for superiority. Both of these
> beliefs have been revealed as being pseudo (sic) (p. 47).

First lie: that certain whites think they worked hard to achieve superiority over other racial groups. She has not established that the white man has superiority over other racial groups. He's got his hands full with the Arabs, and the Africans in Somalia whipped his ass, as "Blackhawk Down" clearly pointed out. Prior to that, he got his hi-tech butt kicked in Vietnam. So there may be an advantage here in America over the people that he outnumbers, but that doesn't mean superiority.

White folks don't brag about working hard with their hands. That's what they've got people of color for. White folks have stolen much of what they've gotten, and they've enslaved entire groups to do their work. Why is Ms. Alexis kissing this devil's ass? Why is she distorting the facts?

Second lie: other races are jealous of the white race. Before coming to that conclusion, why doesn't Ms. Alexis document the jealousy that this powerful white man has of those who are "Minorities"? He wishes he had the suave romanticism of the Latino, the penis size and rapping ability of the black man, and the creativity of the Asian. Some people might be jealous over the power that he has, but few men of color want to be white when power and money are taken out of the picture.

Third lie: other races "thinking they can compete with the white race for superiority." People of color are superior to the white man, which is why he has to sabotage the competition. Why would he discriminate against people of color if he didn't feel inferior? There has never been a fair competition here in America because the white man not only has the numbers, but he hates black people and has sabotaged the competition. Ms. Alexis should know about that: her black ass wouldn't have a job in the public schools were it not for black people like Eddie Chambers, George Westbrook, Lerlean Johnson, and me confronting that racist school board and humanizing them. She ought to keep that in mind before she wastes toner, time and energy exposing her ignorance.

Now comes the clincher. Read it, and weep:

> As so (sic) far as the white race and its purpose is concerned,
> God preordained the white race to lead in love. The Bible says,
> how can you say you love Me (God) who you have not seen, and
> do not love your brother who you have seen? This type of
> behavior the Bible calls hypocritical. Yet, many people of the
> white race practice this type of behavior, daily! Yes, even those
> within the church (pp. 47-48).

How does she figure God preordained the most violent man on the face of the earth to lead in love? How? Has Beauchamp been whispering sweet nothings in her ear? Was this part of her revelation? Again, why would God reveal something to a black woman and have her run and tell the white man? Why didn't God go straight to the source? You know why? Because the shit never happened. She had no "revelation." What she had was some kind of bipolar attack and was hearing voices. And being a sellout, it only stands to reason that what she would defend the white man because that is who she loves. And only she knows why.

Ms. Alexis then has the gall to utter the word "hypocrite." How could she? She need only look into the mirror to get a glimpse of both a hypocrite and a sellout at the same time! She says that "many white people" practice hypocritical behavior and even within the church. If that is true, why does she love them so?

On page 48, she closes down this section of the book – which should have had more to it considering the fact that it's called "Lead in Love." How can the white man lead in love when his definition of love is as sheer and shallow as he is?

Now, bow your heads and try not to barf:

> If I speak with the tongues of men and angels, but do not have love, I have become a noisy gong or clanging cymbal. And if I have the gift of prophecy, and know all mysteries and all knowledge; and if I have all faith, so as to remove mountains, but do not have love, I am nothing. And if I give all my possessions to feed the poor, and if I deliver my body to be burned, but do not have love, it profits me nothing. … But now abide faith, hope, love, these three; but the greatest of these is love (1 Corinthians 13*).*

Calling all squirrels! Calling all squirrels! One of you has a sho' nuff NUT missing!

To God Be The Glory

What she should have called it is, "To the White Man Be the Glory" because to Ms. Alexis, God and the white man are one and the same! Want proof? Let's get busy:

> It is not by might, but by my spirit saith the Lord. It is not by hard work or coincidence that this race is out in the forefront. God has purposed this to be so. For example, most of the trends are set and based upon whites. They set the tone as to what is appropriate business wear, hair wear, weight, and makeup of an individual, just to name a few of the leading orientations. Whites set the tone as to appropriate public behavior, thinking skills and the list goes on.

So God chose the colorless people above all others? This is what Ms. Alexis believes. So now you can see that she has a definite bias, and it is a bias that is so intense that she is willing to bend rules, tell lies and even fabricate fantasies just to give that peckerwood his undeserved due.

For instance, she claims that most trends are set and based upon whites. What? Black people were performing operations on the eye, delving into astronomy and constructing universities when that cracker was living on the fringes of barbarism! Fast forward up to current times: black culture is carrying the cultural load for this nation; from handshakes, greetings and urban wear to the way we talk, that white boy offers nothing. He watches us and once he mimics it and claims its "cool," that is when we know to change up into something else because once he touches it, it becomes the mark of a true "square."

White folks on TV cannot even find songs to fit the mood of their own lovemaking sequences without borrowing from our incredible songwriters: Smokey Robinson, Maurice White, Barry White, and so on. Our music marks the various periods in American culture, even during disco. KC and the Sunshine Band was really about the black horn section and the black bass and drums and the black backup singers. That peckerwood couldn't sing a lick and couldn't even dance to the beat of the music. The list goes on and on, across the culture and across various genre.

The white man sets the tone for the way to wear your hair when he's out, with his woman, trying to get perms? He sets the tone for business wear because they're HIS businesses. And look how stupid and similar these white boys are: ice cream pants, coal miner shoes, navy blue suit coat, a white shirt and some of the ugliest ties ever seen. No individuality or style, whatsoever. They set the tone in weight? How? If obesity is the standard, then maybe she's got a point. But other than that, this stuff is just the sick ranting of a woman who has a slave mentality, pure and simple.

Ms. Alexis claims that whites set the tone for appropriate public behavior, thinking skills and the list goes on. In regard to the public behavior, the tone is called "law"! But "thinking skills"? This woman is supposed to be an educator and she tells a lie like that. Perhaps she has thinking skills confused with IQ tests. The white man can't teach anybody how to think unless it's in a school setting. Let him try to survive on the streets of the ghetto or any barrio for a week. He'd crack under the pressure. So the lesson here is that it's his system and he makes the laws. He creates the tests that reflect HIS way of thinking. But that doesn't mean that he created thinking or that he sets the tone for thinking skills. Ms. Alexis has lost her damn mind, that's what the issue is!

Her love for colorlessness continues:

> Therefore, the white race really has no competition when it
> comes to other races in the arena of leadership.. As I previously
> stated, what God as purposed for each individual or each racial
> group, no other person or race will do.

No competition? What does she think the civil rights movement and the black power movement proved? That the white man could be kicked in the ass if you threatened his financial situation. That is a leadership issue. Going back to Adam Clayton Powell and how he outsmarted them time and time again. Leadership issue. And it goes on at the state and local level in every part of the nation. We just don't hear about it just like the rest of the nation doesn't hear about Senator Ernie Chambers. And speaking of Senator Chambers, he is the smartest politician in this region. That's a leadership issue. Ms. Alexis is a liar, plain and simple.

Now take note of the following piece of drivel:

> Once again, the only way another race can be utilized to fulfill
> the purpose of the white race is if the white race does not concur
> with what God has ordained them to do. The purpose of the
> white race is to lead in a loving positive manner that God may be
> glorified (pp. 49-50).

So all other races are doomed to come in a distant second and the only way that the white man can lose is if he fucks over himself. A white man would not even write these words down – even if he believed it. So what possesses this woman who has children out of wedlock (she told me had six children) and mis-educates other people's kids all over the Omaha Public Schools, to act like some kind of "moral guide" for the rest of us?

Can you believe this? She writes, "The purpose of the white race is to lead in a loving positive manner that God may be glorified." The purpose of ALL people are to lead in a loving way. Why does she therefore only assume and presume that the white race must lead everyone else? Are they supposed to be more loving than other races? That sounds like some shit that Thomas Jefferson wrote in his "Notes on Virginia."

Purpose vs. Status

> As opposed to the white race modeling appropriateness in love,
> they oftentimes demean, display prejudice, discriminate and
> practice unfairness toward other racial groups which (sic) are
> God's children, as well.

The poorly written sentence seems to imply that the white man's racism and discriminatory attitude is only manifested "oftentimes." Try ***all the time,*** dammit!

Continuing:

> ***"Do not judge lest you be judged.***
> ***"For in the way you judge, you will be judged; and by your***
> ***standard of measure, it will be measured to you. And why do***
> ***you look at the speck that is in your brother's eye, but do not***
> ***notice the log that is in your own eye?***
> ***"Or how can you say to your brother, 'Let me take the speck***
> ***out of your eye,' and behold, the log is in your own eye?***
> ***"You hypocrite, first take the log out of your own eye, and then***
> ***you will see clearly to take the speck out of your brother's eye***
> ***(Matthew 7:1-5).***

Bible quotes. For what? If she is an evangelist and if she's acting on what she calls a "revelation from God," then she shouldn't need any Biblical support, should she? But the Bible has been a tool of oppression for centuries, so perhaps its use is appropriate. But Ms. Alexis is so sick, she doesn't really need validation for any of her philosophies or viewpoints. Take, for example, the following one:

> One of the reasons why the white race display (sic) these types of behaviors is because of their erroneous belief that other races can overtake their status. When they realize that God gave them this status, not the world or the money they hold so dear, only then can they operate rightly in their purpose. The purpose of leadership that the white race has the world did not give it to them, and the world cannot take it away. Their status is God ordained (which really is not status, but rather purpose) (pp. 51-52).

The white race feels people of color breathing down their neck, which explains the white paranoia, the white flight from the central cities, the abusive police presence in the black community and a host of stopgap measures intended on keeping black people down. The belief that we will overtake them is a logical one, which they know. This is why they have to cheat, discriminate, lie, steal, manipulate and sabotage. It's really the only way they can maintain that which they are gradually losing.

Secondly, the realization that "God gave them status" is not even a part of the thinking of white folks. You see, they see themselves as God. One even had the nerve to write a book, some years back, titled, God is My Co-Pilot. These white people view God as nothing more than an extension of their own power, as I have stated elsewhere. That is why it is so easy for them to give God human features:

they talk about him hearing and seeing and they talk about God walking with them and talking with them. The white man needs no belief in a Supreme Being. He doesn't have time to acknowledge a greater power, just as the rapist doesn't recognize the word "no," the thief doesn't recognize the "private property" sign, and the killer has no respect for the lives he has taken or plans to take.

Finally, she writes that white status is God-ordained. How would she know? Has she shared these lies with Beauchamp? Why hasn't he condemned her for standing up for his racist fellow whites? There is some conspiracy going on here between this woman, Trinity Church and Les Beauchamp. He knows of her book and yet he has not come forth to deal with the contents (as I have). That is why after I get through dogging out this book, I'm going after Trinity Church and Beauchamp's "shaky" behavior.

Ms. Alexis concludes her defense of her white master, thusly:

> For example, there are many other races that hold the monetary status that is equal to what the white race thinks caused them to be the leading race. Yet, other racial groups, still, do not attain the leadership status purposed by God to the white race. In addition, you will find many white individuals with a lower income than that of another ethnic group. However, a low income white individual would be looked to for leadership more prevalently than a high income other racial individual. Thus, money is not the determining factor as to why the white race is endowed with leadership status, God is (p. 52).

Ms. Alexis lies when she talks of men of color who have comparable monetary status. These men have attained leadership in their communities, but here is what the silly woman doesn't understand: when men of color are leaders, it is based on influence; when the white man has leadership, it is based on power. For instance, Shaq and Kobe, Alex Rodriguez and Samuel F. Jackson all have money and are all well known. Along with that renown comes influence. But none of them have any real power. They are all controlled by the white man. They don't control the gyms they play in, the field they play on or the studios they tape in. This is the main difference. The white man has and seeks power and shares it with his white brother and sisters. Blacks have influence and, in too many cases, don't even want to share that.

When Ms. Alexis claims that a low income white man would be looked to for leadership more than a high income person of color, she is showing how stupid she is. A low income white man lacks education in most cases; a black man with a good education is usually a sellout, much like Ms. Alexis is. So the black man's mind is really more white than that of the low-income cracker. It doesn't have to do with race as much as it has to do with who brings the most cultural capital with them. Generally speaking, a good Uncle Tom is more valuable to the system than a low-income peckerwood.

Finally, since money is not the determining factor for why the white race is "endowed with leadership status" and since God is the reason, answer me this: why is the white man providing such shabby leadership? Why is the white man hated wherever he goes? Why does the white man have to use his television and newspapers to make him appear brave when, in reality, he is a stone coward (just go to the airport and try to take a flight, and you'll have proof of that)

Her defense of her white master continues in the next sub-chapter.

Fear Is Not of God

Speaking for God and lying on him at the same time are grounds for whatever punishment God metes out. Check out this woman's following comments:

> As opposed to looking down on and feeling superior to other races, God has purposed that the white man lead and aid other races into harmony. Yet, the white race, possibly, out of fear that another race may take leadership from them, in a sense, cause (sic) disharmony for other racial groups. This type of behavior is not pleasing to God (p. 53).

And, she adds that,

> Many times we, as humans, get lost and lose sight of our purpose in life. Yet, there is no excuse as to why we cannot get back on track, and fulfill our destiny, today! God is calling of the white race to get back on track to what He has purposed for them to do since the beginning of time.

Since the beginning of time? In the first place, if God has been calling on this honky since the beginning of time, and what we see today is the best this white man can do, then God is not only discriminating against the worldwide majority, but he also must be a moron! Ms. Alexis has no right to lie on God like that! How does she know about the beginning of time; she can barely TELL time!

She concludes with two passages from Psalms, but that's not going to keep her ass from burning in hell – if there is one:

> *The Lord is my light and my salvation; Whom shall I fear? The Lord is the defense of my life; Whom shall I dread? (Psalms 27:1).*
>
> *The Lord is for me; I will not fear; What can man do to me? (Psalms 118:6).*

I'll tell you what man can do in the case of Ms. Alexis. First of all, immediate brain surgery to replace the missing frontal lobe. Secondly, termination as a counselor with the Omaha Public Schools for mis-informing black youth. And finally, a visit from the Drop Squad. They know what to do with sellouts.

Let us now move to the next sub-chapter where she declares that, "Love is the Key."

Love is The Key

In this sub-section we find out just how little studying and reading this woman does in her personal life. She credits a white woman with the metaphor of the salad bowl versus the melting pot when, in reality, that comparison was made decades ago, during the early 1940s. But we'll get to that in a moment.

For now, let it suffice to say that Ms. Alexis' love for the Caucasian reaches its apex in this section of the chapter. She begins by explaining that,

> Not until the white race take (sic) its rightful stance to lead in *love* will we as a nation experience harmony. For if the white race are purposed to lead America, then that makes them leaders of the world. Since, America is leading the nation (sic). Wake up *White American Children of God* and do what you are suppose to do, lead the way with love, this is God's purpose for you. Other racial groups are blocked from fulfilling their God-given purpose due to the disharmony of the races (p. 54—emphasis original).

Still believing that "leading in love" is the rightful stance of the white race, Ms. Alexis then claims that by leading America, the white race will lead the world. Why? Because the other races are "blocked" from fulfilling their God-given purpose because of disharmony. But doesn't this woman understand that in most of those cases, it is the white man that instigated that disharmony? It is the white powers of the world – former colonizers – who created the conditions for disharmony? She acts as if the white man's hands are clean in all this. Only an utter moron would make such an assumption and then put it in a book where the world can see the shallowness of the remark.

In the black community we have this name that we put on people who went to college but come out not knowing their ass from a hole in the ground; they go to college, start hanging out with white folks and internalizing all that bullshit, and then they start thinking like the folks that they studied under. We call them, "educated fools." Ms. Alexis proves this point, and you can see how as you check out the following excerpt:

> I learned in a college course, as well as, read (sic) an article by Joyce Millet (2000) pertaining to two metaphors used to identify racial diversity. The first was like a melting pot. Now, we all know how the white race previously tried to assimilate other racial groups into their way of doing things. That was a good gesture for all the wrong reasons. For instance, the assimilation was like a melting pot where all the races where thrown and enmeshed together. There was no distinction and everyone was to think white, act white, and so forth. This ironclad type of leadership God was not pleased with (pp. 54-55).

The melting pot never applied to black people. It was a phrase concocted by white folks when the people coming into the country were white folks: Jews, Italians, Slavs, Irish and Italians. The melting pot concept was not extended to people of color. And as for Millet getting credit for it, she just borrowed it and probably didn't cite the source. So let's stop crediting white women for things that are not theirs. They get far too much credit as it is.

Secondly, even with assimilation being the dominant theme, when it came to black folks, that sick concept was not applied in the same way. Blacks could assimilate into the economy – from segregated slums. Blacks could assimilate into the workforce – doing menial work and returning to the ghetto at night. There was always a qualifier when it came to black people. There are three general forms of assimilation, and black people have been denied two of the three.

When it comes to marital assimilation, the white man never allowed that and to this day, hates the idea. For instance, when a black man marries his daughter, he cuts off the trust fund. They had a rich white man here to had a daughter and he bribed the brother to leave town for thousands of dollars. The brother wisely took the money – and then took the white girl, too. Although I think the latter decision was a mistake, at least it taught that old racist a lesson.

The second form of assimilation is structural. That's where you join the white man's clubs and seek to be close to him through his organizations. Black people may be allowed in a few clubs, that not many. And the main clubs – like the

Skulls at Yale, for instance – no black will ever get into because these clubs are about white supremacy and power.

The third and final form of assimilation is cultural assimilation, and that is what the white man allows to an extent. As long as you drop your own culture and forget your own history, you can adopt HIS bullshit culture. That is what Ms. Alexis has done. Karenga (1967) once wrote that, "the Negro has been copying white culture so long, and has become so mixed up from doing it, he thinks it is his own." This quote fits Ms. Alexis like a glove.

Furthermore, how does this woman – who apparently knows so little about so many things – know when God is displeased or not? Is she one of God's chosen ones? Does she think she's some kind of prophet?

Continuing on with Ms. Alexis' warped beliefs:

> The second metaphor is the type of leadership that is pleasing to God a type of leading that does not cause disharmony to His creation. Thus, there ought to be a coming together of the races to the metaphor of a tossed salad. In this way, all races can unite in harmony yet maintain their own identity. For example, in a salad we can identify a cucumber, tomato, egg, and so forth,. Although the ingredients are unified, one is able to identify and detect the identity of each particular food. This is how the leading of the white race is to go forth: a common purpose (unified in harmony) with a distinct identity (the races) (pp. 55-56).

The only salad that's been "tossed" is Les Beauchamp's! And he's fronting off in his commercials like he's this committed person who lifts weights and wants to share information about Jesus. He lives in a segregated suburb and the only blacks he associates with are those Uncle Toms up at Salem Baptist Church. That's where he feels "safe." He wouldn't last an hour on the real streets of the same black community that Ms. Alexis was born in and hates so much.

In the next sub-chapter, Ms. Alexis is going to teach us about leadership. This should be interesting.

<u>Leaders Must Be Followers</u>

There is a saying that teaches, "you can't teach what you don't know, and you can't lead where you won't go." Unfortunately for the black community and the people who were duped into reading this book, Ms. Alexis is guilty of both. But she chooses to give advice, anyway. Such as that which follows:

> In order to lead, one must be able to follow. If the white race is to
> lead the other races into harmony, then they must be able to
> identify the path that leads to harmony which is in following
> after God. However, the best way to display unification to other
> races is to first be unified among your own racial group (p. 56).

The white race cannot lead people to a place that it, itself, has never been to! White folks seem to only experience harmony when they are separated from the rest of the world while their fellow race members wreak havoc on the rest of the world. White folks, as a group, are already unified, and only a fool would say otherwise. We have already addressed this topic.

Moving on:

> Most of the time, the white race does manifest unification.
> However, because of their mistaken belief that money gives them
> power to lead, they give some evidence of division among their
> racial group, as well. For example, the one's (sic) with high
> status separate themselves from those in poverty. Once again,
> this is displaying contempt for children of God who, in fact, have
> a purpose and a destiny to fulfill. Hence, the true way to
> harmony is to follow after God (sic) ways. For God and Jesus are
> one, and Jesus is the way, the truth and the light (pp. 56-67).

God and Jesus are one and the same? So God sent himself to Earth to die for our sins? So at one point, that means God was dead? This is bullshit. But since the white man is God's best buddy, that means that God and Jesus are as white as the white man is! How sick is that?

Now, a verse from the white man's autobiography (as Ms. Alexis might believe), the Holy Bible:

> **Commit your way to the Lord, Trust also in Him, and He will**
> **do it**
> **And he will bring forth your righteousness as the light, and**
> **your judgment as the noonday (Psalms 37: 5&6).**
>
> **The steps of a man are established by the Lord; And He**
> **delights in his way (Psalms 37:23).**

She loves the white man, what can I say? She believes in the white man more than she believes in any black man. Is it because brothers have dogged her and left her to raise those kids all alone? This is the classic Jemima – look at how Whoopi Goldberg acted when Ted Danson donned blackface and went on stage and used the word "nigger" a dozen or so times? (Addressed elsewhere in this book) Look at the antics that Sheryl Underwood pulls off, complete with huge Afro (to make sure she's a "coon") daily on the talk show, "The Talk"? Need I say more? Why doesn't this woman, Geraldine Alexis, "come forth and spill thine guts" the way she probably does in church? Oh well, let's move on.

<u>Everyone is Not Qualified to Lead</u>

Ms. Alexis begins this sub-chapter the same way she begins her prayers: by worshipping the peckerwood. Check it out:

> One caveat to this purpose of leadership is that one must be in
> tune with God. Therefore, the God-given purpose of leadership is
> to those who are children of God. How does one determine if
> he/she is a child of God? I'm glad you asked. You must possess
> the spirit of god which shows no partiality to anyone (p. 58).

She thinks she's qualified to give out advice like this? This woman has a personal life that would make Peg Bundy look like a saint. And she's got the gall to serve as a "recruiter" for God? Nigga please! She continues her rant:

> I cannot reiterate enough that God loves us all. No one can have
> that type of love unless he/she is born-again into the family of
> God. The Bible says let the redeemed of the Lord say so. Since
> everyone has not been redeemed, then everyone that is of the
> white race is not qualified to lead. Only those who have been
> redeemed by the blood of Jesus is (sic) capable of leading in love
> (p. 58).

So answer me this: are the unredeemable of the white race STILL superior to the redeemed of the colored races? Or are white people so superior that even their unredeemable are more blessed than our most sacred and pious? She offers a partial explanation in the following passage:

> The relationship born-again believers have with God is liken to that of a
> parent-child relationship. God is the Father and if we have been
> redeemed by the blood of Jesus, then we are his children. God says my
> sheep hear my voice and follow after me (pp. 58-59).

Wait a minute! She said God and Jesus were one and the same. Now this two-faced Troglodyte is saying that they're two different beings! And secondly, I'm nobody's fuckin' sheep. But the churches are full of them, people who are too stupid and gutless to get off their ass and work toward change. So to cover up their cowardice, they hide behind some faggot minister or some cockhounding pastor. They are truly pimps in the pulpit.

Then, Ms. Alexis offers the following nugget of wisdom:

> Therefore, if you are, in fact, a child of God, then you will hear
> His voice calling you to lead all His children with *love,* not hate,
> into a harmonious future. Once the white race comprehends the
> true meaning of leadership, as well as, put (sic) it into action,
> they will then and only then have come face-to-face with their
> purpose (p. 59—emphasis original).

She's asking for too much from the white man. That asshole is not going to change unless somebody puts their foot in his ass. Face it. Moral appeals don't work. When King embarrassed his ass in front of the world and then won the Nobel Peace Prize after he did it, King got croaked in April of 1968. When Malcolm rallied the masses, whitey got some Negroes who think much the way that Ms. Alexis thinks, to shoot him down in February of 1965. These white men killed their own race members: John Kennedy, Robert Kennedy and even George Wallace got maimed. They went international and killed Patrice Lumumba of the Congo and then came back home and killed Meier Kahane, king of the militant Jews.

Now here is where she mentions, by name, the only human male in the entire book. Not her father, no brothers (except televangelist scam artist T.D. Jakes) or none of the men who fathered her children out of or in wedlock. Check it out:

> Since having the opportunity to interact with the white race most
> of my adulthood, I have come to have a love and appreciation for
> their purpose. As previously shared, I am a member of Trinity
> Interdenominational Church. Being a member of this church has
> brought me into constant with one of God's prominent leaders,
> who is qualified to lead, Pastor Les Beauchamp. He displays a
> love for all races of people. With the help of the Holy Spirit, he
> is able to yield to the voice of God which is a real plus! (p. 59).

She "loves and appreciates" the purposes of white people. But she doesn't say their religious or moral purposes. So we have to assume that since she's talking about the white race in general, then that means she loves ALL their purposes! And why? Because they're white, that's why! Nothing else going for them but pale, colorless skin, thin lips and hair that smells like a chicken pissed on itself when it gets wet. This is the race this woman wants to suck up behind and follow.

Secondly, she calls Les Beauchamp one of God's prominent leaders. Let me tell y'all about this silly minister before moving on.

Back in 1995, he was airing commercials about his already-too-large church. He was babbling about how they are out to help people and do God's work. At the time I had a TV show and some friends and I were making the mayor and other white folks around the city look like assholes. We wrote Beauchamp a letter telling him we were fighting against racism and wanted a donation. The charlatan never responded. So we waited about a month and then called. Some woman answered the phone and gave us some shit about, "we're sorry, we're not interested in making a donation at this time."

You see? They all talk that shit hoping that nobody is going to call them on it. It's one thing to help out somebody who you can then turn around and turn into an Uncle Tom – like they obviously did Ms. Alexis. But when you start talking about fighting oppression, people like Beauchamp take it seriously because they know that they are a member of the oppressor class. He lives his life like any other white man does: hidden in suburbia, bullshitting around most of the time and then, on Sunday, leading the mindless flock over the edge of the cliff.

Not only is he shallow, but he's grandiose. As I mentioned earlier, he has these commercials that he airs using different themes. In one he's in a weight room in sweats, talking about getting stronger with Jesus. In another one he's talking about coming to church for Easter because Jesus gave his life. In the latest one, he's hooked up with another asshole from King of Kings Church and they are faking an argument, with Beauchamp doing some over-the-edge acting. Their point is that "people think this is how churches are" (competitive), but in reality, they both share something in common: to lead people to Jesus. What a pair of hucksters.

Anyway, it seems like Beauchamp believes that Jesus is God, because he never mentions the latter name. Could this be where the silly Ms. Alexis got her training? I wonder how much she's putting into that white liar's collection plate on Sunday?

She writes as if she has some kind of crush on Beauchamp. Maybe their relationship is more than she's willing to state. Maybe that's why Beauchamp is taking his time coming out and endorsing this book; maybe he doesn't want to attract attention to himself and this gorgeous black woman who, for some reason, doesn't attend Salem Baptist Church, Mount Moriah Missionary Baptist Church, Zion African Methodist Episcopal Church, Calvin Presbyterian Church or any of the churches in the black community. No, because if she did that, she might meet some black males. And it is clear that there is something missing from this woman's life: what sister in her right mind would put herself on the line by praising the white race in such a manner and worse, by giving props to a middle-aged, Bible-toting, Richard Simmons acting peckerwood like Beauchamp?

You don't think she has a crush? Check out what she has to say about him in the next paragraph:

> There is nothing more admirable than seeing someone with a high status coupled with a humble heart. Only a true child of God can manifest such a beautiful demeanor. No, God is not speaking those who are simply church goers, those who practice religiosity, or those who merely say that they are children of God. If these types of individuals tried to lead, they would cause more harm than good. God is calling for a people who possess His spirit and are ready to get into His purpose for their lives (p. 60).

She's sprung on this cracker, man! Let's analyze her own words.

First off, she says that Beauchamp has a high status but a humble heart. If you're making TV commercials promoting your church, sitting in a weight room so people won't think you're gay, then in my book, you ain't shit. Gays are cool – but admit that you are and then get on with life. Don't be getting married and pretend to dig the opposite sex when, in reality, you're fantasizing about a big hairy set of balls dangling in your mug! High status -- get real!

Secondly, he's got a "beautiful demeanor," according to her – and he could only have one if he was a true child of God. This is a black woman who hides out so her family doesn't know where she is. She doesn't want to live near any black people. Then, out of the blue she writes a book giving praise to the most demonic race in the history of the known universe. Now she's calling one of the true religious hypocrites, Les Beauchamp, a child of God! In the history of the world, has there ever been a white woman who wrote a book giving the black man star status over the white man? Has there? They might fuck us, but that don't mean they worship us! But look what this sister does? She's no ugly duckling, and she knows it. But more importantly – and mock my words on this – BEAUCHAMP knows it.

Third, she moves from glorifying Beauchamp to glorifying God. Why do I get the distinct impression that in Ms. Alexis' pea-brain, these two are one and the same?

Now it's time for Chapter 4 of the book. And if you think this nut was tripping so far, I can't wait to expose to you some of the bullshit she's going to run down in the pages ahead. Stay tuned.

Chapter 4: White Man's Purpose in Relation to Minorities

The title of this chapter proves that Ms. Alexis considers "the world" to be white. If that was not the case, then why have a special chapter that applies the "white man's purpose" to minorities? She's already talked about that purpose as it relates to all humankind – oh, that's right: people of color are not human in Ms.Alexis' mind.

Let's look at what she has to say. She begins on page 61:

Mistakes

> We all make mistakes. This is a part of life. However, just as natural disasters are made and must be cleaned up, so are human errors. We cannot as God's creation turn a deaf ear to what is taking place in our world. For, most of the white race's advantages were capitalized upon beguilement. Deception that has not been cleaned up.

If it is as she says, and most of the white race's advantages have been capitalized upon beguilement (poorly worded; what she means is that most of their advantages are the result of beguilement), then that means that the white race is not deserving of the advantages that they have. That's what I've been trying to tell this nitwit from day one! And if the deception has not been cleaned up – as she says – then where does the white man earn the right to lead anyone? If he is as she says, he is no more capable of leadership than a wino is to drive in the Indianapolis 500!

What happened: did she and Lester "the molester" have an argument? Moving on:

> For example, the Native Americans had American land which through deception was forfeited to the white race. Blacks were enslaved to work American land, build and construct, as well as rear white children without pay. Furthermore, other races were employed for cheap labor as they immigrated into (sic) America. Not to mention, the poor whites who were used as indentured servants in America (p. 61).

Ass backwards concepts yield ass backwards conclusions. Look at the preceding passage: loaded with asinine concepts. Let's take some time out for analysis.

First of all she has the script twisted when she writes that, "Native Americans had American land which through deception was forfeited to the white race." The land was not American – as far as the natives were concerned, the land belonged to no man, only to God. So get that straight. The natives couldn't understand this white man's obsession with something he could never really own.

But whitey knew what he was doing. And yet this is the man she wants us to follow. The land was not forfeited by the native brothers – but she hates to tell the truth when it's about her white master. It's easier to write "forfeit by Native Americans" than it is to write "stolen by peckerwoods." This brings to mind a native name for Ms. Alexis: "Dances With Thieves."

Although she is right about black people being enslaved, she never says by who. SO again, she protects her white master. The does the same thing when she talks about other races being employed for cheap labor – but she doesn't mention who the number one exploiter of those laborers was. Why is she so protective? *She acts as if she's married to Beauchamp.* Hmmm.

She talks about the "poor whites" who were used as indentures servants, but there were blacks who were as well. And who was the "master" of those indentured servants. Her buddy, the white man.

Probably by now realizing how stupid she sounds, she wants to give up but she's in too far. She's the disease and her white buddies are the cure. She continues with her litany of lunacy:

> With all due respect, I speak to the former statements as not to point the finger, but rather to highlight truth. Most of the beguilement that took place among the races happened in past-times (sic). For, (sic) the originators of these errors, racial biases, discrimination, segregation, and the like, between racial groups, are dead and gone. However, like a cancer, the mark made by these pioneers continues to spread throughout generations (p. 62).

Now she seeks to absolve the master racist for what he's done. And she has to know she's lying about all this stuff. This woman has a Master's degree (or so she claims) and therefore must have had some kind of classes dealing with the glass ceiling of today that keeps women trapped, or the system-wide discrimination against black men. And yet she creates this fantasy world where the criminals are transformed into disciples!

She claims, for one thing, that she is trying to highlight the truth. Trust me: this woman wouldn't know the truth if it snuck up behind her and bit her on her ass! You can't highlight what you can't recognize!

Secondly, the claims that the beguilement of the past and the people who are the originators of discrimination, segregation and the like (white folks, in other words) are dead and gone. Is Beauchamp dead and gone? How about former mayor Hal Daub? What about current governor Mike Johanns? And former Husker football coach Tom Osborne? All these men have something in common: they are all white, they are all stupid and they are all racists. What Ms. Alexis has to learn is that racism and discrimination are alive and well and both are being perpetrated right up under her nose. But since her nose is always up Beauchamp's ass, she can't see the reality of the situation!

She is willing to admit that these problems spread through generations. What she really means is that they spread FROM one generation to the next. Of course it does; one racist hands down his beliefs to his son and, as Gil Scott once said, "we are the ones, who link our fathers to our sons." And that's the way it is with white folks, which is why it seems like they never change. Why can't Ms. Alexis see that?

Finally, the sub-chapter is about to end. But first a word from the white man's best friend, Aunt Jemima:

> As you know, if you suspect that you have cancer and make an appointment to meet with a doctor for a checkup, the familiar word that leaps from his/her lips are questions about past family members with this disease. Hence, it is common that generational error breeds error. Yet, it does not have to be this way, because we as humans have the choice to follow after God's way as opposed to familial ways. What is your choice today? Will you continue in error or choose a new way of life. Once again, the choice is yours (p. 62).

Generational error breeds error. You see? She's apologizing for those white boys again: claiming that what they did was by error. No, it was intended, planned and designed. These white devils are racist, and they are only concerned about maintaining their own positions of power. They hand their racism down to their children, and they know they can only do that in a segregated set of conditions. Why? Because they can't maintain the myth of white supremacy if there are black people around. So they keep their neighborhoods "sanitized" so that they can spread their lies to their gullible children ("say nigger and I'll let you use the Porsche").

Ms. Alexis might think she's doing crackers a favor by kissing their ass, but she'll find out the hard way that they don't give a shit about her, either. Once those breasts start sagging and that ass drops, once that pretty face gets some wrinkles in it, she'll be dropped faster than a hot potato. In some cases, a brain might save a woman from being ditched, but Ms. Alexis, as you can see, doesn't have to burden herself down with brains. Talking out of her asshole will do just fine.

Relinquish the Past

Like the hits on a hot radio station, the lies just keep on comin'! Ms. Alexis asserts that,

> The irony of the entire situation revolving around past mistakes
> among the races is that the white race continues to relive the
> past. The white racial group's position of enthronement,
> dovetailed by some misgivings of other racial ethic groups, has
> caused whites to become somewhat callous. For, we all know the
> law of the land which is "what goes around comes around."
> Hence, I believe that the white racial group fear this very thing.
> Yet, the Bible says that fear is not of God. Thus, if you are
> operating in fear, then you ought to check yourself, to see if, in
> fact, you are a child of God (p. 63).

She says that the white race has a position of "enthronement." What she should be calling it is "self-enthronement." Nobody voted those assholes in and they sure didn't earn it. They just stole it and then used what they stole to get more and more. Like the playground bully, they get all they can when they can because sooner or later, those kids you bullied are going to grow up. And they're not going to forget what you did on the playground. That's what 911 was all about.

Secondly, she writes of whites "becoming somewhat callous." That's like saying that Jeffrey Dahmer was "slightly pissed." Come off it! These are people that used to cut off black men's dicks and then display them in the store. These are men who raped black women and snatched black children from their families and sold them for casks of rum! "Somewhat callous"? Did the treatment of those prisoners in Iraq look like a roll in the hay? Did the bombing of that black church in Birmingham – when four little black girls died – sound like a day at Disneyland? The more she stands up for that white man the more she shows how much she hates herself, her race and her history.

Third, she says that the white race fears payback. She is right. But again, she makes it sound as if payback is not deserved. The white man deserves all that's coming to him. He bought it all upon himself. And to this day, he shows no signs of remorse for what he did to black people. And all of this is something that Ms. Alexis doesn't want to accept or deal with. Well, as far as I'm concerned when whitey burns in hell, she can have her luscious, cocoa-brown ass right there with him, handing him the suntan oil.

Now that she's shown how little she knows about her own history and the white man's role in it, she now moves into dealing with the American Indian. Let's check out what the female version of Stepin Fetchit has to say:

> I remember a few years ago I was selected to participate in a
> group that would do a study of the Native American lifestyle. We
> studied their tribal names, locations, and so forth. Then, we took
> trips to their reservations, I was surprised to learn that the
> superintendents of these reservations' schools were white males.

I was totally taken aback. My understanding was that Native
Americans refused to assimilate, therefore, choosing to live on
reservations separated from whites (pp. 63-64).

Let me get this straight: somebody was stupid enough to select HER to participate in a group that would study native lifestyles? It must have been because she was black, and the person must have had LAST choice! What does she have to offer other than an inherent bias against those poor people? She hates skin color, period. It should be clear, although I doubt she shares these stupid beliefs in public because if she did, she'd get laughed out of the classroom, even by her own fellow whites. If ANYBODY knows that the white man ain't shit, it's the white woman and younger white males. They can see it all around them – but their tradition of cultural arrogance keeps them believing in the hype.

She says they took trips to "their reservations." Those are the white man's reservations, just as the ghettos and barrios belong to him as well. They are concentration camps where they hole us up while they cavort in the suburbs. She says she was surprised to learn that the superintendents of those reservation schools were white men. Did she say anything about it? Did she speak out about her concerns? Probably not. She just kept it all inside and probably fell in love with one of the superintendents on top of it.

How can she be "taken aback" about white boys running reservation schools but not be equally shocked at the foolishness of her silly "vision" and the crap that she wrote about in her book? Her understanding, she writes, was that the natives refused to assimilate and therefore CHOSE to live on reservations separated from whites.

From whence did she get this "understanding"? From an Archie and Jughead comic book? Did she spread this fucked up viewpoint to the students in her classes, the way she earlier spread lies about what a ghetto was? The natives were FORCED into white boarding schools and some rejected it. But the education on the reservation is just like the public school system – the same sick bullshit about how great the presidents were, about how their people were "massacred" and about how life is now better for them than ever before.

The trick from Trinity Church continues:

In addition, I really don't recall all Blacks ever holding a grudge
against whites despite their ill treatments. Blacks are
intermarrying with whites, moving into neighborhood where
whites reside, befriending white, and the list goes on and on.
Furthermore, other racial groups display respect/honor to the
white race, as well.

This woman must have a brain tumor. Black people don't go around wearing, "I Hate Whitey" t-shirts (although I have some for sale) because black people know what that means in a society that already hates their guts. But that doesn't mean that black people have forgotten what white people are about (except for Ms. Alexis, of course).

Then a subject she loves: evidence of "integration." The first thing on her list: intermarrying with whites. Not a house in a neighborhood, not sharing a job. But getting married to them. Also on the list is "befriending whites." Can you see where her mind is?

Then, to add even more insult to a growing list of injuries, she claims that "other racial groups display respect/honor to the white race, as well." Does she think that marrying white people, being their friends and moving into a white neighborhood are signs of respect and honor? What's wrong with this woman? No matter what the subject area, she is going to see to it that somehow, people of color are on their knees paying homage to this honky!

I don't know of a single black person I've met in all my years who ever said that they wanted to pay respect or honor to a white person. I'm not saying they haven't done it (we are all forced to during some of their bullshit holidays), but no one has said it. So where does Ms. Alexis get off making that claim about displaying honor and respect to the white race?

Then she flip flops, changes the white man from the savior to the non-forgiver. Take note:

> Why is it that the white race continues to hold on to past conditions? Why is it that other racial groups reach out to make amends with the white race, yet, the white racial group refuses to call a truce? This will ultimately cause the white race to lose out on their purpose. Once again, this negative attitude is not just among the secular white group, but yet, (sic) within the church as well (pp. 64-65).

Why should white folks "call a truce" when they have stolen all they need to retain power – for now? If the white boys have to choose between their "purpose" and money – they are going to pick the money, hands down! They don't give a shit about world peace or racial harmony or any of that "kumbaya" bullshit! They want theirs right now, and they are sure in the hell going to get it.

Now, a word from our Biblical sponsor:

> A man who hardens his neck after much reproof will suddenly be broken beyond remedy. When the righteous increase, the people rejoice, but when a wicked man rules, people groan (Proverbs 29: 1&2).

That's not the way this passage is supposed to read! Come on: if you're going to pretend to be religious, at least have the sense to quote the traditional scriptures from your book of bullshit. Here is how the passage should read, "He, that being often reproved hardeneth his neck, shall suddenly be destroyed, and that without remedy. When the righteous are in authority, the people rejoice: but when the wicked beareth rule, the people mourn."

And what do you see the masses doing today? They're in mourning, but they're also angry. Ms. Alexis' white pals invading country after country, lying about what they're doing, cutting back on assistance to the poor and elderly, denouncing people's sexual choice and so on. This is the kind of riff-raff that Ms. Alexis associates with and craves to follow. And she wants us – you and me – to follow these crackers as well. In that way, the rest of the world will hate us, too.

Finally, the words you've probably been waiting to hear: "the conclusion." Reading this book has been like being on a bad acid trip while you've got diarrhea! I don't know how she did it, but if you notice, by rebuttal is longer than her bullshit book! And if I hadn't properly single-spaced it, it would have been TWICE as long!

<u>Chapter 5: Conclusion</u>

Well, just when you think you've come to the end of taking a shit, there's that little turd still aching to get out. And so we have a similar situation with this book. The closer we get to the end, more bullshit seems to come our way. So let us not tarry; let's dive into the final few sub-chapters of this lesson in self-hate.

The first hunk of bullshit is where she seeks to quantify the works of God. She's already blasphemed him, insulted him and lied on him. Now she's going to define his actions. Let's check it out.

<u>God Works in 3's</u>

She begins the onslaught with more jabs against people of color and more kudos for white folks:

> White people/race can go ahead and breathe, because they really
> have no competition as so far as the other races are concerned
> when it comes to leadership. Children of God have learned that
> God works in 3's (sic). For example, we have the Father, the
> Son, and the Holy Spirit. We have Abraham, Isaac and Jacob.
> Hence, God has named three distinct groups as leaders of the

world which are the following: Man, the White Race, [and]
America (pp. 66-67).

There is a group of three that Sis. Alexis could have easily belonged to, based on the way she thinks; that group, which consisted of Moe, Larry and Curly Joe: the Three Stooges!!!

But seriously, she says white folks have no competition as far as the other races are concerned. Whose cars are they driving? Whose music and dance styles are they stealing? Who taught them medicine and the use of herbs? Whose tacos, burritos and enchiladas are they scarving down in the name of "eating Mexican"? Whose diet are they trying to copy even as they still learn how to use chopsticks? And why is he kissing the asses of Middle eastern countries so he can bring his gas prices down? The fact is, he's got competition on every front, and that's why he's so damn paranoid. Even Ms. Alexis has to concede that he can "breathe easier." When somebody says that, it means that you'd better NOT breathe easier.

As an example of God working in threes, she uses "the Father, the Son and the Holy Spirit." But earlier, she said that God and Jesus were one and the same. Is she forgetting to take her medication or what?

And finally, as part of this lesson in white ass kissing 101, she lists how her road dawg, God, has named three distinct groups as leaders of the world: Man, the White Race, [and] America. Ain't this a bitch? Let's look at how Ms. Alexis justifies THIS shit.

First Leadership

As if attacking and putting down her own people was not enough, now she goes after her own gender. Take note of the following case study in female-based misogyny:

> First, men were named or preordained as the leaders of gender.
> God made creation (sic), yet, he made man to be the ruler over all
> creation. Men are to be the heads of households. They are to follow
> after God and lead their families. All of this is to be done in love.
> For the Bible says men are to love their wives as Christ loves the
> church (p. 67).

Men were named or preordained as leader of the genders? By whom were they so named? By other men, perhaps? And on what basis would they lead? Superior strength? More hair? Karenga (1967), during his truly sexist days, once wrote, "we say that male supremacy is based on three things: tradition, reason and acceptance." These words sound great, but the criteria that REAL humans are judged by are areas where the woman wins, hands down.

For instance, creation of life, nurturing, compassion, problem-solving, manual dexterity – all her domain. Contrary to popular belief, males are just as emotional as women, but white boys like the ones that Alexis adores want to say that women are emotional –in that way he can keep them out of leadership positions. Like he does blacks whom he envies and fears, he places a glass ceiling over women so that they can't advance. If he was so superior, why does he constantly have to stack the deck and rig the game?

Men are to be heads of households. Then where is HER man? The point is that first of all, men are not made to be anything other than what they are. The female has ALWAYS been the head of the household because he was always out hunting, gathering, fishing or fucking some poor sheep in the ass. Like the white race, males want to lead but don't know how. All we know how to do is start wars and talk shit. Meanwhile, women raise the children and take care of the home front.

She says men are made to follow after God and lead their families. What about women? She puts down her own gender just to appease the white man. Then she quotes an anti-female excerpt from the Bible: "men are to love their wives as Christ loves the church." Christ or God? Are they one and the same? What gives?

But more profoundly, why does the woman have to be your wife in order for you to love her? Can't women learn to love women, period? Or do you have to have a license signed by some white man in order to be considered "valid" or "legit"? If Christ loved the church so much, why would he put a devil like Beauchamp in charge of one?

Third Leadership

She appears to be getting sicker and sicker as the book progresses! Take note of the following contentions:

> Next, God has made America as the leading nation. Thus, as
> America allows this nation to freely worship and serve God, then it
> is fulfilling its purpose as He has predestined it to. It is not a
> coincidence that America is looked to for leadership. America is a
> place where God can reign. Hence, God is calling for America to
> lead in love as so far as freedom is concerned (pp. 67-68).

America the leading nation? Yeah, it's in first place among the nations that are headed for the scrap heap. This modern day Sodom and Gomorrah has plagued the rest of the world, raped and stolen. It is time that whitey get his comeuppance. God is no respecter of persons so why would he love America any more than any other nation? Why would he love a country that was stolen away from its native inhabitants? Why would he love a country that is using up more than half the world's natural resources while polluting the rest? Why would he make this place the leading nation when it is fucking its children in the butt, putting people out on the street, invading nation after nation in the name of "democracy" and basically destroying the environment? "God shed his grace on thee" my ass!

America is looked to for leadership only by those who are desperate. The rest of the world knows that America is going to get it. Only blind folks like Ms. Alexis think America's best days are ahead of it. The statement that, "America is a place where God can reign" is a lie – unless she is once again implying that God and the white man are one and the same.

Freedom, in America? Probably when compared to some fascist right-wing dictatorship. But what about black folks? Are we really free? Look at the segregation we face in almost every major city. Look at the way the banks treat black people, even the ones that have good credit. And of all people, Ms. Alexis should know that she's not free because she had to apply for a "minority scholarship" when she was at UNO. Since she thinks she's white, why didn't she apply for the "regular" scholarships? The answer is clear: she is white mentally, but it takes more than that to be "free" in America. You have to have the pink skin, as well.

Linking Leadership

Did they forget about the second place "ranking" of her buddies in the white race? Of course not. She explains the "link" below:

> We all were fully aware of the first and third forms of leadership
> endowed upon man and America, by God. Yet, as previously
> stated, God works in 3's more than not. Therefore, the second
> form of leadership God is revealing, at this appointed (sic) time
> in history, is that His children that are called by His name fulfill
> their purpose (p. 68).

No, we are not "fully aware of the first and third forms of leadership endowed upon man and America." We are aware that there is this beautiful black woman who BELIEVES in this shit. With that out of the way, we can now go to the third form of leadership:

> Hence, the last form of leadership or the missing link between
> man and America is the white race. The white race is to step up
> to the plate and lead God's children in love. God has predestined
> this since the beginning of time. If you are a child of God, then

allowed God's will to be done. Have faith over fear. For perfect
love, rids (sic) all fear (p. 68).

Pitiful. Even Clarence Thomas would read this shit and say, "Damn, this woman is a bigger sellout than me!" Condoleezza Rice would say, "Gosh, and I thought I had an inordinate amount of love for the Caucasian race." Can you believe there's a woman out there providing counseling to young children while at the same time, hating herself and her race so much that she stoops to writing a book so she can share her gooniness with the world?

In the next sub-chapter, she explains to us how all these "truths" were revealed to her. Here come de pain!

God's Revelation

I know that God works in mysterious ways, but telling an imbecile about white folks being destined to rule is a bigger mystery than who shot JFK! Ms. Alexis offers the following as an explanation:

> I know you are wondering how is it (sic) that god would reveal
> something of this magnitude to a Black woman as (sic) myself.
> Well, I wondered the same thing when I learned that a dynamic
> male preacher who goes by the name of T.D. Jakes could reveal
> what thus saith the Lord unto females (p. 69).

T.D. Jakes is as big a fraud as Beauchamp is. Take notice that the only black man she mentions is one that's making money and would have nothing to do with her. And he has to be doing something that supports her views – no compromising for Ms. Alexis. Check out the following:

> As I listened to him, truth rang from his lips. I would ask myself
> how could a man tell a woman what God's will is for her life?
> How is it that what he speaks sets many a (sic) women who were
> formerly held captive, free? Then, the answer was shared with
> me. In the beginning, God created man. Then, He made woman
> out of the rib of man. Thus, man was first, then woman. Why
> would man not know about his own rib? (p. 69).

If the sick shit that Jakes is feeding people is that Adam's rib crap, then only a total moron would accept it. People like Ms. Alexis get talked out of their panties because of this kind of crap. She's weak-minded, and it's reflected in the preceding paragraph. Let me give you an example from an old story that I shared with my children and one that was shared with me.

A man was reading to his child one day and the child turned to him and asked, "Father, you always tell me that the lion is the king of the jungle, but in each of the stories you tell me, the man wins. Why is that, father?" The father looks at his son and says, "That's the way it will always be – until the lion learns how to write."

Men write stories that make them look infallible and wise. White men write stories that make them look universal. A woman came from the rib of man – yeah, right. Let's see it happen now. Why doesn't she tell Beauchamp to pluck out one of his ribs so that she can have a girlfriend to talk to. You know why it ain't happenin" Because it isn't supposed to. And if it can't happen now, it didn't happen then. The Bible is a story book with some history in it, but other than that, it's just as full of shit as anything written by a man. And if it was inspired by God, it would be flawless, and not the mistake-riddled tome that it is. Got it?

The same women that just subscribed to the Adam's rib myth now flip flops and tries to turn into Sis. Clara Muhammad! Check it out:

> It stands to reason, the human race originated in Africa. Thus, the Black race is the first race of the earth making them the mother of all races. Per science, all other races originated from Blacks, then why would God not reveal His word unto a Black woman the mother of all races? In addition, I am a Black woman born and raised in the heart of America, Nebraska (p. 69-70).

If the human race originated in Africa, then doesn't that throw her God created man/Adam's rib thesis out of the window? If the black race was the original race, then why didn't her God choose THEM to lead the rest of the race? Makes sense to me! But she's selfish: she's saying this because she wants us to believe that she, like the women in Africa, is the mother of all races. She is a black woman raised in Nebraska, so she has some kind of "attraction" that prompted God to choose her as the vessel to use to "reveal" his (God's) teachings.

Her fantasy continues:

> As I prayed in regards to the white race and I shared with others what God had revealed unto my spirit, the first question many would ask is, "Then, what purpose do other races hold"? My answer to this is God reveals in seasons. Hence, it was not revealed to me the purpose of other races, not even my own. Yet, God confirmed many times, to me, this revelation was, in fact, from Him (p. 70).

She says that after she "shared" her revelation with others, they would ask what purpose other races hold. She must have been doing the bulk of her sharing with white people. Because the first question a black person would say is, "Bitch, have you lost your fuckin' mind?" The second question would be, "What white man are YOU fuckin'?"

She claims her answer to the question is that "God reveals in seasons." So she must have passed through the fall of foolishness, the winter of wooziness, the summer of stupidity and the spring of being "sprung" (on Beauchamp, that is) and arrived at the conclusion that "it was not revealed to me the purpose of other races, not even my own." So God tells her what the white man is supposed to do, but doesn't tell her anything about her own race? She has no proof, no facts, no hard evidence – just the word of a dingbat that God "talked" to her.

Then, to make things worse, she claims that God "confirmed many times" to her that the revelation came from him. What did he do, hit star-69? How did God confirm it and why would an all-knowing, omnipresent God have to "confirm" anything with an ignorant human? Is she trying to claim a status that is more than earthly? She must be: God talked to her, he then confirms his revelation to her, and she has the job of spreading the word about the white man's being born to lead. The thinks she's one of the disciples, and wants us to agree with her. She's a disciple, alright.

Satan's disciple.

God's Confirmation

You see, to a nut, anything can be anything. In this case, she is trying to describe the confirmations that she got from God. Following is how she explains one of them:

> As I was completing this book, I really needed a confirmation from God that this is a word from Him. So, I prayed for some sort of sign or confirmation that I was, indeed, hearing from Him. A day before I finished my first draft, several flyers were distributed to white neighborhoods in Nebraska by a white radical group practicing hate stating, "Non-whites are causing Nebraska to become a third world slum … send them home! (pp. 70-71).

She doubted God! She wanted a confirmation and God, being obedient to her, gave her one. Do you expect us to believe this bullshit? Why would God need to give her confirmation – isn't his Word good enough? She says she prayed for a sign and claims it came when white boys passed out racist literature. The only thing that is a sign of is what I've been saying all along. SHE is the one that said they were destined to "lead in love," remember. Well they're leading alright: they're rallying their anti-black troops and preparing to come after us.

And she compounds the lies with statements like the one that follows:

> This was a confirmation that YES God is calling for white
> individuals to practice love. More importantly, YES, God has
> revealed a prominent word to a Black woman residing in Omaha,
> Nebraska. As I previously stated, God looks at the heart, and
> Nebraska is the Heartland; the heart of America (p. 71).

If God looked at the heart, what would possibly make Ms. Alexis think that she had something so special that God would make her "the chosen one"? She's already sinned by having children out of wedlock. She's blasphemed God and put other Gods before him. She's coveted her neighbor, and she's lied. These violations make her "typical" as far as the American norm is concerned!

But wait – Mommy Dearest has more!

> Another confirmation God shared with me is that He wants to
> communicate with those who are unable to hear, as well as those
> who cannot speak. For, what I am sharing in this book is no
> secret. Yet, many people of the white race are either turning a
> deaf ear to God, or not speaking what they know to be truth. It is
> written in the Bible that a man after given much reproof and still
> does not take heed will be broken beyond remedy (pp. 71-72).

Why is she so concerned about white folks turning a deaf ear to God? Hasn't she been looking at them in action? They don't believe in God! They worship themselves and, like her, they put all their faith and trust in their priest, rabbi and minister! Sure, they'll shout out, "Oh my God!" when they have their flat asses in a sling, but other than that, you don't see them banging tambourines, doing the hully-gully in the aisles and talking in tongues like Porky Pig! The time she's spending worrying about the salvation of the white race could be better spent with a psychiatrist trying to find out why she hates herself so much.

Take my word for it: most of the people in this society are "broken beyond remedy." Slavery alone was enough to put white folks on any Supreme Being's shit list. But then add to that the oppression of women, the maltreatment of the American Indian and the broken treaties, the abuse of the Latinos, especially those who are coming across the border, the cutbacks of social services that aided the most critically poor, the hatred of homosexual and the handicapped, the neglect of the elderly, and the wanton pollution of the environment. Trust me: America is doomed, and so is everybody in it who isn't fighting for chance. That includes Ms. Alexis, Les Beauchamp and all of those racists in those white suburban churches who are walking around trying to act like they're moral leaders.

The book is now at an end. Her work is done. She offers one last verse from the Bible where she quotes, "Those who have ears let them hear what the Spirit of the Lord is saying to the church! (p. 72).

Now the Lord is saying it to the entire church. Of course, her church is almost all peckerwoods anyway, so what difference does it make? It's just her, her white pals, her "mentor" Les Beauchamp and the rest of the white race. And where does that leave black folks. In the same place as Ms. Alexis.

On the outside looking in.

My Conclusion/Closing Remarks

Well, there you have it: too sickeningly inaccurate to laugh at, and to shallow to cry about. Geraldine Alexis is physical evidence that all that glitters is not gold: looks galore, somehow managing to infiltrate the public school system and even incredibly earning a Master's degree. All this – and not a sound thought in her head.

As I make clear, her problem is that she was vulnerable and remains that way. She is also a beautiful black woman who has probably received compliments form men her whole life. She has given up the bootie to guys who then probably betrayed her. This made her frustrated and bitter. But her ego continues to make her susceptible to bullshit from all kinds of places: her "friends," probably most men and mainly so-called "Reverend" Les Beauchamp, an effeminate white man who lifts weights (in order to feign machismo) and makes some of the cheesiest "come to my church" commercials ever conceived.

So she searches and she wonders why someone like her is having such bad luck. She's desperate, but too backwards to delve into her own situation. So she reaches out – but since she hates her family and her own race, she turns to white folks, a race of people that have always been close by. Beauchamp meets her and gives her some fucked up advice and the next thing you know, she thinks she's Samantha on "Bewitched."

This has truly been a lesson in brainwashing, buffoonery and anti-black blasphemy. This woman has been brainwashed by shrewd white men in the name of "Christianity," so much to the point where she now exposes sheer buffoonery in her actions to "save" the white race and in her subsequent moronic statements regarding race relations. Finally, she blasphemes her own ancestral greatness by claiming that God favors white folks. Despite all their crimes, she still believes that the white race was "born to lead" all others.

Most people, black and white, who read this book, will understand how sick Ms. Alexis is. But most of them will not take the time to write down their ideas in an attempt to "balance" the anti-black venom that this woman spews forth as she praises the enemy of our race. Somebody had to do it. A much shorter review of the book will appear in the Omaha Star newspaper in the weeks ahead. It will not be nearly as harsh because I wish Ms.Alexis no public harm. But I have a philosophy: whatever my enemies do to my people, I'm going to do to them. By the choice of her own words and her decision to publicize those words, Ms. Alexis has clearly shown whose side she's on.

I, therefore, could do no less. To this day, neither Pastor Beauchamp or Ms. Alexis have responded to my counter-document. I suppose the truth speaks for itself.

CONCLUSION

The myth of the Black rapist. The myth of sacred white womanhood. The myth of the Black superwoman. The myth of the universal white male. All of these are rooted in the white male's mentality and are reflected in his attitudes, values, policies and laws. All of these serve as the basis for why this society cannot solve its political and social problems: it must first solve its personal and psychological hang-ups. At present, these hang-ups are evident in the customs, morals, practices, policies and institutions that guide and direct this society. Many of these have been accepted by the majority of people who deem themselves "Americans." But just because the majority says gives something legal or normative status, ***does not necessarily mean that it is right.***

Two black women write books that essentially lie on black men. One woman, claiming to have acquired the highest degree in the academe, believes that black men "choose" white women. This basic misconception is given book form and distributed all over the nation. A second woman, younger than the first, claims to have had a "vision" and that vision told her that the white pastor of her suburban church was some kind of "messenger" from God and that black people should fall in line and follow white folks, in general. She, too, has an advanced degree (Master's) from an American university. Unfortunately, she is also in a position to counsel and advise young, impressionable children in a major public school system.

Finally, a white woman and a woman whose name implies that she is a Muslim, co-write an article that claims that white women and their long-time violations of their marriage vows is somehow a "secret" and that their lasciviousness is "on the rise." Not only do these two women have degrees from accredited universities, but they also possess journalistic experience, background and credentials and therefore should know the value of researching a subject before arriving at myopic and white supremacy-laden conclusions such as the ones shared in the *Newsweek* piece.

All three of these pieces have something in common. They are all evidence of the insanity rampant in American society and, as their backgrounds show, the sickness is not only among the poor, illiterate and ignorant; it is shared by and with people who should know better. Again, insanity is essentially a relatively permanent disorder of the mind. What makes it "permanent" however, is the fact that these people hand the distorted beliefs down to upcoming generations. This is how racism, gender bias and the misconceptions that these writers share with the public become accepted as "facts."

Even as these words are being finalized, ABC's "The View" airs a segment on what they call "arm candy." Along with their commentary, the women display pictures of old white men with young, model-looking white women. Once again, the majority population, in being segregated and locked away from everyday reality, is a day late and a dollar short. Akin to the so-called "trophy wife," these kind of women have been in existence for a long time. Older black men, from way back, would "date" these younger women who were single, paying them for their company. And it still goes on today in any black community you might visit.

And black men don't have a monopoly on it. The concept of "arm candy" is as old as the millionaire who wanted to appear as if he still had his youth, even after he entered his sixties or seventies. The answer? Find a lovely young woman and make her an offer she couldn't refuse. There may not even be sex involved, just that she be available to travel the country or the world with him, treat him as if he was the only man alive, and be on her best social behavior. This is an old story but once again, as it was with "secret lives of wives," these people want to try to re-define history or re-name social reality when, at the root of these alleged "trends" or "fads," are long histories of the exploitation of women in a male-dominated society.

The fact that those being castigated and corrected are women in no way means that they have a monopoly. In fact, there are white men (pseudo-scientific racists) and "negroes" (Shelby Steele, Glen Loury, Thomas Sowell, Alan Keyes, to name a few) who paved the way and contributed to misconceptions that many of us accept today. But this book is about the female bootlickers of the species and although I've hand-selected several for this book, can there be any doubt that this woman, Geraldine Alexis – green contact lenses and all – is the prototype of the sellout?

The fact is, at the core of our humanity are first, skin color and its attendant social definitions and, secondly, the family. If we limit our belief in family and love to issues of monogamous marriage, romantic love and "free sexual choice," we are lost. Our race is in trouble. We have to begin thinking about who we want to be the last person we look at before we close our eyes at night and the first person we see in the morning. This is no call for racial hatred; it is a call for perpetuation of OUR race and for the development of conscious young black men and women who will join the struggle against oppression and keep resistance alive.

Geraldine Alexis is (was) a counselor in Nebraska's largest school system, the Omaha Public Schools. One quarter of those students are black. What are they learning or gleaning from a lovely black woman who bats her eyes at them and the color of those eyes are as fake as her graduation certificate probably is. The role of the Jemima is therefore secured, and white folks don't care because the mistakes made will only serve to benefit their system. We need to speak truth to power and fight the powers that be.

That is what this book is committed to. As Dr. Frances Welsing once wrote, "sometimes we may be wrong. But many times, we will be right."

STAR PARKER

Some of you may have heard of this beauty, and some may not. But trust me: when it comes to Jemimas there are few who make statements like the ones she makes and still have the gall to consider themselves part of the black community.

She considers herself a "political writer and commentator." But there's more than that, as we are informed by Wikipedia (2018):

> **Star Parker** is an American syndicated columnist, Republican politician, author, and conservative political activist. In 1995, she founded the Center for Urban Renewal and Education (CURE), originally the Coalition on Urban Renewal and Education. In 2010, she was the unsuccessful Republican nominee for the United States House of Representatives in California's 37th District.

By the way: when she ran for that Congressonal seat she only got 22.7% of the vote. After that ass kicking she probably figured she had enough name recognition to launch some semblance of a career. So that's when she got the idea for an organization called CURE.

Why would you "found" an organization that is named after one of the most unsuccessful urban "experiments" in American history? In my view this is a way to let her "listeners" and "followers" know that she is the kind of "negro" who believes more in the system than she does in black people. But there are other signs as well. After all, urban renewal "changed" black communities and the lives of black people by destroying both; perhaps that is one of the goals of Star Parker.

For instance, note that she ran for office as a Republican? I am the type of person who thinks that this system is corrupt no matter what party you are a member of. But she thought she would morph her writing and syndication into a political career. And it didn't quite work. She did her best to win the sympathies of supporters, however. For instance, check out the following pity party:

> Parker was born in Moses Lake, Washington; she was raised in a nonreligious home by **often-absent parents**. She lived in Japan for three years and returned to the U.S., moving to **East St. Louis, Illinois,** at twelve … She said that after **one arrest for shoplifting, her white high school guidance counselor told her "not to worry about it, because I was a 'victim of racism, lashing out at society …** After attending church at the behest of her friends, **Parker became a Christian and reformed her life …** She enrolled in Woodbury University, graduating with a degree in marketing … She began **advocating for conservative social and political causes,** and founded CURE in 1995. After she was **laid off from her job as a program host** on Los Angeles radio station KABC (after the outlet was purchased by Disney), Parker devoted her efforts to CURE full-time (Wikipedia, 2018 – emphasis added)

What you just read is the most pitiful attempt at a "leeching resume" that I have ever read. Wikipedia is an international internet source, so whoever put this together needs their ass kicked. Perhaps she wrote it and just faxed it in to the editors, who knows? What I do know is that what you just read is the basis for a "poor girl turned her life around" stories that Jemimas like Whoopi Goldberg and the others tend to use when they want to curry favor with their white "master." Let me break it down for you with six (6) concerns I have about this Jemima.

First, the "often absent parents" statement. What the hell does that mean? Either they were there or they weren't. If there were two of them then her upbringing was no different than most other youth who have a mother and father, perhaps one who works and maybe both are employed. If that is the case, then that means that these kids also have "often absent parents." Now were they absent for nine hours a day and then came home or were they absent for weeks and months at a time. I believe the former: I believe this "often absent" bullshit is one of those "I was born the son of a sharecropper" stories that these coons use to curry favor with their white master.

Secondly, she came back to the States from Japan and landed in East St. Louis. Why is this significant? How do you go to Japan and return with parents unless you are a military brat? And if that is the case and you come back with some semblance of security, how in the hell do you end up in East St. Louis, the capital of black-on-black gunfire? Again, to mention East St. Louis lends itself to the "poor black kid growing up" story that Parker is working into her life story of "rags-to-riches."

Third, when did a single arrest for shoplifting merit inclusion on Wikipedia? That's like putting down that you got ticketed for jaywalking as a teen! I'll tell you what she's trying to do: she's trying to establish some middle-of-the road street cred! Not REAL street cred like fighting in school, being put in juvenile hall, dealing drugs, or busting a cap in somebody's ass. No. That would scare her white master. So she "shoplifts". And the fact that the statement says "single arrest" further qualifies the crime: she was only caught one time and learned her ways. "You see – she's not like the rest of the niggers."

Fourth, why mention that her high school counselor was white and then played the "racism" card as a form of advice? By being "turned off" by the advice, she is telling her white handlers that she rejects the victimization route! She's snitching off on a white liberal while at the same time implying that she doesn't see racism as a part of her life. That is what Jemimas do: they publicly deny the existence of racism the way that Raven-Symon, Ezola Foster and Stacey Dash do.

Fifth, it says "she became a Christian and reformed her life". Oh, just like that? Does becoming a Christian lead to reformation? I think not. Look at all the Christians who are still screwing up: Rev. Jesse Jackson, Congresswoman Bernice Johnson, Rev. Ben Chavis, Rev. Al Sharpton and so many others. But by placing this in her "resume," she can win over more conservatives who will relax because white folks know that black people are religious and will therefore be no threat to them. This brings us to the sixth point, akin to this one.

Sixth, then she decides to advocate for conservative social and political causes." Is there a link between the Lord and being a conservative? Of course there is! To be Christian is to be conservative. Conservatives want to conserve the existing way of life. That is why they are anti-abortion and don't want any niggas in their neighborhoods. To be conservative is to sit back, get on your knees and never worry: "God will handle it," or "Jesus will find a way." That is the black version of conservatism. The white conservative simply picks up a gun and busts a cap in yo' black ass!

Her conservative views are described briefly on Wikipedia:

> Parker supports welfare reform measures, claiming that welfare has become like a government plantation, which creates a situation where those who accept the invitation switch mindsets from "How do I take care of myself?" to "What do I have to do to stay on the plantation? … She believes stable families and strong moral values are the key to ending poverty. She has asserted a moral objection to abortion and claims that rampant abortion has hurt black families. She opposes abortion, divorce, homosexuality, same-sex marriage and birth control …

She's a Christian, alright! In 1998 she wrote a book called Pimps, Whores and Welfare Brats: From Welfare Cheat to Conservative Messenger. I wonder who she's talking about? The snippet of the book on Amazon.com reads, "Star Parker tells the inspirational story of how she turned her life around from a world of drugs, crime, and welfare to success as an entrepreneur, founder of the Coalition on Urban Affairs, and spokesperson for African-American conservatives." Really. So that's why the mention of East St. Louis was so important: she wanted to paint herself as a "victim of circumstance."

The Barnes and Noble website goes into more detail. Check it out:

> She was a delinquent teenager, mixed up with crime and drugs. In the 1970s, Star Parker came to Los Angeles with a dream of dancing on *Soul Train* — and ended up an unemployed single mom, barely literate, and living on welfare. But life on county aid was far from impoverished — she was able to lounge in her own jacuzzi, party at Venice Beach, bring in extra income with under-the-table jobs, and take the system for all it was worth. It was the power of Christianity that turned her life around. But it was Star's no-excuses attitude of self-empowerment that firmly positioned her on the fast track of conservative politics, speaking out against welfare as the cause of urban America's moral and economic decline — and in favor of taxpayer vouchers for private school education, banning abortion, and condemning condom distribution in public schools."

The bullshit gets deeper as the snippet adds:

> Guided by her faith, Star has broken the "code of silence" among blacks to speak out on:

- Affirmative action: "What we haven't told our people is that they can start their own businesses. Entrepreneurship works for everybody."
- Equal opportunity: "Capitalism doesn't have any racial boundaries."
- The death penalty: "How many murders do we have to read about before we get serious?"
- Black rage: "Blacks cannot cry racism every time something doesn't go their way."
- The Los Angeles riots: "After three decades of handouts...they had evolved into a group of government-dependent, out-of-control, racist monsters."
- Liberalism: "White liberals are afraid. That monster they created in their socialist lab has gone crazy on them....Their liberalism has backfired."

> Speaking her mind and taking control of her life, Star Parker has forged a bright future. And while she'll always stir up controversy, there's no disputing that her rise from public assistance to public prominence is proof that the American dream is alive and well — for all of us.

The American Dream is alive and well for all of us – the mantra of the Aunt Jemima. "Guided by her faith"? And what faith would that be – devil worship? These Jemimas all talk about being Christians and believing in the Lord. They might even go to church every once in a while. But all of them have something in common: they would rather screw a pastor than listen to one.

Furthermore, can you see the similar threads? They want to be black only as children and then they have "changed for the better" the closer they get to white values, mores, belief systems and dogma. Then they latch on to a public forum – television, newspaper, radio, social media – and work to make a name for themselves by finding a niche with white people who don't mind "working with the nigra people."

Her name is Star Parker and she's a "star" alright. But when it comes to relevance to black people, she's a "falling star."

WHOOPI GOLDBERG

Whoopi Goldberg is 62 years old and dresses like a pre-teen hobo fresh off the train from Greenwich Village. No slouchier a Jemima than she, that's for sure! Her real name is Caryn Elaine Johnson and she claims her mother told her to change her name to Whoopi Goldberg so she would be able to get tight with the Jews. Who knows if it's true or not, but the part about her hanging with Jews most certainly is. And Jews are about as white and racist as you can get when it comes to exploitation and making money off of black people (witness the music and film industries).

As a Jemima she has been well compensated, being one of only a few women (another one is Rita Moreno) to win an Oscar, a Grammy, an Emmy and a Tony. And there is another one she would win if it was awarded and that would be "Female Bootlicker of the Decade."

Most of her movies were bullshit except when she played the abused young sistah "Celie" in "The Color Purple," which was written by Alice Walker but directed by a Jew, Stephen Spielberg. By 1992 did you know she was the highest paid actress of that time?

But back to that name thing for a minute. According to one source:

> She has stated that her stage forename ("Whoopi") was taken from a whoopee cushion; "When you're performing on stage, you never really have time to go into the bathroom and close the door. So if you get a little gassy, you've got to let it go. So people used to say to me, 'You're like a whoopee cushion.' And that's where the name came from" … She said in 2011, "My mother did not name me Whoopi, **but Goldberg is**

> **my name, it's part of my family, part of my heritage. Just like being black."** (Wikipedia, 2018 – emphasis added)

Really? Not according to another sellout, Henry Louis Gates, Jr., Check out the following:

> Henry Louis Gates Jr., in his book *In Search of Our Roots: How 19 Extraordinary African Americans Reclaimed Their Past*, **found that all of Goldberg's traceable ancestors were African Americans, that she has no known Jewish ancestry, and that none of her ancestors were named Goldberg** … Results of a DNA test, revealed in the 2006 PBS documentary *African American Lives*, traced part of her ancestry to the Papel and Bayote people of modern-day Guinea-Bissau.
> Her admixture test indicates that she is of **92 per cent sub-Saharan African origin and of 8 per cent European origin** (Wikipedia, 2018 – emphasis added).

And there we have it, one more component of the Aunt Jemima repertoire, that "of denial." Just as the young Butterfly McQueen shouted out in "Gone With the Wind," "Ah don't know nothin' 'bout birthin' no babies!", coons like Goldberg find a way to make an association with whiteness: Stacey Dash is green eyes, Geraldine Alexis is fake green contacts and a white minister, all have a gimmick that links them with white folks. We can add Halle Berry, Venus and Serena Williams, Iman and a host of others to that list.

But this is about Whoopi, and her "Aunt Jemima" moment came during an event held for her at a Friar's Club roast. Following is the text of someone who attended although what happened made national news. I use the following excerpt because you get to see the words of the "tommish" Goldberg.

The article comes from a website called "Is It Funny or Offensive?" The title of the article: "The Roast of Whoopi Goldberg: A Look Back At Ted Danson's Blackface Performance." My analyses will filter in and out.

The article starts off with the sub-heading, "Friar's Club Flop?"

> May 18th, 2017 – Whoopi Goldberg and Ted Danson made a lot of headlines back in the 90s but perhaps none were more hard-hitting as those that followed October 8th, 1993. That Friday night, the two entertainers, who were recent co-stars and lovers, were in attendance at the Friar's Club roast held at the New York Hilton Hotel ballroom. Danson was roasting Goldberg. His makeup was blackface and his jokes included over a dozen uses of the n-word.

A dozen times with Whoopi sitting in the first chair right next to the podium where Danson was clowning up a storm, uttering the word "nigger" in a huge room full of entertainers, celebrities and corporate types. Nobody shouted him down. Nobody said, "Get your racist ass of the stage." The best that Montel Williams (another favorite "coon" of the establishment) could do was take the hand of his white wife and walk out.

Continuing:

> Noted film critic Roger Ebert covered the event, opening his <u>October 10th column</u> with: **"It's a tradition of the celebrity roasts at the Friar's Club that everything goes – that no joke is in such bad taste that it cannot be told. Friday, that tradition may have ended, as a roast for Whoopi Goldberg turned into such a tasteless display that some audience members hid their faces in their hands, and others left."** (emphasis original)

Ebert is right, and remember: he was married to a black woman, so you know he was pissed. Goldberg, the Jemima in question, just sat there. But worse than that, she defended the actions of Danson. Let's move on:

> More than 3,000 people were in attendance and the star-filled dais had over 100 celebrities including Halle Berry, Vanessa Williams, Anita Baker, RuPaul and Mr. T, Michael Spinks, Sugar Ray Leonard, and New York Mayor David Dinkins. Most reporting sets the reception of jokes at "stone faced" or "cringing" with talk show host Montel Williams turning his back and eventually leaving the event.

Look at all the toms and Jemimas who were present. I have no idea what RuPaul thinks he/she is, but whatever it is it's nasty. But Sugar "the coke head" Leonard was present, as was Michael "take the money and run" Spinks, former governor David "bootlicker"Dinkins, Halle "the zebra" Berry, and foxy and sweet Anita Baker (they ain't all bad). The thing is, nobody said a damn thing while Danson was acting a fool at the expense of black people.

And while all this was going on, guess what Aunt Jemimia Whoopberg was up to?

> Goldberg, however, smiled and laughed during Danson's roast and defended him both on the dais and in statements after extreme fallout from the *Cheers* star's decision to cross the line. **"Let's get these words all out in the open. It took a whole lot of courage to come out in blackface in front of 3,000 people. I don't care if you didn't like it. I did,"** she said at the roast. **"If they knew me,"** Goldberg said the week after the roast, **"they would know that Whoopi has never been about political correctness. I built my whole career destigmatizing words like 'nigger.'"** (emphasis added)

Look at those fucked up explanations for her tommishness. It didn't take a whole lot of courage for Danson to come out in blackface, no more than it takes that slouchy bitch to appear on the view five days a week looking like she just got gang raped by Ali Baba and the Forty Thieves! She said she liked it. That goes back to the "self-hate" section of this book and proves, once again, that black celebrities hate being black and only do so because they get paid for it. The only roles that black people get are roles reserved for them (with the exception of Denzel Washington, and he'll do anything for a dollar, just like Samuel L. Jackson).

She has never been about political correctness. I didn't like that term when I first heard it. Call me a nigga and I'm gonna kick your ass and I don't care what the conventions or social protocols of the time dictate. Social correctness? Calling us nigga IS socially correct for most peckerwoods, which is why the word is still being used! She claims she spent her entire career "destigmatizing" words like nigger, which is a damn lie: Her career is filled with nigger-like roles and stereotypes. Want proof?

How about flicks like "Ghost" (1990) where she played a spook (which is what they used to call black people back in the day), "Jumpin' Jack Flash" (1986), where her character admittedly "doesn't fit in" with the bank she works at, "Burglar" (1987) which is self-explanatory, or "Boys on the Side" (1995), playing a lesbian on a cross-country road trip with two white bitches? In most of her movies she just does walk-ons and plays herself. Now that must be for comic relief. If that ain't a Jemima-related job, then I don't know what is. She's never worked to "destigmatize" anything; if she has accomplished anything it is that she has brought utter shame to the locks that she wears, but that's just part of her "po' me, po' me" gimmick. Remember, all Jemimas have a gimmick.

Back to Danson and his being defended for appearing in blackface by the truly backwards Whoopi Golderg:

> Goldberg also defended the routine by sharing that **she had written some of Danson's remarks as a satirical piece** and tried to re-focus the attention to what he said at the beginning of the roast. "**Ted prefaced his remarks by saying to me, 'I love you, I'm proud of you, and I love being with you.' That's all being left out by people.**"

A truly sick bitch. She collaborated with his peckerwood to poke fun at black people. And then she falls for the okey-doke when he says that he loves her, is proud of her and loves being with her. That's the same thing that these white people utter to their pets at home; that's what the dickless corporate cockhound utters to his mistress before handing her a fistful of hundreds. He didn't love her because as you will see later, this bitch don't believe in marriage. And yet everyone she marries is a white man. Sounds a lot like Geraldine Alexis and some of the others, doesn't she?

But "Jemimas of a feather, flock together." Check out who got in on the act: "African-American model Beverly Johnson also defended Danson and the intent behind the roast. **"If you can't see the humor at a place where there's supposed to be over-the-line jokes, then there's something really wrong" ((emphasis added). Say what?** This is the same bitch who was wining about the white man doing black models wrong when it came to covers of magazines, remember?

And since she wanted to poke her nose in the shit, let's look at what she has to say about race and racism before we move on with Whoopi's bootlicking ass. In an October 2014 internet article the beautiful super model Johnson said,

> "I lived a very sheltered life," she shared. "Of course, I'd been called the n-word riding my bicycle through the wrong neighborhood, but I really wasn't that aware of just the centuries of struggle that my ancestors had."Still, Johnson asserts, **it doesn't offend her when young stars like Raven-Symoné speak about eschewing the label African American**, saying, "I think it's freedom of speech. I think it's her opinion of herself and who she wants to be." (Sprankles, 2014 – emphasis added)

Johnson was a culturally deprived "negro" and grew up the same way. She learned about her blackness late and how she skipped over the "Black is Beautiful" movement of the '60s I don't know. I do know that she was the first black woman to ever grace the cover of Vogue magazine and that didn't take place until 1974, more than enough time to know what Malcolm X, the Black Panther Party and Martin Luther King, Jr., were fighting for. Some Jemimas mature late; but even now she sides with the likes of Raven-Symone (you'll read about her elsewhere) and that can't be a good sign. That "she's who she wants to be" bullshit is one way that the majority of black people continue to get bamboozled by the white media elite. As Karenga (1967) once wrote, "Individualism means being yourself at the expense of others."

Moreover,

> Johnson also empathizes with Raven-Symoné in a way, as she knows firsthand how a seemingly simple statement with no agenda can be blown out of proportion. "I just remember doing this radio show, and they immediately said, 'Well, how does it feel to be the top black model?' And I said, **'Excuse me, I'm really the top model in the nation!'"** she said, laughing. (Sprankles, 2014 – emphasis added)

Another element of "Jemima-ism": the belief that "we're all Americans and by golly we need to pull together." That kind of bullshit is what keeps black people trapped in mythology. And with that "I beez an American" belief system linked to that mythology of Christianity, can there be any doubt as to why black folks are so miffed and mummified in their dealings with each other?

The top model in the nation? That's like saying "I'm the head nigger on the plantation." The answer to both is, who owns the modeling agency, the magazine and the promotional elements? Who pays you to lay back, gap your legs, change your clothes in dressing rooms that are most likely "bugged" by horny white boys, and who are you modeling for? Black women can't afford that bullshit that those white boys have you trying on! Like any other prostitute, she sells herself and her body. And she loves it.

She adds,

> "You know, because I was on the cover of *Glamour*, *Vogue*, Italian *Vogue*. And after that, it was this big hoopla. So I understand how the things that you can say can be taken out of context and that she's merely speaking what she feels — **that she wants to be labeled a human being," said Johnson.** (Sprankles, 2014 – emphasis added)

She shouldn't want to be "labeled" at all. If it's up to the white man, the only label you will be wearing is "human being/nigger." He defines things the way he wants them to be. And he gets people like Whoopi Goldberg (and Beverly Johnson, for that matter) to act the way he wants them to act. People like Raven-Symone say and do things assuming that they are "above" other black people. And in Raven's specific case, she's half peckerwood – just like Halle Berry, Barack Obama, Blake Griffin, Stephon Curry, and a host of other "celebrities" who get a break because they are part cracker.

But it's only "half a break" because you're considered "mixed race," and remember what Dr. Welsing said about that term "non-white." It means the absence of whiteness. So these Jemimas may be dancing jigs now, but their time will soon run out when a new nationality (Asians and Middle Eastern women, for example) come into vogue with just enough skin color, their own hair, and a willingness to do anything, and that mulatto will be replaced with the quickness.

Back to the Goldberg-Danson debacle:

> *The New York Times* interviewed Richard Greene, owner of Crown and Glory Hair Salon, for their coverage of the roast to get his take on how Danson and Goldberg's decision was playing at his predominately black, female business. **"A lot of people feel she's just covering up for Ted and not looking at it as an insult to a race of people," he said. "She may say, or think, that comedy has no limits. In reality it does, and what they did exceeded those limits."** (emphasis added)

You can explain it any way you want to. Whoopi Goldberg is a sellout and that night, in particular, made that fact crystal clear.

So acceptable is she by the white establishment that they made her the new co-host of ABC's "The View" in 2007 when Rosie O'Donnell was canned. She learned quickly that even as America's favorite Jemima, there were limits to what she could say. Wikipedia (2018) documents a couple of incidents:

> Goldberg has made controversial comments on the program. Her first appearance included statements taken by some to condone football player Michael Vick's dogfighting … In 2009, she opined that Roman Polanski's rape of a thirteen-year-old in 1977 … was not "rape-rape" … later clarified that she had intended to distinguish between *statutory rape*("unlawful sexual intercourse with a minor") and *forcible rape* … Goldberg was a staunch defender of Bill Cosby from the outset of his rape allegations, asserting he should be considered innocent until proven guilty, and questioning why Cosby had never been arrested or tried for them … After learning that the statute of limitations on these allegations had expired and thus could not be tried, she called for Cosby to answer the allegations, and began advising women to come forward if they are raped.

She was wrong in every instance, defending black men who also thought they were above the law (Vick was a multimillionaire quarterback who couldn't stop hanging with his 'homies' and doing gangsta shit like dog fighting and got busted, Cosby drugged and raped those women and thought no one would ever find out, and "rape is rape"). Her voicing those views also shows that she thinks she's above the law – the basic belief of one Jemima after another.

The next Jemima is also in love with the media and is a self-made public speaker.

CANDACE OWENS

You're never too young to sell out it seems. You may not have heard of this sistah but like Star Parker, she's a staunch conservative and uses every means at her disposal to promote it. According to Wikipedia (2018), "Candace Owens … is an American conservative commentator and activist. She is known for her pro-Trump commentary and her criticism of Black Lives Matter and of the Democratic Party … She is the Director of Urban Engagement at the conservative advocacy group Turning Point USA."

Another Jemima who wants to get involved in urban life (remember Candace Parker?). These bitches don't seem to understand what it takes to run an organization or start a movement. The only component they have is the "communications" element. They are still missing the ideology – which is the white man's way of thinking and that's not going to be of benefit to them in the long run; they're missing resources because they scrounge to sell articles and speaking gigs to get chump change to pay for their draws and keep the lights on. Living on a bologna and cheese economy when they're in a caviar and prime rib environment.

Who is she? Check out her resume and get ready for yet another "po' li'l black girl who made it big" story:

> Born to an African American family and raised in Stamford, Connecticut,[5] Owens is a graduate of Stamford High School … She was raised by her grandparents **after her parents divorced** … In 2007, while a senior in high school, **Owens received hurtful and threatening racist phone calls that were traced to a car in which the 14-year-old son of then mayor Dannel Malloy was present** … Owens' family sued the Stamford Board of Education in federal court alleging that the city did not protect her rights, resulting in a **$37,500 settlement** … Owens was pursuing an undergraduate degree in journalism at the University of Rhode Island **but left school after her junior year** … Afterwards, she **worked for** *Vogue* magazine … In 2012, she took a job as an **administrative assistant** for a private equity firm … (Wikipedia, 2018)

Ain't this a bitch? Her scratch-and-claw journey up the ladder to public renown is almost as pitiful as her educational background. But let me not get ahead of myself. Let's break down six (6) concerns I have with the previous excerpt.

First, the fact that her parents divorced. What is the purpose of mentioning that when indeed, her grandparents did an adequate job of raising her? What this tells me is that she had chance to give up booty and take over her own growth and development because the elders couldn't keep up with her. That's how it usually goes.

Secondly, that lawsuit about a threatening racist phone call being "traced" to a 14 year old. So fuckin' what? Traced to whom? Is a call like that the basis for an actual lawsuit? Making terrorist threats is nothing unique or sui generis! But when you're a Jemima and you're trying to establish enough street cred to convince the white man that you are worthy of hiring and trusting, then this is the kind of shit that you capitalize on.

Third, the size of the settlement – chump change! Just like that nickel and dime payments doled out to Diamond and Silk. These white people know that if they can't buy a nigga, they can sure enough rent one! But that was probably the money that she used to get into Rhode Island, and she couldn't even hack it there.

Another "well I went to college" story without stating that you never finished college, which was the whole purpose. The degree – remember, heifer?

Fourth –and a continuation of point number three - she never finished school. You know I find that interesting about Facebook as well. When these so-called successful people are asked about their education, they merely put that they "attended" this college or that university. Just like these negroes who are leaders – "I went to college." So what? The question is, did you finish and what did you do while you were in college to positively impact on black life?

Fifth, it says she "worked for Vogue." Name the position. Name the job responsibilities. Who did you report to? Were you a janitor? Did you work in the mailroom like Damon Wayans (another sellout) did in the 1992 movie that he did with a fellow Jemima Stacey Dash ("Mo' Money"). Was she just a token hire or a fake ass "intern"? Was it college work study? What? What? What?

Sixth, the was an administrative assistant at "a private equity firm." Which one was it – Dewey, Cheatem and Howe? How big was the firm? As an administrative assistant, was all she did was type and take messages? To far too many black people this is an impressive list of credentials. To me – this woman couldn't be a leader or advocate of any kind of movement I was involved in unless it was a bowel movement!

And like the other script-flipping Jemima types, she starts off one way, smells money to be made, dumps what little values she had, and becomes a lackey for the system:

> Prior to 2017, Owens ran a website that frequently criticized conservatism and mocked then-candidate Donald Trump … By 2017, she had become prominent in conservative circles for her pro-Trump commentary and for criticizing liberal narratives around structural racism, systemic inequality, and identity politics (the kind of content that her website previously trafficked in).(Wikipedia, 2018)

She starts off as a critic of the right wing and Donald Trump. But that was BEFORE 2017. Once he got in office, she saw there was money to be made, and like most Jemimas – Diamond and Silk, Omarosa Manigault and Candace Parker to name but a few – they flipped and ran behind the white man. These Jemimas have a common trait: they are willing to make themselves look like hypocrites and coons in exchange for some radio, television or newspaper time. That's what it's all about, because even notoriety translates into cash when all is said and done.

Continuing:

> In 2015, Owens founded the website Degree180 … The website frequently posted anti-conservative and anti-Trump content, **including mockery of his penis size …** Owens said in one of her postings that it was "good news" that the "Republican Tea Party … will eventually die off (peacefully in their sleep,

Making fun of a white man's dick usually doesn't bother him because he knows it's true. But in the case of the ultra-sensitive Trump, she's lucky she wasn't locked up. Then she lied on Buzzfeed the same way that Diamond and Silk had lied on Facebook. No evidence, no proof – just allegations. But she was a long way from being "done" with her Jemima mission:

These Jemimas wait in the wings until the white man inevitably gets his nuts in the wringer. Then he needs a token, a "coon" who can be marched out to claim that he's not a racist or guilty of racism. That's what Omarosa did in her early days with Trump, and that's what Star and Diamond do. Ms. Owens is no exception as you can see. She promotes "Black conservatism" which is not in itself bad. Black people ARE conservative on a lot of social issues because of that Christian tradition, a dogma that teaches black people not to upset the apple cart.

And she got her appointment as "director of urban engagement." Another long title along with a set of keys that probably didn't fit anything. Just like Omarosa was appointed to a "created position" called "Assistant to the President and Communications Director for the Office of Public Liaison," and at the same time Her title was assistant to the president and communications director for the Office of Public Liaison and was placed in charge of the White House Office of HBCU Initiatives out of the Department of Education. It was placed into the Executive Office of the President.

The "urban engagement" is just a fancy of saying "nigga issues." That's what these white boys do: they appoint people to handle issues that are majority black and then deny the same people the resources to do the job properly. That is what is going to happen to Dr. Ben Carson, another lackey who doesn't know his ass from a hole in the ground, who is in charge of Housing and Urban Development.

Only when Turning Point was charged with being racist did Ms. Owens get marched out. But toms stick together, even across industries:

> In April 2018, Kanye West tweeted "I love the way Candace Owens thinks."[17] The tweet was met with derision among some of West's fans … In May 2018, President Donald Trump stated **that Owens "is having a big impact on politics in our Country...**She represents an ever expanding group of very smart 'thinkers,' and it is wonderful to watch and hear the dialogue going on...so good for our Country!" (Wikipedia, 2018 – emphasis added)

Trump was then and continues to be a lying sack of shit. That woman didn't have any "big impact on politics" by any stretch of the imagination. Influence peddlers don't get things done – only power brokers do. Owens was and remains a Jemima and gets paid for doing just what she does: intellectually masturbate and talk to the gullible masses.

It's only a matter of time before these Jemimas overstep their rhetorical boundaries and begin delving onto areas that they have no business discussing. Just like Whoopi did when it came to defining "rape" and just like Stacey Dash did when (along with Raven-Symone) somehow became experts on black culture and black history month, Owens committed a similar act. Check out the following:

> In May 2018, Owens suggested that **"something bio-chemically happens" to women who do not marry or have children**, and she linked to the Twitter handles of Sarah Silverman, Chelsea Handler and Kathy Griffin, saying that they were "evidentiary support" of this theory … Silverman responded, saying "It seems to me that by tweeting this, you would like to maybe make us feel badly. I'd say this is evidenced by ur effort to use our twitter handles so we would see. My heart breaks for you, Candy. I hope you find happiness in whatever form that takes." … Owens responded, accusing Silverman of supporting terrorists and crime gangs. (Wikipedia, 2018 – emphasis added)

What Owens was basically saying was that a woman is nothing without a man to marry or children, provided by the man. This is akin to Barbara Acklin's 1968 jam, "Love Makes a Woman" or Aretha's "You Make Me Feel Like a Natural Woman." This is all derived from that bullshit theory of Adam and Eve and Eve supposedly being formed out of Adam's rib. Ain't that a bitch?

But her views are what keeps her going. For instance one source documents the following:

> By 2017, Owens had become a pro-Donald Trump conservative commentator … *The Guardian* has described her as "ultra-conservative", the *Daily Beast* has described her as "far-right", the *New York Magazine* and *Columbia Journalism Review* described her as "right-wing", and the *Pacific Standard* described her as "alt-right" … Prior to 2017, she ran a website that frequently criticized conservatism

<blockquote>
and mocked then-candidate Donald Trump … She has characterized
Trump as the "savior" of Western civilization … She has argued that
Trump has neither engaged in rhetoric that is harmful to African
Americans nor proposed policies that would harm African Americans
(Wikipedia, 2018)
</blockquote>

When you find a black woman who is deemed "ultra conservative," you have a true, full-fledged Aunt Jemima on your hands. When you consider a psychotic like Trump to be the savior of Western civilization, that is a trap. People know that Trump is so bitch-like that if you give him a compliment, it will go straight to his head and he will let you into his fold. She is sending a message to that racist that she loves him more than he loves himself.

And, like most Jemimas, she is a pathological liar. In my book Donald Trump as White Male Prototype, I list a plethora of lies that Trump has told, and that was a year back, before the New York Times revealed that he had told more than 3,000 lies since his inauguration! So we know that Owens is an opportunist and, like Omarosa Manigault, will say and do anything to curry favor with the white power structure.

And these Jemimas also turn against their own race in a direct way. For instance,

<blockquote>
Owens did not vote in the 2012 and 2016 elections, saying in June 2018,
"his is the first time I've been politically inclined and active." … She
has called for the imprisonment of Hillary and Bill Clinton, former FBI
director James Comey, and special counsel Robert Mueller, as well as
TV anchors such as Jake Tapper, Rachel Maddow and Anderson Cooper.
(Wikipedia, 2018)
</blockquote>

Now we know who ran for President during this period: none other than Barack Obama. But some reason this Jemima didn't vote, which is her right. But then to turn around and shower someone like Donald Trump with hosannas of praise is going too far. Like the white conservatives she calls for the imprisonment of Bill and Hillary Clinton (both of whom are two-faced peckerwoods who did black people a grave disservice), and like Trump, calls for locking up James Comey along with members of the media. Whatever Trump says, she does. He says "jump, nigger," and she asks, "how high?"

And her views on race are equally jejune, although some of them I tend to agree with even though it is for different reasons. Let's go through a few of them. To begin with,

<blockquote>
Owens is known for her criticism of Black Lives Matter … She has
described Black Lives Matter protesters as "a bunch of whiny toddlers,
</blockquote>

> pretending to be oppressed for attention" … Owens has argued that
> African Americans have a "victim mentality" and often refers to the
> Democratic Party as a "plantation … She has argued that the American
> left "like black people to be government-dependent" …. Owens has
> argued that black people have been brainwashed to vote for Democrats
> (Wikipedia, 2018).

Some of the things that this woman is opposed to are areas where I have similar concerns – just for different reasons. I am skeptical of black groups that make generic appeals to white people's non-existent morality. Black lives have always mattered, but when you make the fact a slogan to generate social interest, you are basically saying that black lives don't matter and we need white approval to affirm black humanity. Besides that, they appear to be linked to the homosexual lobby and that is a group with a whole different set of issues and I think black people need to iron out our own problems and leave the rump roasters to fend for themselves.

But it just seems in the case of Owens that whatever Trump opposes is what she opposes. Black people do have a "victim" mentality and that is because we are victims. But pointing it out to the culprit – the victimizer – is like running from the wolf to the fox! In fact, the Jemimas I 've mentioned have exponentially increased the victims mentality to the point where they act and sound like handicapped lab rats. They are the ones constantly looking for a conservative/white cause to "adopt" them.

And she is right when she says that black people have been brainwashed. But not just by the Democratic wing – by white people in general. Look back to enslavement and study the 350 years of dehumanization that black people were exposed to. If that wasn't a cultural brainwashing of sorts, then I don't know what is. But it gets worse:

> She has argued that police violence against black people is not about
> racism … According to *The Guardian* and the Daily Beast, Owens has
> referred to police killings of black people as a trivial matter to African
> Americans … (Wikipedia, 2018)

What?! If shooting unarmed black men in the back is not about racism, then what is it: some kind of new police bullet disposal project? And if she says what she is cited as saying about black people thinking that those shootings are a trivial matter, then she is as out of touch with the black community as most Jemimas are. The white man knows all this – he just needs to re-direct black ire from his racist ways and words to someone else stupid enough to promote his policies – and Jemima will bail him out every time!

Moreover,

> After the 2017 Unite the Right rally in Charlottesville, Virginia, Owens
> said that **concern over rising white nationalism was "stupid"** …
> Owens rejects the scientific consensus on climate change … **She has
> called climate change a lie used to "extract dollars from Americans."**
> … Owens described the #MeToo Movement - which was an
> international movement against sexual harassment and assault - as
> **"stupid" and said that she "hated" the movement** … Owens wrote
> that the #MeToo Movement was premised on the idea that "women are
> stupid, weak & inconsequential." … **She is critical of feminism**.
> (Wikipedia, 2018 – emphasis added)

She is towing the conservative line and backing up everything that the racist President Donald Trump believes in. At a time when the nation is seeing its own racist past in full view (sans denial), here comes some Jemima marching out and claiming that concerns over rising white nationalism was "stupid." I'm sure the Jews thought the same thing before Hitler marched them into the concentration camps and gas chambers.

Climate change is real to anyone who is alive and breathing. And in my view it appears to be getting worse. The worst expenditure that can be made by a television station is to hire a full-time weather reporter. Part-time maybe, but full time is a waste of funds. And some of these stations carry three and four meteorologists. Weather is too unpredictable and can even avoid detection by Doppler Radar and those other gadgets. To doubt that global warming is a lie flies in the face of reality.

According to the December 6, 2017 issue of the **Huffington Post**, 14 cities "could disappear over the next century because of global warming." Which ones are they? Miami (FL.), Fort Lauderdale (FL), Boston (MA), NY, Atlantic City (NJ), Honolulu (HI), New Orleans (LA), Sacramento (CA), San Diego (CA), Los Angeles, (CA), Charleston (SC), Virginia Beach (VA), Seattle (WA) and Savannah GA). That's right. So if they "could disappear" in a century that means that the actual process of disappearing is taking place even as we speak. And yet people like Candace Owens are out there calling this reality "a lie."

I agree with her about the MeToo movement because white women have co-opted it from the black woman who began it all. Feminism is also the white woman's domain for the most part. But Owens is a woman who backs the Trump agenda and he doesn't even consider women to be human beings who are worthy of respect! Not only has Owens missed the proverbial boat, but I think that one of the blades from the boat motor may have sheered one of her brain stems!

Continuing:

> **She has said that abortion is "extermination" of black babies** … She has advocated for **an end to all welfare programs** … She attended the opening of the United States embassy in Jerusalem … She is critical of the press and open borders policies … **She has called for the immediate deportation of all undocumented immigrants** … In May 2018, Owens praised Louis Farrakhan's tweet endorsing Donald Trump with a description of "a really big deal" and "relevant." … Afterward, Owens received **criticism from conservative figures** for praising Farrakhan - who has a history of anti-semitic remarks - Owens deleted the tweet (Wikipedia, 2018 – emphasis added)

And so it goes. Abortion is about the extermination of the control that men want to have over women's bodies, period. It is an option when two people in hedonistic and sex-crazed America make a major mistake concerning bringing a life into the world. As for deportation of all undocumented immigrants, that is a racist policy and it should begin with people like Donald Trump's wife who got to the U.S. by way of Canada through a series of manipulations of the immigration system.

When Owens praised Farrakhan, that is when she tore her panties. Even if Farrakhan endorsed Trump (for reasons different from hers), she forgot one thing: Jews control the electorate and their money and the power of AIPAC (the American Israeli Public Affairs Committee) dictates who says what and when they say it. That means that the previous paragraph statement about "conservative figures" criticizing her actually meant "Jews criticized her." And they also control the radio waves, the major TV stations, the film industry and social media.

The Jemimas just keep on coming. Candace Owens, like some of the others, is a true beauty. But we all learn, sooner or later, that "all that glitters ain't gold." The only thing about Candace Owens that is remotely related to gold is that when it comes to being opportunistic, she is a "gold digger."

IMAN

Another confused beauty that clearly falls into the category of an "Aunt Jemima."

My dealings with her relate to something I read about three decades ago, around 1979 or 1980. Iman had just married one of my favorite basketball players, Spencer Haywood. I admired Haywood because he sued the NBA and won. But that's not the issue here. In an interview, I read where Iman was asked about her relationship with Haywood, with whom she has a daughter, and she said he was "tall, dark and handsome." And then this dumb bitch told this white reporter that "he had the biggest penis I had ever seen."

I share this with you because it clearly establishes the mindless lengths that a Jemima will go through as she works to curry favor with the white establishment. She has changed her beautiful Somali name from Zara Mohamed Abdulmajid to its current form, given to her by her grandfather.

At any rate this woman is now deemed a "pioneer in the ethnic-cosmetic market" and is the widow of English rock musician David Bowie, the white man she married in 1992. The second mark of a Jemima. Supposedly she is a Muslim and can speak five languages, which are Somali, Arabic, Italian, French and English. Notice that of the five three are European – as are her values, mindset and orientation as you will see.

She has been thoroughly "whitenized." Put another way,

> While still at university, Iman was **discovered by American photographer Peter Beard**, and subsequently moved to the United States to begin a modeling career … Her first modeling assignment was for *Vogue* a year later in 1976. She soon landed some of the most prestigious magazine covers, establishing herself as a supermodel …During her 14 years as a high fashion model, Iman also worked with many notable photographers, including Helmut Newton, Richard Avedon, Irving Penn and Annie Leibovitz …Iman credits the **nurturing she received** from various designers with having given her the confidence to succeed in an era **when individuality was** valued and model-muses were often an integral part of the creative process (Wikipedia, 2018 – emphasis added)

Her assimilationist track has landed her a major cosmetics business and clothing line, as well as her highly regarded charity work. She has appeared in some very forgettable movies, but what I remember are the times she appeared on NBCs "Miami Vice" and clearly showed that she could not act worth a damn.

At any rate, she continues to make zany remarks. She was married at age 18 to a black man who was a Hilton executive, then was divorced two years later. When she got to the states she used to date Warren Beatty, then married Spencer Haywood, had a child with him and after two years f marriage they split, then she marries Bowie and becomes stepmother to Bowie's son, Duncan Jones.

She's a Jemima, but less so that the others. She fought against blood diamonds that were being mined in Africa, for instance. She's a Muslim which to me, is just the flip side of the coin, with Christianity being the "religious scam" on the other side. She was married to Bowie for 24 years and in my view, the fact that she is always surrounded by white folks is what influences much of her thinking.

But another dimension of Iman's selling out has to be mentioned: her African background. These sistahs, no matter where they hail from, can be seduced by the glitz and glamour of all that the white man and his racist nation, America, have to offer. Most black people seem to fit this mold – the lure of the filthy lucre. Iman has no real talent but, like Beverly Johnson and Naomi Campbell, gets by on her natural beauty. But a Jemima is a Jemima is a Jemima.

EZOLA FOSTER

Ezola Foster is the only one of the Jemimas in this book who actually had a shot at a high-ranking political office. But the man she ran alongside was as racist and backwards as President Donald Trump. You've heard of him – Patrick Buchanan. A veritable redneck, he chose her as his vice-presidential running mate, but let us not get ahead of ourselves. Her comments and views are what makes this Jemima one of the higher-ranking sellouts on my list.

Now it gets really interesting. This white man who talks all that shit about minorities being the problem decides that he's going to choose a black running mate! Check it out:

> As his running mate, Buchanan chose African-American activist and retired teacher from Los Angeles, Ezola B. Foster. Buchanan was supported in this election run by future Socialist Party USA presidential candidate Brian Moore, who said in 2008 he supported Buchanan in 2000 because "he was for fair trade over free trade. He had some progressive positions that I thought would be helpful to the common man" ... On August 19, the New York Right to Life Party, in convention, chose Buchanan as their nominee, with 90 percent of the districts voting for him.

Let me state at this juncture that when white people select black people as running mates, it means that the black person is mentally as white as the white person. Ezola Foster was certainly no exception. As one source documents it,

> Pat Buchanan selected Foster as his running-mate after several other candidates such as Jim Traficant of Ohio and Teamsters Union president James P. Hoffa declined his offer. Foster, who had supported Buchanan's campaigns in 1992 and 1996, quit her own speaking tour to join the race. While Buchanan was hospitalized during part of the campaign, Foster was the ticket's mouthpiece, campaigning through television and radio appearances. This was the first time in history that an African-American had been nominated for Vice-President by a Federal Election Commission-recognized and federally funding political party, and the second time a woman had accomplished this (Democrat Geraldine Ferraro being the first) … (Wikipedia, 2016).

Rarely have such "Jemimas" see the public in such a manner other than Hollywood. When a black woman is "trusted" enough to be a mouthpiece for a conservative white boy, you know she has to be a sellout, a water-carrier, a flunky – a willing thrall.

Check out Foster's "credentials":

> Foster was chosen because of her conservative credentials and speaking ability; she called Lyndon B. Johnson's Great Society social policy "Marxist". Buchanan critics saw her as an affirmative action selection because she had never held a political office and is African American …(Wikipedia, 2016).

Throughout our history as a people there has always been some crazy ass "nigger" who the white man dubs a savior of our people. The more insane or stereotypical the person was, the more whitey propped him or her up. In our recent history the names Ward Connerly, Clarence Thomas, Michael Steele, Alan Keyes, and Dr. Ben Carson come to mind. Ezola Foster is of that ilk. If you think that today's black conservatives are backwards, their predecessor was this black woman, Ezola Foster. Known for saying dumb shit, following are some of the positions she's held. To begin with,

- Left Democrats & GOP because of differences of belief. (Aug 29)
- In the race to win. (Aug 29)
- Encourages attending John Birch chapter meetings. (Aug 29)
- No rift in Reform Party; no change in platform. (Aug 29)
- Worker's Comp claim not based on real mental disorder. (Aug 24)
- Foster was president of California John Birch Society. (Aug 14)
- Calls black leaders "snake-oil peddlers". (Aug 12)
- Foster denies reports of divorce filing. (Aug 12)
- Ran for office as both Democrat and Republican. (Aug 11)
- Strongly defends "family values". (Feb 14)

It should be clear that this is one confused bitch. But it gets worse. Check out her record as it relates to civil rights:

- Homosexuality is biologically & psychologically damaging. (Aug 29)
- Racism is out of govt; now focus on people. (Aug 29)
- Supports display of Confederate flag in southern states. (Aug 12)
- Against racial preferences. (Aug 12)
- Confederate battle flag should be honored. (Aug 11)
- Against gay rights & women in military. (Aug 11)
- Accuses Jesse Jackson campaign of using fascist slogans. (Feb 14)
- Democratic party policies are motivated by racial hatred. (Feb 14)
- Reparations bill for descendants of slaves is socialist. (Feb 14)

- No pro-gay groups & no AIDS educaiton at RNC. (Feb 14)

Just like Trump had the sellout Ben Carson and then hired beautiful black female Amarosa Manigault (for window dressing), the point is that she joined a long list of white men and "negroes" who literally had been throwing herself at him ever since she appeared on "The Apprentice." Others like Herman Cain often come out of the woodwork, as did Paris Denard, Michael Steele and a number of sick reverends and celebrities like NFL Hall of Famer Ray Lewis, rapper LL Cool J and former boxer Mike Tyson.

Like Candace Owens, we have a Jemima who has "flipped" several times. Prior to 1984 she was a Democrat; from 1984 to 2000 she was a Republican, and from 2000-2002 she was a member of the Reform Party. Now the name of her party is the Constitution Party – whatever the hell that is.

She started off like some of the others, as a "conservative political activist and writer. She was president of a group called Black Americans for Family Values, which I equate with the existence of the 2018 version, Blacks For Trump." She literally started from the bottom before dragging her way up the conservative system. As Wikipedia (2018) notes:

> Foster was born and reared in Maurice in Vermilion Parish in southwestern Louisiana and earned a master's degree from Texas Southern University in Houston, Texas. In 1960, she moved to Los Angeles, California, where she was employed as **a public high school teacher for thirty-three years**—teaching typing, business courses, and sometimes English classes. She had sought public office prior to 2000—as a Democrat in the 1970s and as a Republican candidate for California State Assembly in 1986. (Wikipedia, 2018 – emphasis added)

All the time she was a political wannabe, but my concern is how many black minds did she poison by slipping her views into the curriculum when she taught for just over three decades. Like other Jemimas, she flips back and forth until she finds an ideological outlook or rich white man who will "adopt" her.

Moreover,

> In the 1980s, she became an outspoken opponent of pornography, sex education, AIDS education and gay rights and **founded "Black Americans for Family Values."** She has been affiliated **with the John Birch Society,** founded after World War II by the late Robert W. Welch, Jr., to the dismay of Moderate Republicans. She was arrested in 1987 with several other women while disrupting the California state Republican convention to protest its recognition of the Log Cabin Club, an organization of gay Republicans. In 1992, **she was a staunch**

defender of the police officers in the Rodney King beating case and organized a testimonial dinner for Laurence Powell, one of the convicted officers, in 1995. (Wikipedia, 2018 – emphasis added)

So this woman is not only a homophobe but she's out of her damn mind as well. Some of the stuff above I can understand because I understand the nature of the Jemima. But when she backed the officers who beat the shit out of Rodney King, this is evidence that her mindset and thought process is as white as they come.

But it is clear to me why she is involved in all this. She wants to stick out in the crowd. There are whites who, of course, hold the positions that are outlined above. But when a black woman does it, attention can be gained. And that is what she is all about: like most Jemimas they crave the television camera and the media and it is almost as if they can't live without it. That is why some of them begin as writers and bloggers, while others still seek some way to get on television or, as in the case of Whoopi Goldberg, walk about looking like the mate of "Manimal."

She seems to hate black people and other people of color as well – just like her white conservative "masters." Check it out:

In 1994, while teaching at Bell High School in Bell, California, Foster was a public advocate of Proposition 187, a California ballot initiative to **deny government programs of social services, health care, and public education to illegal immigrants**. Her position was extremely unpopular at the school where she taught, **which was 90 percent Hispanic.** In 1996, after she argued on PBS's *MacNeil/Lehrer NewsHour* that illegal immigration was responsible for the low quality of Los Angeles schools, **some of her colleagues at the school condemned her in an open letter.** Two days later, she attended an anti-illegal-immigration rally where several of her supporters **were attacked by members of the Progressive Labor Party, who allegedly wanted to harm Foster herself.** (Wikipedia, 2018 – emphasis added)

These Jemimas send up these kinds of "smoke signals" with their actions and statements that are aimed to document their commitment to the conservative movement. They know the white man will pick up on it and the conservatives are in need of "activist coons" who can show America that they are not the lily-white "no niggers allowed" party that they appear to be. Look at Ezola's visible (and life-threatening) positions.

She opposes social programs and other assistant for immigrants. They are not "illegal" because the white man says so. HE is the illegal immigrant, the great-great-great grandson of a slew of white illegal immigrants who came here and murdered off First Nation people. Now he points the finger at people of color whose ancestors were here before he was. And that is what Ezola is counting on: a white man who sees her for the brave "negress" that he can count on.

Foster was doing all this work in an context that was predominantly Hispanic. She was risking her life to defend the white man against her brown brothers and sisters. Now that's what I call true "Jemima-ism" – white nationalism in blackface.

As for the John Birch Society it is described by the Dictionary of Politics as, "an ultraconservative organization, founded in December 1958 by Robert Welch, Jr., chiefly to combat alleged Communist activities in the U.S." I have also heard that during the riots of the 1960s these were white boys who opposed the black movement because they felt that the turmoil was inspired by "communists." What is she doing hanging out with these dangerous white folks? And why would they accept her unless it was to use her for their own political ambitions?

And,

> Shortly thereafter, she left her job, **which she calls a necessity resulting from her treatment at work.** She went on **speaking tours for the John Birch Society** and took workers' compensation for an **undisclosed mental disorder**—which she describes as "stress" and "anxiety"—until her official retirement as a teacher in 1998. (Wikipedia, 2018)

How can you do the things this woman has done and make the decisions that she has made without feeling or experiencing "stress and anxiety" the entire time? And as for leaving her job, she did that because she didn't want those Hispanics to start kicking her off in the ass! And finally, how can a black woman go around on speaking tours for the John Birch Society and do it with a straight face? Maybe the pressure behind all these anti-black contradictions is why she developed an "undisclosed mental disorder" – *paranoid schizophrenia!*

As is in the cases of most of the other Jemimas, the white media ate it up. They know that controversy is what people want to see and hear, so they bring this clown on their shows to say that no sane person, let alone a black woman, would ever say:

> Foster has appeared on *Larry King Live, CBS This Morning, CNN & CO., Nightline, NewsTalk Television, CNN Live*, MSNBC, *Politically Incorrect*, and various CBS, NBC, and ABC newscasts. (Wikipedia, 2018)

And so with national appearances that clearly exposed her conservative views (and consequent anti-blackness) this black woman was finally spotted, and history was about to be made:

> Pat Buchanan selected Foster as his running-mate after several other
> candidates such as Jim Traficant of Ohio and Teamsters
> Union president James P. Hoffadeclined his offer. Foster, who had
> supported Buchanan's campaigns in 1992 and 1996, quit her own
> speaking tour to join the race. While Buchanan was hospitalized during
> part of the campaign, Foster was the ticket's mouthpiece, campaigning
> through television and radio appearances. **This was the first time in
> history that an African-American had been nominated for Vice-
> President by a Federal Election Commission-recognized and
> federally funding political party,** and the second time a woman had
> accomplished this (Democrat Geraldine Ferraro being the first).
> (Wikipedia, 2018 – emphasis added)

All these black "firsts" and our people wear them like a badge of pride, as if they're saying "we'ze finally made it." You haven't made shit; how long did it take you before you became "the first," how many of our people died or were locked up in order to get that "first" to become a reality, and finally and most importantly, what good is it to be "the first" of anything in a system that only rewards cowardice, backwardness, acquiescence and "Aunt Jemima-ism"?

So Ezola got what she wanted: a chance to actually be a serious part of the electoral process. Her name is in the history books next to a man who was one of the staunchest anti-black conservatives to ever run for public office. But to the Jemima, even bad publicity is good because it's STILL publicity.

Why was she selected? One source claims,

> Foster was chosen **because of her conservative credentials and
> speaking ability;** she called Lyndon B. Johnson's Great Society social
> policy "Marxist". Buchanan critics saw her as **an affirmative
> action selection** because she had never held a political office and is
> African-American (Wikipedia, 2018 – emphasis added)

And there you have it. Of course she and Buchanan got their asses kicked and she continued to make one of herself when she appeared on several talk shows promoting the values of what was called the Constitution Party. But even Buchanan's co-hosts on the PBS program, "The McLaughlin Group", snickered at him and realized that he was just using this black woman to push his right-wing politics.

Ezola Foster is the prototype Jemima. Her last book, titled *What's Best for All Americans*, was co-written with another conservative and had a forward written by another conservative coon, Walter Williams. And so it goes.

SHERYL UNDERWOOD

To begin with, she's overweight and has more black gums than a pack of Black Jack. I normally prefer darker skinned sistahs and my newsletter voted Viola Davis "the most beautiful woman on television. But this ebony freak is a whole different story. It seems that Underwood considers herself a comedian and an actress but it known more for her role on the CBS daytime talk show, "The Talk," which has won several Emmies and which is led by Julie Chen, the Asian American wife of CBS President Les Moonves, who was just busted for sexual harassment. But the joke is on her: she's a Jemima through and through and increasingly larger numbers of people are beginning to see it.

Underwood is a walking stereotype. She has every drawl, cliché and southern twang down to an art form. She is fat, dark-skinned and the type of black woman that white people simply drool over. Why? Because she hails back to the days of Butterfly McQueen and Hattie McDaniel; she is a modern-day Beaulah (remember that 1950s show about the overweight black maid?).

> **Sheryl Patrice Underwood** (born October 28, 1963) … is an American comedian, actress and television host. She first rose to prominence in the comedy world as the first female finalist in 1989's Miller Lite Comedy Search. She is well known for hosting *BET Comic View* and is currently one of the five hosts on the daytime chat show *The Talk* on CBS, a role she first stepped into in the autumn of 2011. (Wikipedia, 2018)

Jokes. And that's what she's good at. She makes a few CBS cameo appearances every now and then, but other than that her roles are those of a "coon." That is what she does best. With her pearly white teeth, bright pink gums and her beautiful dark skin, she is the prototype of the "darkey" image from days gone past. If she would drop about 60 pounds she would be a beauty. But for now she's just Sheryl - a Jemima and on the following pages, you will find out why.

> Underwood revealed that she was born with a twin that didn't survive. She went on to say that she had been lied to by her mother, who said that her father murdered her sister. Underwood admitted to carrying her sister's birth certificate around with her. She even stated that her mother stabbed her father, who survived, after Underwood had gotten close to her father, which her mother wanted to prevent after she lied to Underwood about her father being a murderer. (Wikipedia, 2018)

Here we have the vintage "coon story." Note that most of these Jemimas have a hard luck story, one that they use to appeal to the white man or any other prospective benefactor. Her mother supposedly lied on her father, her father supposedly killed her sister but he really didn't but then again that's alright because her mother stabbed her father after Sheryl and "Pops" got close. So this is the tragic story that endears her to those who might want to see her as more than just a joke teller. And it's a good way to curry favor with those who have the power to "give a sistah a break."

Continuing:

> After graduating college, she served in the military . .. She later gained public notice as the first female finalist in the Miller Lite Comedy Search in 1989 … She won the BET "Funniest Female Comedian on Comic View" award in 1994 and the BET Comedy Awards' Platinum Mic Viewers Choice Award in 2005 … Following her stand up success, Underwood took a number of minor acting roles including Bad Mouth Bessie in the 1998 film *I Got the Hook Up,* and Catfish Rita in the 2005 film *Beauty Shop.*Underwood was the host of BET's *Comic View* and executive producer and host of the limited run comedy/variety series *Holla* (September 2002 – January 2003). (Wikipedia, 2018)

Remember earlier when I said she played "coon" roles? I wasn't lyin.' Just read the previous excerpt once again. Other than winning comedy competitions which the writers refer to as "stand up success," she got roles that clearly define her as a person: as "Bad Mouth Bessie," and how about "Catfish Rita." These are the names that will appear in the credits at the end of the movie and this is what children will see. This is what she will boast about on her resume. This is what white people do to their "coons": they first enlist their services to test their loyalty (e.g., Omarosa, Diamond and Star) and then they "tag" them with stereotypical and public roles that will forever reserve them to perpetual servitude.

With a face that I say is "made for radio," she then moved to that medium for a few years, or so it would appear:

> Underwood was a contributor on the nationally syndicated *Tom Joyner Morning Show* until June 2010 when she jumped ship to *The Steve Harvey Morning Show*to be their contributor … She briefly hosted her own radio program, *Sheryl Underwood and Company* for Radio One-owned Syndication One News/Talk and XM Satellite Radio's Channel 169 (The Power) … On Tuesday nights, Underwood hosts *The Sheryl Underwood Show* on Jamie Foxx's Sirius Satellite Radiochannel, The Foxxhole (Sirius 106) …

Jamie Foxx – another "coon" who will do whatever the white man asks him to do, from wearing a dress to making fun of black women by poking out his lips and wearing a huge pillow on his butt to perpetuate the myth to chasing after any white woman that gives him th e time of day, Foxx is much like the Wayans

Brothers - a negro sellout who will do whatever it takes for visibility. But that's for another book.

Back to the pink-gummed Underwood where we are informed that, "In 2011, , she joined the daytime show *The Talk* in its second season replacing Leah Remini … I would call myself a sexually progressive, God-fearing, black Republican."(Wikipedia, 2018) How can you be "sexually NON-progressive"? Is that another way of saying that she's a slut? Because all she seems to want to talk about on that show is her so-called sex life. And if a white man comes on the show that she thinks is attractive, she is all over him including kisses on the lips.

Why is she so silly? She's been well trained in Anglo American values 101. Check it out:

> She holds a Bachelor of Arts degree in Liberal Arts from the University of Illinois at Chicago and master's degrees in Media Management and Mass Communication from Governors State University … Underwood once served in the U.S. Armed Forces, and frequently makes jokes about "all the creative places you can get busy on a military base." Underwood is a lifelong Republican … (Wikipedia, 2018)

Do you see what I mean when I say that she wants to flip everything into some kind of "sexcapade"? If she was having sex in the military, and she looked the way she does not, she was nothing more than a sperm spittoon for some racist white boy(s). But she's well educated and seems to have a Chicago orientation with that education. She seems to want to be "black" in many respects. For instance,

> However she campaigned for Barack Obama's re-election in United States presidential election, 2012 … Underwood also campaigned for Hillary Clinton in the 2016 election "because we have to protect the legacy of President Obama. Low voter turnout benefits Donald Trump and the Republicans. He can't win … (Wikipedia, 2018)

What the previous passage proves is that Underwood, an advanced college student and military person, is fully aware of what she does and what she does is based on what she strongly believes in. She can be self-deceiving at some points (I believe she thinks she's far more physically attractive than she actually is), but it is clear she is intelligent. That means that when she makes an ass out of herself the way she does each day on "The Talk," then it is part of a design, which further means that her actions and statements are intentional.

Part of the reason for her uncle tomfoolery could be her involvement in the Greek fraternity system – a sorority. I have written extensively on how these black people divide the race with their beliefs that they are somehow "elite" and better and above other blacks. My book, *From Fear to Fraternity*, documents how the fraternity system itself clings to Greek symbolism and slogans and in doing so places "blackness" in a secondary category, having only been formed after it was clear that the white students on college campuses had a clear "no niggers allowed" policy when it came to their fraternities and sororities.

Specifically,

> **Underwood is a lifetime member of Zeta Phi Beta sorority, first joining in 1990 ...** She served as **president of the organization's Omicron Rho Zeta chapter**, as the **National Chair of Honorary Members, National Executive Board Chair and International Grand Basileus ...** She also **chartered a graduate chapter of Zeta Phi Beta in Inglewood, California ...** Underwood was **elected as the 23rd International Grand Basileus (President) during Zeta Phi Beta's biennial business meeting in Las Vegas, Nevada in 2008**. Her election as Grand Basileus was disputed, but District of Columbia Superior Court Judge Gerald I. Fisher dismissed a lawsuit against the sorority and Underwood that asked the court to unseat her ... **Her election made her the first professional entertainer to hold the highest elected office of a National Pan-Hellenic Council organization** (Wikipedia, 2018 – emphasis added)

There you have it: Underwood is not only a member of a sorority, she is engulfed in fratdom! This "we're black Greeks" bullshit is a key component of her thought process. And this, dear reader, speaks volumes. The groups she belongs to of a social or political nature are of a conservative bent:

> In addition to the Zeta Phi Beta sorority, Underwood is also a **member of the National Council of Negro Women and the NAACP ...** She also founded the **African-American Female Comedian Association ...** In the fall of 2011, Underwood revealed that after dating seven years, her husband—who might have suffered from clinical depression—**committed suicide after they had been married three years**. (Wikipedia, 2018 – emphasis added)

The statements says "might have suffered from clinical depression." That is no sane medical diagnosis. He might have had crabs too, but that doesn't mean that it killed him! He was married to her after dating her seven years – that's enough to drive anybody batty! She was so locked into her Greekness, her military background, telling her "I got fucked here" and "I got fucked over there" stories as part of her standup comedy routine and on television, the brutha probably just got fed up.

Sheryl Underwood is probably the most relevant of the Jemimas because it is clear that she knows better. But as long as she's surrounded by those crazy white bitches and that assimilated Chinese co-host on "The Talk," she will say and do whatever it takes to get a laugh at black people's expense. And this forever solidifies her place in "Jemima-dom."

STACEY DASH

Jemimas Assemble! Old and young alike. It's not the age it's the point of view. And here is a classic example of a younger sellout.

In my view Stacey Dash is the most physically attractive woman on this list. Not because she has green eyes or dyed red hair, but because of the symmetry of her face, her hour-glass figure and the way she carries herself. That's from the physical aside. But as the saying teaches us, "all that glitters ain't gold," and Stacey Dash proves this in spades. She is clearly psychologically damaged and her positions on certain social and political issues proves the point.

Let me demonstrate. Like many of the Jemimas featured herein, she began as a Democrat and then flipped to being a Republican. Like many of the Jemimas featured herein, she draws from an alleged traumatic experience and makes sure that it is a part of her public resume. Can you say "pity party"?

> **Dash has spoken openly about past traumas in her personal life.** She has at various times revealed that **she was molested as a child by a family friend,** was **addicted to cocaine in her teens and 20s**, and has a history of **being with physically and emotionally abusive partners** … Dash has attributed her openness with such topics to her desire to be honest with her children, feeling that being honest is the best way to protect them, **and to let them and others know that she is not a victim but a survivor** … She is supportive of the right to keep and bear arms, crediting a gun with saving her life **after being sexually assaulted at gunpoint by an ex-boyfriend, because she was able to retrieve her own weapon, a .22 revolver, and shoot at him, scaring him away**. (Wikipedia, 2018 – emphasis added)

So being a true Jemima, we begin with her views about Black History Month. In January of 2016 she began her attacks through an article by Kendall Fisher which appeared on Entertainment On Line under the headline, "Stacey Dash Doesn't Think Black History Month Should Exist, Wants to take BET Off the Air." Following are her comments and my analysis of them:

> Stacey Dash has her own opinions amid the controversy stemming from the all-white Oscar nominations this year.The Clueless actress sat down with Fox News' Fox & Friends and not only called the outrage over the Oscars "ludicrous," **but she also said African-American-targeted institutions—such as BET, the Image Awards and holidays honoring black history—should no longer exist, calling them an unprogressive "double standard."** (Fisher, 2016 – emphasis added)

What would this bitch know about that which is "progressive" when every woman in Hollywood is at the mercy of "auditions" that are conducted by lecherous white men? When their very profession is based on pretending to be someone else? If she has an opinion on anything "black" it is as an outsider, and what you just read is the opinion of someone who may have dark skin but who is definitely outside of the race. When she describes herself she does so by placing her ethnicity and nationality BEFORE her racial background. That means that she is ashamed to be considered black. And that shame is evidenced by the comments you just read.

For her to believe that Black Entertainment Television (BET), the Image Awards and holidays are "African-American targeted" is a mistake. These black institutions and symbols are aimed at white advertisers, convincing them that by taking out ads aimed at the black community, you should do so by promoting them on programs that CLAIM to be black. But the fact is that these are not aimed at African-Americans; they are aimed at white people who, in one way or another, have bitten and bought into the black cultural market. Everything that's black ain't black.

And look what she does: she runs to the enemy of the race and degrades what she considers to be black institutions. Who would do that but a traitor, a "Jemima"? And it apparently gets worse:

> She explained, "**We have to make up our minds. Either we want to have segregation or integration.** And if we don't want segregation, then **we need to get rid of channels like BET and the BET Awards and the Image Awards where you're only awarded if you're Black**. If it were the other way around, we would be up in arms. It's a double standard."Later, she added, **"Just like there shouldn't be a Black History Month. You know? We're Americans. Period. That's it."** (Fisher, 2016 – emphasis added)

As I wrote earlier, this bitch doesn't know the difference between segregation and separation. Segregation is what led to the need for things like BET and Black History Month, although both definitely fall short. Segregation is what led to the need for black businesses and black institutional arrangements. White people imposed the ghetto upon black people and we responded by doing for self. Separation was something that was an ideal by groups like the Nation of Islam and the Republic of New Afrika. But black people were so tommish – much like Stacey Dash – that we didn't want to "separate from that good ol' white man." So we settled for a segregated reality because it was the law of the land.

Now, having begged for inclusion and integration, the black community has to look up and deal with this green-eyed, high yellow bitch complaining about what few institutions there are that have the courage to put "black" in their name. While no threat to the white system, they are at least making an attempt at representing a symbol of pride. What does Stacey Dash do in that regard? She joins in with a movie that carries an indicator of what she is: "clueless.' She teams up with a white girl in a flick where she is basically the white girl's tagalong lackey. And then she joins the Fox Network, which hates both women and blacks, and then has the nerve to critique Black History Month?

Even white people have a problem with what she was saying. Check it out:

> The show's host, Steve Doocy, clarified: "Are you saying there shouldn't be a Black History Month because there isn't a white history month?" To which Dash replied, **"Exactly. Exactly."**After the Internet erupted over her commentary, she took to her blog and stuck to her word, promising she is "right" and again reiterating, "There should be no Black History Month." (Fisher, 2016 – emphasis added)

There is a white history month. And a white history year and a white history century. This country re-writes history every day of the year to make it appear as if it is greater than it really is. Just recently even Governor Andrew Cuomo of New York made the statement that "America is not so great." He said what black people already knew (as is usually the case with these white talking heads). Specifically what he meant was described as follows by the *New York Times*:

> Gov. Andrew M. Cuomo mocked President Trump's ubiquitous "Make America Great Again" campaign slogan on Wednesday, quickly drawing the ire of Republicans from New York to the White House for saying that America "was never that great." "We are not going to make America great again. It was never that great," Mr. Cuomo said. "We have not reached greatness. We will reach greatness when every American is fully engaged." Mr. Cuomo made the comment at the end of a 20-minute speech that focused heavily on Mr. Trump. The event was ostensibly a bill-signing ceremony for new penalties for sex trafficking in New York. (Goldmacher, 2018)

So who is closer to being right: some beauty who makes her living acting out lies on screen or the governor of the largest state in the union? Both are liars for the most part, but I'm going to lean with Cuomo's analysis of the situation, especially where it relates to race.

And she's just as anti-female as she is anti-black:

> Of course, her controversial remarks shouldn't come as much of a surprise … A few months later, in April, Dash also told Meredith Vieira **she doesn't believe that a pay gap exists between the sexes.**"I feel like it's an excuse," Dash explained to the audience. "It's the same thing with race, it's an excuse. Stop making excuses." **She continued, "If there are opportunities, seize them and be prepared for them and be the best if that's what it takes. If you have to be extraordinary, then be extraordinary…**If you want to be pissed off about it, then be pissed off about it and **work harder for it**. I don't think us complaining about it because there is a law passed that we get equal pay." (Fisher, 2016 – emphasis added)

How sick can one bitch be? What's she's saying is if the audition (in her profession) calls for you to suck dick, then do it! Cave in to the perverted whims of those Jewish directors, producers and script writers. And in that way you land the part and nobody feels "used." That's the unspoken message and, unfortunately, there are a number of "actresses" who cater to such a sick Sargeant Schultz "I see nuthink!" philosophy.

A similar article appeared on MSN.com with the heading, "Stacey Dash Becomes Her Own Joke at 2016 Oscars" as Chris Rock sarcastically introduced her as "the director of our new minority outreach program." She came out and fed into the sarcastic moment saying, "I cannot wait to help my people out. Happy Black History Month!" The sarcasm was deeper than most people realize: for Dash to refer to blacks as "her people" was an inaccurate statement based on what this Jemima has said about black people in recent years.

A month later, during a February 28, 2016 airing of Entertainment Tonight On Line, Dash began her litany of lunacy for the world to see. Following is the news report with my analyses filtering in and out.

The article, titled, "Stacey Dash Speaks Out on Oscars' Lack of Diversity: 'It's Ludicrous,'" focuses on comments made regarding the 2016 Academy Awards, began as follows:

> Stacey Dash has a lot to say about the lack of diversity among this year's nominees. On Wednesday, the *Clueless* actress and Fox News contributor expressed her outrage over the fact that, once again, only white performers made the cut while chatting with Steve Doocy on *Fox & Friends*."I think it's ludicrous," she said. **"Because we have to make up our minds. Either we want segregation or integration."** (ETonline, 2016 – emphasis added)

Ignorant black people are continually put in front of the microphone to spew forth specious and spurious opinions which are then pawned off as fact. In this case, Stacey Dash shows she doesn't understand racial issues even though she is a black woman in a white-dominated society and white-oriented Hollywood culture.

More specifically, you can see where she puts the black condition in the hands of her white master. When she says "Either we want segregation or integration," what she should be saying is that "either we want SEPARATION or integration." Segregation is decided by white folks and imposed on blacks, as is integration. Separation is what WE decide to do. Most Jemimas, like the title of one of Dash's movies, are "clueless" when it comes to political vision and therefore they should keep their mouths shut.

RAVEN-SYMONE

The March 18, 2015 publication Business and Politics reported a story under the headline, "Actress sparks firestorm defending Michelle Obama-Planet of the Apes reference on 'The View': 'Some people look like animals'. The article, written by Carmine Sabia, documented the following:

> Actress Raven-Symoné infuriated many African-Americans by defending the Univision host Rodner Figueroa over comments he made **comparing a makeup artists impersonation of Michelle Obama to a cast member from "Planet of The Apes" — comments that got him fired from his job.** Symoné appeared as a guest co-host on ABC's "The View" Monday when she made the controversial remarks. "He said that he voted for her later," the actress who played Olivia on "The Cosby Show" said. "I don't think he was saying it racist." (Sabia, 2015 – emphasis added)

When you read something like this, the only sane response is, "You stupid bitch!" I mean, comparing the beautiful Michelle Obama to an ape is like comparing an apple to a car engine! And if the peckerwood who said it believes that, then what could he possibly think of other black people? And what else could the comment be other than racist?

But it gets worse. Check out the following:

> That's like saying I'm not a racist but I have black friends," liberal co-host Rosie Perez fired back. "Michelle, don't fire me from this right now," Symoné said, joking about the first lady's possible role in Figueroa's firing. **"Some people look like animals**. Is that rude? I look

like a bird! **So can I be mad if somebody calls me Toucan Sam?"**
(Sabia, 2015 – emphasis added).

This little yellow bitch has always been precocious, since the days when the Cosby show exploited her. What happened was that she "auditioned" and her parents probably played up how "cute" she was. Cosby saw the skin color and the attitude and marched that little girl out there and gave her lines that made her sound like a miniature adult. Now she's grown and the bitch is walking around with multi-colored hair and is as confused as ever. She is a true sellout.

Before her stint on "The View" (she is no longer there), she had this show called "That's So Raven." The show should have been called "Check out them titties" because this bitch was built like a brick shit house. And she played it to the hilt! That show exploited the shapes of both Raven and her white co-host, Chelsea Daniels (played by Anneliese van der Pol) amidst all the hijinks and foolishness that permeated every show. It stayed on for four years, but don't ask me how.

OMAROSA MANIGAULT-EDWARDS

As is the case with the traditional paranoid schizophrenic, there are "two sides" to Omarosa: the side that entered into the world of conservative politics and Donald Trump (both pre-and post-Apprentice) and the one that launched a conniption and turned on him after being canned. As the line from the 1697 William Congreve poem taught, "Heaven hath no rage like love to hatred turned/Nor hell a fury like a woman scorned."

Entrance Into Trump World

She was prepared all along for her Jemima role, beginning with a stint on NBCs "The Apprentice" where a group of us watched and observed this woman's sluttish behavior, especially when it came to flirting with Donald Trump.

Before he even took office she was quite literally kissing his ass. In September of 2016 she was quoted as saying that Trump's critics would be "bowing down" to him. According to Zimmerman (2016),

> Former "Apprentice" contestant and top Donald Trump cheerleader
> Omarosa Manigault is warning his critics they will soon be bowing down
> before him.**"Every critic, every detractor, will have to bow down
> to President Trump,"** she said. "It's everyone who's ever doubted
> **Donald**, who ever disagreed, who ever challenged him. **It is the**

> **ultimate revenge to become the most powerful man in the universe."**
> (Zimmerman, 2016 – emphasis added)

Referring to him by his first name only? Kissing his ass to this incredibly grandiose extent? Am I alone or does it sound like she was screwing this old white man? She sure came off that way during several episodes of the apprentice. Like the slavemaster of old he despised black people (witness his calling black football players "sons of bitchs" and calling Omarosa a "dog" after she turned on him), but though blacks are deemed an "inferior race," we were always good enough to rape, ravage and use as sex toys. That is the attitude of Trump's father and he passed his racism down to his colorless son.

> Manigault, Trump's **director of African-American outreach**, made the
> prediction in an interview for a PBS "Frontline" special on the 2011
> White House Correspondents' Dinner.It has been reported that President
> **Obama's mocking of Trump over his "birther" stance during the
> dinner prompted the real estate magnate to run**. (Zimmerman, 2016l-
> emphasis added)

How petty of this white man. Obama cracked on him and embarrassed him but this peckerwood knew he wouldn't be facing Obama in any election. So he ran against lesser quality opponents and then got his booty-buddy in Russia, Vladimir Putin, to lend a hand in sabotaging the election.

> Recalling the dinner and watching Trump get "hammered" by Obama,
> Manigault told PBS she thought, "Oh, Barack Obama is starting
> something that I don't know if he'll be able to finish." "Inside the Night
> President Obama Took On Donald Trump," part of "Frontline's"
> ongoing political series "The Choice," will air Tuesday at 9 p.m. EDT on
> PBS. (Zimmerman, 2016)

A true Jemima.Even going so far as to take the side of an inferior white man over a black man who had always achieved and who was married to a lovely black woman the same color and hue as Omarosa! But she knew that Trump was vulnerable to flattery and she won him over with words and who knows what other "actions" were taken behind closed doors?

Fast forward less than a year later.

By the time Trump won the office of the Presidency Omarosa was right there, singing his praises. To back up this statement I quote from a March 21, 2017 article that appeared on the Atlanta Buzz website right after Omarosa entertained all of the presidents of the Historically Black Colleges and Universities (HBCU). The article was headlined, "Omarosa Praises Trump's Actions on HBCUs, Other

Topics." Following is that article, my analyses and then we move on to the exit (read: expulsion) just over a year later.

Continuing:

> Reality show personality turned Donald Trump **operative** Omarosa Manigault praised the president's actions on historically black colleges and universities and other issues, saying, "Every single promise he made we've outlined and we are checking off one by one." In February, Trump met with HBCU leaders from around the country, including Atlanta, **and signed an executive order aimed at signaling his commitment to the institutions, saying that those schools will be "an absolute priority for this White House."** (Brett, 2017 – emphasis order)

An executive order signed by a man who would go on to tell more than 3,000 lies during the first year in office is an order may hav well be written on a piece of toilet paper with a pen made of dog shit. How can you hate the root of a tree (the black race) and not hate the tree itself? Omarosa mistook "tolerance" for "concern" and that is all tolerance is supposed to do – enable you to exhibit the power to "put up with" those you deem inferior. Omarosa thought she was seductive enough to call the shots. But don't forget that the Jemima, like the Uncle Tom, was made and manufactured in America.

On that day full of black presidents of black colleges and Kelly Conway sitting on a couch with her legs gapped, Omarosa should have felt right home. According to one account,

> Afterward, Morehouse College President John Silvanus Wilson Jr. offered a muted assessment and mentioned U.S. Education Secretary Betsy DeVos' clumsy praise of historically black institutions, calling them **"pioneers when it comes to school choice."** "HBCUs were not created because the 4 million newly freed blacks were unhappy with the choices they had," Wilson wrote in an open letter to the college community following the White House meeting. **"They were created because they had no choices at all. That is not just a very important distinction, it is profoundly important."** (Brett, 2017 – emphasis added)

Sellout black men who live off the checks provided by the United Negro College Fund and who, on more than a dozen occasions, have pilfered the money, gotten caught and then transferred to other black schools to begin their chicanery all over again. More than a few black colleges were closed down because of this type of "minister-like greed."

> Speaking with "Extra's" **AJ Calloway**, Omarosa (usually known by
> solely her first name) **had nothing but high marks for her former
> mentor on "The Apprentice" and "The Celebrity Apprentice**. ""You
> look at what we have accomplished to date, **everyone knows that we
> are going to do exactly what we said we were going to do," she
> said**. "We started to bring jobs to areas and identifying companies that
> would keep their business here in the United States. **The first 30 days,
> already we have done so much and we have so much to go."** (Brett,
> 2017 – emphasis added)

"We," she says as she lies and embellishes. But it is ironic because her phraseology brings to mind a lesson taught by MalcolmX, the one about the house negro who identified with his master more than the master identified with himself. Here are those words from Malcolm X's 1964 "Message to the Grass Roots" speech:

> If the master's house caught on fire, the house Negro would fight
> harder to put the blaze out than the master would. **If the master
> got sick, the house Negro would say, "What's the matter, boss,
> we sick?" We sick! He identified himself with his master more
> than his master identified with himself.** And if you came to the
> house Negro and said, "Let's run away, let's escape, let's separate,"
> the house Negro would look at you and say, "Man, you crazy.
> What you mean, separate? Where is there a better house than this?
> Where can I wear better clothes than this? Where can I eat better
> food than this?" **That was that house Negro. In those days he
> was called a "house nigger."** And that's what we call him today,
> because **we've still got some house niggers running around
> here**. (emphasis added)

This can be seen in present-day terms, not only in the guise of "black Republicans" who carry water for the system, but even for the so-called leadership that continues to talk about black people and "our" system and talking about what we should do "as Americans." Is there any wonder why those people from other parts of the world who have it in for this country and its racist history now include US as a part of the problem? With the white-run media promoting images of us has happy and satisfied, the people of the world who suffer have begun to hate us as much as they hate the white man. They now lump all "Americans" into the same mold and it's because of that "house nigger" mentality that the black people who get on television continue to display. As far as the world is concerned, "the friend of my enemy is my enemy."

Malcolm's description continues:

> **This modern house Negro loves his master**. He wants to live
> near him. He'll pay three times as much as the house is worth just
> to live near his master, and then brag about "I'm the only Negro out
> here." **"I'm the only one on my job." "I'm the only one in this**
> **school." You're nothing but a house Negro** …(emphasis added)

And Omarosa was "the only one" in the White House inner circle. And she loved it and she coveted it. She was "one of them." And then she went too far and brought her wedding entourage to the White House to "show off." Suddenly the "we" that she felt was shown to be "them," and those white folks moved with the quickness.

Exit From Trump World

During the December 13, 2017 telecast of "CNN Newsroom with Brooke Baldwin," the news came heavy and hard about the "drama" around Omarosa's "resignation" from the White House. It didn't sound like a resignation to me.

This is the same bitch I saw on "The Apprentice" and when I saw her for the first time I said to myself, "she's sucking Trump's dick." Later on, after Trump had won the presidency she was on television and said something to the effect, "Every critic, every detractor, will have to bow down to President Trump. Everyone who ever doubted Donald, whoever disagreed, whoever challenged him. It is the ultimate revenge to become the most powerful man in the universe."

There is no doubt that this woman has "game." She can seduce any man by appealing to his ego, which is probably how she trapped Michael Clark Duncan, that huge Uncle Tom who appeared in such degrading movies as "The Green Mile" and then played the Kingpin in the Ben Affleck flop, "Daredevil." After he croaked she has apparently latched on to some other hapless coon, John Allen Newman who is, get this: a pastor from west Florida. One pimp marries another.

She had her wedding at the Trump Hotel and then had the nerve to bring her wedding entourage to the White House for photos. More on that debacle later.

General John Kelly was brought into the White House to screen Trump's visitors. Even cabinet members had to go through Kelly and when I heard that I immediately knew that Omarosa's days were numbered. And sure enough, Kelly – on the record for not liking black women – made it clear that she was persona non grata and asked what she actually did to earn her $180,000 a year salary. More on this second situation in a minute.

According to April Ryan of Urban American Radio Network, General Kelly said he had "a tense exchange with her twice." When a white man says that it means that she was cussing his white ass out and he became afraid because as quiet as it's kept, white men are far more afraid of black women than they are of black men. They consider black men as sissies because of the degrading things they have been able to get black men to do. They have no respect for them. But that black woman, that sassy fireball – that's what the spineless white boy, regardless of rank or status, is truly afraid of. So he fired her.

According to Ryan, " It was a dual firing resignation." Ryan said that General Kelly grew tired of Omarosa's antics. Since the days of former sissy Rance Priebus, nobody really knew what Omarosa's duties were. She told Priebus at one point that she didn't have to listen to him. In other words there was something going on between her and Trump that gave Omarosa the impression that her shit didn't stink, that she was above the rules and protocols. And recall my initial impression of her: she and Trump had a salacious background while she was on "The Apprentice".

April Ryan, in her report, said that her White House sources told her that Omarosa "stirred things up." She said that Omarosa was a "mood changer." If Trump was doing something, Omarosa would march into his office, show him a newspaper clipping or say something that would set him off. On the streets we call this an "instigator." In black politics we refer to her as a "provocateur." Omarosa's "walk right in" access to Trump and the Oval Office was changed when General Kelly was brought in.

In addition, it was reported that Omarosa "did not have warm feelings with others, and she would cause problems within the White House. She would come and go whenever she wanted to. Now back to the wedding.

Not only did this bodacious bitch get married in the Trump Hotel (I doubt if she got a discount), but then had the gall to bring the bridal part into the White House to take pictures. She didn't ask permission and violated every protocol and one source said she "trivialized the White House" in doing so. Hell yeah: a bunch of black folks walking around taking pictures like they were at Disneyland, all on the invite of a woman who didn't have a lick of juice.

During the back-and-forth after her resignation she was telling reporters and anyone dumb enough to show interest in her story that she "helped elect Donald Trump" and that she "brought the black vote." That bitch didn't deliver a single vote except for her relatives and that dumb hallelujah huckster who was dumb enough to marry that slag. Black people didn't even like her. In fact, after the Charlottesville incident where Nazis and the Klan waged war on regular citizens, Trump defended the Nazis and Omarosa defended Trump!

Then there was the escapade at the National Association of Black Journalists meeting where she got into it with Ed Gordon, the moderator. She was heckled throughout by black people who knew she wasn't about shit. She embarrassed herself and even in front of all those black people she continued to kiss Trump's ass. Trump didn't show up, but he had a more than willing thrall ready to mock his every word.

And if America saw her as a villain when she was on the apprentice, why assume that black people couldn't see through her as well? We have a bunch of lyin' ass bitches in the 'hood who do the same shit that Omarosa was and continues to try to do.

On MSNBC's "Deadline: White House," Symone Sanders said that "high drama individuals are tolerated, but not her." Of course not. She's black. Despite her belief that she is some kind of "exception," nothing could be further from the truth.

With that having been said, let's dig a little deeper and get another look at one more Trump hire that got into a position and immediately began to think that they were not only above the law, but in Omarosa's case, could do what they wanted to do because she was "Friends" with Trump (read: concubine).

According to reports, after being told she was canned, Omarosa tried to go to Ivanka Trump (Donald's daughter) and ask her if she could keep her job. Ivanka must have told her to fuck off because then Omarosa tried to go straight to Trump, through the President's quarters. Alarms went off and from there she was escorted off the premises and had her security access revoked. The key words here are "escorted off the premises." She claims that she will continue to be paid through January, but if her security clearance is revoked, that means that she's being paid with taxpayers dollars for doing absolutely nothing.

Meanwhile, Sarah Huckabee Sanders, the lying bitch who has the unenviable task of defending Trump's antics, said she didn't know how many African Americans are in White House, but was quick to add that, "We have a truly diverse team, we always want to continue to grow the diversity. She also claimed, "I don't have a number directly in front of me, [but we have] … a diverse team at WH and in press office. We strive to grow to be more diverse …" Such bullshit and it's not even convincing bullshit.

According to MSNBC, the 22 highest paid people at the White House are white and Omarosa is the only black woman on the list.

Now she's going around claiming that she has "a story to tell." She's talking about what she heard and saw at the White House and how much of it disturbed her and her alleged concerns for "my people" and "my community." This bitch doesn't consider herself a member of the black community, in the same way that Vanessa Williams turned her back and was dating white boys. But when that bitch did that Penthouse layout, butt naked, and white folks stripped her of her Miss America title, that cute green-eyed, yellow bitch came running back to black people.

Omarosa is either shopping a book deal, a reality TV show or some kind of movie. She's just as egocentric as Trump, but as a black woman she's going to have to take another road. She's pretty enough to go into movies, but her attitude is going to alienate her from the decision makers. She probably figures that if she gives them head then the least they can do is allow her into the hallowed halls. She still hasn't learned yet that white men are duplicitous – just like she is.

In the movie "Outlander," these Scottish assholes are supposedly immortal and down through the years they may meet and battle one another to the death. Their motto? "There can be but one." This seems to be the philosophy of white folks in general but in this case, the doctrine of Donald Trump when it comes to black people in high places. If there are going to be any at all they have to be easy to control, willing to jump through hoops and willing to turn their backs on their own people. And even those of this misguided ilk are suspect, which is why, "there can be but one."

The exit was as messy as the entrance had been quiet. According to an August 10, 2018 article under the headline, "Omarosa Manigault Newman says she refused hush money, pens White House memoir calling Trump racist," the following was reported:

> Omarosa Manigault Newman was offered a **$15,000-a-month contract from President Trump's campaign to stay silent after being fired from her job as a White House aide** by Chief of Staff John F. Kelly last December, according to a forthcoming book by Manigault Newman and a document viewed by The Washington Post. (Dawsey, 2018 – emphasis added)

So she must have known something that the white men didn't want to get out. But a Jemima, once betrayed, can be a formidable adversary. The story of Omarosa the Jemima continues:

> **But she refused**, according to the incendiary new book, "Unhinged: An Insider Account of the Trump White House," **which also depicts Trump as unqualified, narcissistic and racist.** Excerpts of the book were obtained by The Post. After she was fired, Manigault Newman wrote**, she received a call from Trump campaign adviser Lara Trump, the president's daughter-in-law, offering her a job and the monthly contract in exchange for her silence**. (Dawsey, 2018 – emphasis added)

Omarosa had learned well from her white "handlers." From her days on "The Apprentice" she took over the show by assuming and them mastering the role of the "villainess," the black seductress that everyone loved to hate. And she used that role to get close to Trump and then was able to finagle a position in the White House once he got elected.

Continuing with Omarosa's exit from Trump World:

> A nondisclosure agreement attached to the offer, which was reviewed by The Post, said Manigault Newman **could not make any comments about President Trump, Vice President Pence or their families or any comments that could damage the president.** It said she would do "diversity outreach," among other things, for the campaign. "**The NDA attached to the email was as harsh and restrictive as any I'd seen in all my years of television," Manigault Newman writes in the book.** (Dawsey, 2018 –emphasis added)

Yeah – but she signed it. That's the point. All of a sudden she gets this profound epiphany about Trump, about how crooked and racist the White House staff is and about the "harshness" of a non-disclosure agreement that she only violated when she got treated like a dog (which Trump even called her) and got rejected by the man whose ass she used to kiss. Her credibility was ruined because she was a cheerleader for Trump and his way of life but when she got rejected and thrown out she now sings a different tune. A Jemima is always going to be lacking in credibility but as usual, black people forgive and forgive those who betray us (e.g., Tiger Woods, Vanessa Williams, Rev. Eddie Long, Jesse Jackson, Marion Barry, etc.)

For instance, Omarosa knew that, "Throughout his career as a businessman and politician, **Trump has repeatedly used nondisclosure agreements to quiet critics and accusers,** including adult-film star Stormy Daniels. The Trump campaign did not respond to a request for comment Friday."(Dawsey, 2018 – emphasis added) She knew what she was getting into but, as is the case with many a Jemima, she over-estimated her value and under-estimated the racist system that would enlist and employ those of her misguided ilk.

Now the White House was on the attack:

> In a statement, White House press secretary **Sarah Huckabee Sanders said the book "is riddled with lies and false accusations."** She added, "It's sad that a disgruntled former White House employee is trying to profit off these false attacks, and even worse that the media would now give her a platform, **after not taking her seriously when she had only positive things to say about the President during her time in the administration."** (Dawsey, 2018 – emphasis added)

Several points can be made here.

First of all, if Sarah Huckabee Sanders were black, she would fit the mold for the perfect "Jemima." She is a liar and a lackey for Trump and will do whatever he tells her to do and defend whatever he does. So her credibility is lacking as well

Furthermore, she does have a point: when Omarosa was kissing Trump's ass, the same media that now listens when she (Omarosa) castigates the President is the same one that knew better than to accept those hosannas of praise that she was heaping on him previously. Even white people could see what type of person Omarosa was. Her sluttishness and gold digging preceded her even before her appearance on "The Apprentice." Remember she was married to "actor" Michael Clarke Duncan, a giant of a man and a giant of a tom as well. This nigga would make Stepin Fetchit look like a militant. Some of the bootlicking roles he made major money playing include the role of dunce in the following movies: "Daredevil," "The Green Mile," "The Whole Nine Yards" and he played a gay virgin in the 1999 bomb, "The Underground Comedy."

They were married in 2010 and were still married when he died of a "heart attack." The reason why I have it in quotes is because I have my doubts because this is how it was reported in the Los Angeles Times:

> On July 13, 2012, Duncan was taken to Cedars Sinai Medical Center after suffering a heart attack … **Media reports suggested that his girlfriend, Omarosa Manigault, had tried to save his life by performing CPR …** Duncan's publicist, Joy Fehily, issued a statement on August 6 that read he was moved from the intensive-care unit but remained hospitalized following his heart attack … On September 3, Duncan died in Los Angeles (emphasis added)

Yeah, I'll bet. I wonder who got the money from Duncan's estate? The wife, of course. At any rate she is known as the only person ever fired twice on "The Apprentice" and became known all over America as "the woman America loves to hate." She played on it and this brought attention to the show, which meant ratings which meant Trump was pleased.

The exit however, was much quicker than her entrance into Trump World:

> Manigault Newman **does not offer evidence for some of her most explosive charges** but extensively recorded her conversations in the White House. The Post has listened to several of the recordings made by Manigault Newman, which match quotations recounted in the book excerpts. The existence of some recordings was first reported Wednesday by the Daily Beast. (Dawsey, 2018 – emphasis added)

The fact that she was taping the conversations shows that she knew something was wrong with what was taking place and she knew,all along, that she was working for a snake. The fact is that like most Jemimas, she over-estimated her worth. She thought she was "accepted" by the white establishment. For instance,

> White House aides have long described Manigault Newman as a problematic employee who tried to stage a wedding photo shoot at the White House, exploded at other West Wing aides and left shoes strewn around the West Wing. For months, they accurately feared that she was taping conversations inside the building. **In the eyes of many around Trump, the book is another publicity-grabbing stunt from someone known for them.** (Dawsey, 2018 – emphasis added)

How is anyone with any pride going to leave shoes strewn about in a business they work in? Again, she over-estimated her value and she ended up paying for that mistake. How can you stage a wedding photo shoot at the White House without the proper paperwork being done? These are reasons why I believe that this woman sounds like someone who was having sex with Trump, sounding very much like a jealous and overlooked "mistress" than a professional member of the staff.

She was a nut and so was he, an allegation she is just now willing to make public:

> **She questions Trump's mental state, describes him as unstable and portrays him as unable to control his impulses**. She recounts the extensive lengths that staff members have gone to in attempts to keep him in line. "All we need to remember is that Trump loves the hate," she writes in the book. "He thrives on criticism and insults. **He delights in chaos and confusion.** Taking to Twitter to call him names only fuels him and riles his base. **To disarm him, starve his ego; don't feed into it."** (Dawsey, 2018 – emphasis added)

What she just described makes it sound like she knew this all along, that she just kept it inside so she could collect a check. And that is why she kept on kissing his ass, feeding his ego, bringing him newspaper clippings to further feed into his "uncontrolled passions" and to instigate wherever she could.

Moreover,

> According to her account, Kelly comes into the room and begins by saying, **"We're going to talk to you about leaving the White House.""The integrity issues are very serious," Kelly continues. "If this were the military, this would be a pretty high level of accountability, meaning a court-martial. . . .** If we make this a friendly departure, you can look at your time here in the White House as a year of

service to the nation. You can go on without any type of difficulty in the future relative to your reputation." (Dawsey, 2018 – emphasis added)

So she was threatened – she claims. Not only that, but:

> Manigault Newman then **demands an explanation for why she is being fired and whether Trump knows.** Kelly tells her it is nonnegotiable and soon leaves the room after mentioning "serious integrity issues." "The staff works for me, not the president. So after your departure, I'll inform him," Kelly told her, according to the book. "With that, I'll let you go." (Dawsey, 2018)

This Jemima had the unmitigated gall to "demand" an explanation? It was clear that both Trump and Kelly had a special kind of hatred for African American women and that Omarosa must have believed she was the exception. So then, why was she shit-canned? Her version of the story is that,

> She was kept in the Situation Room for more than an hour, according to her telling in the book, with her husband waiting outside. She fights with Passantino, who tells her **she is being fired for abusing the government car service. She tries to explain why she used the car each time — for official government business, in her telling — to no avail.** "It's not a fight that is winnable," says Uttam Dhillon, another lawyer. (Dawsey, 2018 – emphasis added)

Using a government car? After all the hundreds of thousands of dollars that were abused as was reported on March 8, 2018 by National Public Radio. Among some of the abuses are:

> At least seven current and former officials in Trump's 24-member Cabinet have faced accusations of abusing the perks of their office.

> Tom Price, the former head of the Department of Health and Human Services, lost his job after it was revealed that he took charter flights costing nearly half a million dollars.

> Interior Secretary Ryan Zinke used helicopters to avoid Washington's notorious traffic. In one case, he took a helicopter to Yorktown, Va., to visit the battlefield, which is maintained by the National Park Service, and then flew back to go horseback riding with Vice President Mike Pence.

> And the way Treasury Secretary Steven Mnuchin explained it, his request for a military plane for his European honeymoon actually came

from his staff. "They put in a request to consider the use of an aircraft —
not so much just for flying, but effectively it was a portable office," he
told Politico.

All this money and all these perks and the best they could come up with was
that she abused a "car"? According to Omarosa,

> Trump told Manigault Newman that he had no idea she was ousted the
> day before, according to her account. "I just saw on the news you were
> thinking about leaving!" Trump says. "What happened?"Manigault
> Newman responds that Kelly told her, "You guys wanted me to leave."
> Trump expresses his displeasure. (Dawsey, 2018)

There is no way that Kelly would be firing this woman without Trump's say
so. And the entire Trump family is skilled at lying, as we now know:

> Manigault Newman said the call from Trump was followed by a call
> from Jared Kushner, Trump's son-in-law, and Ivanka Trump, his
> daughter, who said she "really loves" her and would do anything for
> her"Call us anytime," Kushner says on the call, according to the
> book. (Dawsey, 2018)

How can you be a racist and "really love" the focus of your racism? Moving
on,

> Then, Lara Trump called and reiterated how much the president and the
> family loved Manigault Newman, offering her the job and wanting to
> make sure "everything is positive." "If you come on board, we can't
> have you mention that stuff," she added, referring to interviews
> Manigault Newman gave immediately after her firing. (Dawsey, 2018)

Omarosa is not finished because she's good at what she does. And when it
comes to kissing ass, telling lies and towing the company line, Omarosa is one
Aunt Jemima who reigns without rival.

CONCLUSION

The first thing out of the mouths of black women who learned about and
read this book is, "why don't you write about the black male sellouts." The fact is,
that is what I write about most of the time because in my view, there are far more
male traitors than female. But the males who are married are married to women

who KNOW that they are uncle toms and do nothing about it; that makes those sisters and "others" quite culpable.

In addition I devoted a book to *The Black Athlete as 21st Century Slave*. On the cover of that book are none other than Charles Barkley and Michael Jordan. Another who could easily have made that cover is Karl "The Mailman" Malone. But this book was more about definition of what constitutes an Aunt Jemima because sisters are more subtle and tend to ease under the radar with their antics. I am about to complete another book, *Made and Manufactured in America*, where I list some of the top black "sellouts" in the nation. In addition, I have pointed out a number of them in this book.

There is going to be a sharp increase in the number of Aunt Jemimas both in the media and in politics. The ideology of the female sellout is going to strike home to a group of women who have been the strongest on the planet for the past 400 years and then again before that in Africa. The time has come for them to look around and make a decision about what to do about all these black men chasing white bitches, engaging in "down low behavior", and getting locked up and of course, stopping the bullets of police officers. They have families to care for and the time has come for them to forget that "the man is the head of the household" bullshit. That has long been gone.

It is akin to what the late journalist Bill Moyers once said: "In one way or another, this is the oldest story in America: the struggle to determine whether 'we, the people' is a spiritual idea embedded in a political reality – one nation, indivisible – or merely a charade masquerading as piety and manipulated by the powerful and privileged to sustain their own way of life at the expense of others."

REFERENCES

Alexis, Geraldine (__) The **White Man's Purpose**. Kearney, Nebraska: Morris Publishing.

Brett, Jennifer (2017, March 21). Omarosa praises Trump's actions on HBCUs, other topics. Atlanta Buzz. Retrieved from https://www.ajc.com/blog/buzz/omarosa-praises-trump-actions-hbcus-other-topics/yZCmFgrSCsXKY4DcczYUnM/

Dawsey, Josh. (2018, August 10). Omarosa Manigault Newman says she refused hush money, pens White House memoir calling Trump racist. **Washington Post**. Retrieved from https://www.washingtonpost.com/

Doneghy, Sarah (2018, January 30). Aunt Jemima: It was never about the pancakes. Black Excellence. Retrieved from https://blackexcellence.com/aunt-jemima-never-pancakes/

Fisher, K. (2016, January 20). Stacey Dash doesn't think Black History Month should exist, Wants to take BET off the air. Eonline. Retrieved from http://www.eonline.com/news/732690/stacey-dash-doesn-t-think-black-history-month-should-exist-wants-to-take-bet-off-the-air

Goldmacher, Shane. (2018, August 15) Cuomo Says America 'Was Never That Great' in Jab at Trump Slogan. **New York Times**. Retrieved from https://www.nytimes.com/2018/08/15/nyregion/cuomo-maga-trump-.html.

Hollowverse (2018). The religious and political views of Diana Ross. Retrieved from https://hollowverse.com/diana-ross/

Olu, Yolanda (2017, May 19) One cause of black self-hatred. **Gary Crusader** Retrieved from https://chicagocrusader.com/one-cause-of-black-self-hatred/

Murphy, D. (2016, January 20). Stacey Dash Speaks Out on 2016 Oscars Boycott: 'It's Ludicrous'. Entertainment Tonight. http://www.etonline.com/news/180458_stacey_dash_speaks_out_on_2016_oscars_boycott_its_ludicrous/

National Endowment for the Humanities. (2014, October 8). Frederick Douglass's "Narrative:" Myth of the Happy Slave. Retrieved from https://edsitement.neh.gov/lesson-plan/frederick-douglasss-narrative-myth-happy-slave.

Romano, Nick (2018, August 10). White House says Omarosa book 'riddled with lies' after claim that Trump used N-word. Entertainment Weekly News. Retrieved from

Sabia, C. (2015, March 18). Actress sparks firestorm defending Michelle Obama-Planet of the Apes reference on 'The View:' 'Some people look like animals.' Biz Pac Review. Retrieved from http://www.bizpacreview.com/2015/03/18/actress-sparks-firestorm-defending-michelle-obama-planet-of-the-apes-reference-on-the-view-some-people-look-like-animals-187862

Sprankles, Julie (2014, October 24) Beverly Johnson on overcoming racism in Hollywood. She knows.com. Retrieved from https://www.sheknows.com/entertainment/articles/1055195/beverly-johnson-interview

Thomas, Michael (1973, February 1)) Diana Ross goes from riches to rags. **Rolling Stone.** Retrieved from https://www.rollingstone.com/music/music-news/diana-ross-goes-from-riches-to-rags-165274/

Watkins, B. (2010, July 23). The evolution of the sellout in Black America. Madame Noire. Retrieved from http://madamenoire.com/103165/the-evolution-of-the-sellout-in-black-america/

Zimmerman, Neetzan (2016, September 23). Omarosa: Trump's haters will be forced to 'bow down' to him. **The Hill.** Retrieved from http://thehill.com/blogs/in-the-know/in-the-know/297430-omarosa-trumps-haters-will-be-forced-to-bow-down-to-him